BLACK+DECKER

The Complete Guide to
PLUMBING

Updated 6th Edition

Current with 2015-2018 Plumbing Codes

COOL
SPRINGS
PRESS

Inspiring | Educating | Creating | Entertaining

Brimming with creative inspiration, how-to projects, and useful information to enrich your everyday life, Quarto Knows is a favorite destination for those pursuing their interests and passions. Visit our site and dig deeper with our books into your area of interest: Quarto Creates, Quarto Cooks, Quarto Homes, Quarto Lives, Quarto Drives, Quarto Explores, Quarto Gifts, or Quarto Kids.

First published in 2015 by Cool Springs Press, an imprint of The Quarto Group, 401 Second Avenue North, Suite 310, Minneapolis, MN 55401 USA. T (612) 344-8100 F (612) 344-8692 www.QuartoKnows.com

Cool Springs Press titles are also available at discount for retail, wholesale, promotional, and bulk purchase. For details, contact the Special Sales Manager by email at specialsales@quarto.com or by mail at The Quarto Group, Attn: Special Sales Manager, 401 Second Avenue North, Suite 310, Minneapolis, MN 55401 USA.

ISBN: 978-1-59186-636-7

Cataloging-in-Publication Data on file with the Library of Congress

Printed in China

15 14 13 12 11 10 9

Acquisitions Editor: Mark Johanson
Design Manager: Brad Springer
Layout: Danielle Smith-Boldt
Technical Reviewer: Bruce Barker

Photography: Rau + Barber
Photo Assistance: Brad Holden, Alexandra Burniece, Natalie Williams

The Complete Guide to Plumbing
Created by: The Editors of Cool Springs Press, in cooperation with BLACK+DECKER.
BLACK+DECKER and the BLACK+DECKER logo are trademarks of The Black & Decker Corporation and are used under license. All rights reserved.

NOTICE TO READERS

For safety, use caution, care, and good judgment when following the procedures described in this book. The publisher and BLACK+DECKER cannot assume responsibility for any damage to property or injury to persons as a result of misuse of the information provided.

The techniques shown in this book are general techniques for various applications. In some instances, additional techniques not shown in this book may be required. Always follow manufacturers' instructions included with products, since deviating from the directions may void warranties. The projects in this book vary widely as to skill levels required: some may not be appropriate for all do-it-yourselfers, and some may require professional help.

Consult your local building department for information on building permits, codes, and other laws as they apply to your project.

Contents

The Complete Guide to **Plumbing**

Contents  (Cont.)

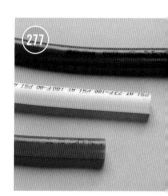

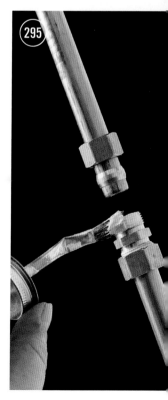

Introduction

*P*lumbing is a large and varied DIY category. As you explore it, you'll find that the tasks you encounter can differ in difficulty, just as taking a pop quiz in math differs from getting a PhD in physics. Fixing that drip in your sink drain might be as simple as tightening the compression nut on your P-trap: about a ten-second job. But running new lines for that extra bathroom you've been wanting in the basement? You're looking at jackhammers, dumpsters, multiple inspections, and many weeks of hard labor. But as variable as the jobs we lump into the "plumbing" category are, they have one important thing in common: doing the job yourself can save you a ton of money.

The key to doing the work yourself is twofold: you need ambition, and you need good information. The ambition is pretty much up to each homeowner, but when it comes to information, we're here to help. For more than a decade, *BLACK+DECKER The Complete Guide to Plumbing* has been the leading plumbing manual for do-it-yourselfers. Now in its updated 6th edition and boasting one million copies sold, it is the clearest and most complete plumbing book you can own. From its easy-to-understand explanations of how modern plumbing works to its clear how-to photos of the most common home plumbing projects, this is the only plumbing book you'll need to become master of your home plumbing system.

This edition of *The Complete Guide to Plumbing* has been revised and updated to conform to national plumbing codes in effect from 2015 through 2018. National plumbing codes change every three years, and we pay attention to what's new so you don't have to. The truth is, though, most of the national code updates are aimed at large commercial buildings and multi-unit dwellings, not single-family homes. Many code changes apply only to new construction. But codes also change for a reason, and the reason is almost always to improve safety. That's why we think monitoring the changes and reporting them back in the form of updated editions of our book is so important. Your municipal building department may not have adopted the changes yet, but we think you should. When it comes to the safety of your family, we always urge you to fall on the side of "code-plus."

It isn't codes alone that prompt us to make sure our DIY books stay as current as possible. It's also convenience. Every year, manufacturers and toolmakers come out with new products and ideas that are specifically designed for the home DIYer. Some are better than others, but we watch them closely, and when we see a better way to accomplish your goal with a greater likelihood of success, we'll show it to you. Take flexible supply tubes, for example—it wasn't long ago that appliances and fixtures were supplied with water and gas in rigid pipes. Rigid pipes (and even so-called flexible copper tubing) is reliable, but every time you move your dishwasher or bump your water heater, you risk breaking the connection or kinking the tubing. Because most codes now allow flexible gas and water supply tubing for hook-ups, we've taken care to show how hook-ups are being made with these simple products wherever it makes sense. That's why we're confident that when you use this book as a guide for any home plumbing job, you can be assured that you're getting the latest and best information.

The Home Plumbing System

Because most of a plumbing system is hidden inside walls and floors, it may seem to be a complex maze of pipes and fittings. But spend a few minutes with us and you'll gain a basic understanding of your system. Understanding how home plumbing works is an important first step toward doing routine maintenance and money-saving repairs.

A typical home plumbing system includes three basic parts: a water supply system, a fixture and appliance set, and a drain system. These three parts can be seen clearly in the photograph of the cut-away house on the opposite page.

Fresh water enters a home through a main supply line (1). This fresh water source is provided by either a municipal water company or a private underground well. If the source is a municipal supplier, the water passes through a meter (2) that registers the amount of water used. A family of four uses about 400 gallons of water each day.

Immediately after the main supply enters the house, a branch line splits off (3) and is joined to a water heater (4). From the water heater, a hot water line runs parallel to the cold water line to bring the water supply to fixtures and appliances throughout the house. Fixtures include sinks, bathtubs, showers, and laundry tubs. Appliances include water heaters, dishwashers, clothes washers, and water softeners. Toilets and exterior sillcocks are examples of fixtures that require only a cold water line.

The water supply to fixtures and appliances is controlled with faucets and valves. Faucets and valves have moving parts and seals that eventually may wear out or break, but they are easily repaired or replaced.

Waste water then enters the drain system. It first must flow past a drain trap (5), a U-shaped piece of pipe that holds standing water and prevents sewer gases from entering the home. Every fixture must have a drain trap.

The drain system works entirely by gravity, allowing waste water to flow downhill through a series of large-diameter pipes. These drain pipes are attached to a system of vent pipes. Vent pipes (6) bring air into the drain system to prevent suction or pressure that might allow the trap to lose its water seal. Vent pipes usually exit the house at a roof vent (7).

All waste water eventually reaches a drainage stack or a building drain (8).

NOTE: In a two or more story house there is usually more than one drainage stack. There is no stack in a one-story house. The stack or building drain becomes a sewer line (9) that exits the house near the foundation. In a municipal system, this sewer line joins a main sewer line located near the street. Where sewer service is not available, waste water empties into a septic system.

Water meters and main shutoff valves are located where the main water supply pipe enters the house. The water meter is the property of your local municipal water company. If the water meter leaks, or if you suspect it is not functioning properly, call your water company for repairs.

(7) Roof vent

(8) Drainage stack and vent

(6) Vent pipe

(5) Trap

(4) Water heater

(3) Branch line

Main shutoff valve

(2) Water meter

Branch drain line

Hot water supply lines

Cold water supply lines

Drain lines

Vent lines

Floor drain

(1) Main supply line

(9) Sewer line

Water Supply System

Water supply pipes carry hot and cold water throughout a house. In homes built before 1960, the original supply pipes were usually made of galvanized steel. Newer homes have supply pipes made of copper. Beginning in the 1980s, supply pipes made of rigid CPVC plastic became more commonplace, and the more recent plumbing innovations find PEX pipe widely used and accepted.

Water supply pipes are made to withstand the high pressures of the water supply system. They have small diameters, usually ½" to 1", and are joined with strong, watertight fittings. The hot and cold lines run in tandem to all parts of the house. Usually, the supply pipes run inside wall cavities or are strapped to the undersides of floor joists.

Hot and cold water supply pipes are connected to fixtures or appliances. Fixtures include sinks, tubs, and showers. Some fixtures, such as toilets or hose bibs, are supplied only by cold water. Appliances include dishwashers and clothes washers. A refrigerator icemaker uses only cold water. Tradition says that hot water supply pipes and faucet handles are found on the left-hand side of a fixture, with cold water on the right.

Because it is pressurized, the water supply system is occasionally prone to leaks. This is especially true of galvanized iron pipe, which has limited resistance to corrosion.

For some houses in older neighborhoods, the main supply line running from the street to the house is made of lead; this once posed a health hazard. Today, however, municipalities with lead pipes often add a trace amount of phosphate to the water, which coats the inside of the pipes and virtually eliminates leaching of lead into the water. If you are concerned about lead in your water, check with your local water supplier.

Hot water supply lines

In from municipal water supply

Cold water supply lines

In from municipal water supply

Drain-Waste-Vent System

Drain pipes use gravity to carry waste water away from fixtures, appliances, and other drain openings. This waste water is carried out of the house to a municipal sewer system or septic tank.

Newer drain pipes are plastic. In an older home, drain pipes may be cast iron, galvanized steel, copper, or lead. Because they are not part of the supply system, lead drain pipes pose no health hazard. However, lead pipes are no longer manufactured for home plumbing systems.

Drain pipes have diameters ranging from 1¼" to 4". These large diameters allow waste to pass through efficiently.

Traps are an important part of the drain system. These curved sections of drain pipe hold standing water, and they are usually found immediately after the drain tailpiece in the drain opening. The standing water of a trap prevents sewer gases from backing up into the home. Each time a drain is used, the standing trap water is flushed away and is replaced by new water.

In order to work properly, the drain system requires air. Air allows waste water to flow freely down drain pipes.

To allow air into the drain system, drain pipes are connected to vent pipes. All drain systems must include vents, and the entire system is called the drain-waste-vent (DWV) system. One or more vents, located on the roof, provide the air needed for the DWV system to work.

Vent

Vent lines

Trap

Drain lines

Out to municipal sewer or septic tank

Shutting Off the Water

In case an emergency requires you to replace or repair a faucet, fixture, or appliance, knowing how to shut off the water is imperative. The photos on this page show the most common types of shutoffs. If you don't feel completely confident about finding your home's shutoff points or how to turn them off, contact your local water company for information.

There are two basic types of valves, which shut off in two different ways. To turn off many older valves, rotate the handle clockwise (remember "lefty loosey; righty tighty") until it stops. To turn off many newer valves, rotate the handle one-quarter turn only.

Some outdoor shutoffs require the use of a special tool, often referred to as a "key." Keep your key within easy reach in case of an emergency. To turn off, slip the key over the valve and rotate one quarter turn, so the handle is at a right angle to the pipe. The outdoor main shutoff shown below is an example of a shutoff that requires a key. If you lack a key, a meter valve can usually be turned with a wrench or channel-type pliers.

An outdoor main shutoff may be as simple as an exposed valve that you turn by hand. Or it may be buried in a housing that is sometimes called a Buffalo box. In this example, both the meter and the main shutoff are housed in the Buffalo box; in other cases, the meter is located inside the house.

Meter

Key-operated shutoff (open)

You may have an inside main shutoff, usually located near the point where the main supply pipe enters the house near the water meter. Many homes have both a Buffalo box and an indoor main shutoff. There may be a valve on each side of the meter; turn off either one of them to shut off water to the house.

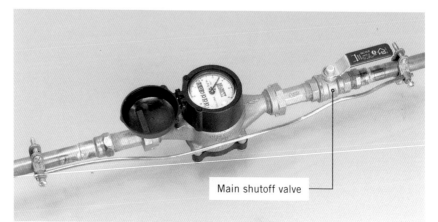

Main shutoff valve

Partial-house shutoffs are often found in medium- to large-size homes. They control water flow to large areas of the house. They are found in pairs, one for hot and one for cold water. Turning off a pair of these may shut off water to a floor or to an entire bathroom or kitchen.

Fixture shutoff valves, also called stop valves, control water to a specific faucet, toilet, or fixture. They are also usually found in pairs, one for hot and one for cold. However, toilets, icemakers, and other cold-water-only fixtures will have only one stop valve. If you live in an older home that lacks stop valves, it's a good idea to install them.

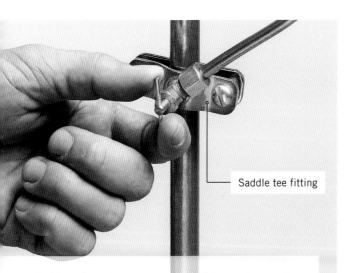

Saddle tee fitting

Saddle valves often are used to tap into a water supply pipe to bring water to a low-demand fixture, such as an ice maker or a hot water dispenser. Some municipalities do not endorse saddle valves, but most do (although the vast majority of professional plumbers do not like to install them because they tend to leak). The saddle valve handle appears to be a shutoff but it is not—if a leak develops at or downline from a saddle valve, find the closest shutoff valve between the water supply and the saddle if you need to stop the water flow.

Built-in shutoff valves

Integral shutoffs are sometimes found on tub-and-shower faucets and other fixtures. This arrangement allows water to be turned off to the fixture only, so water remains available for the rest of the house.

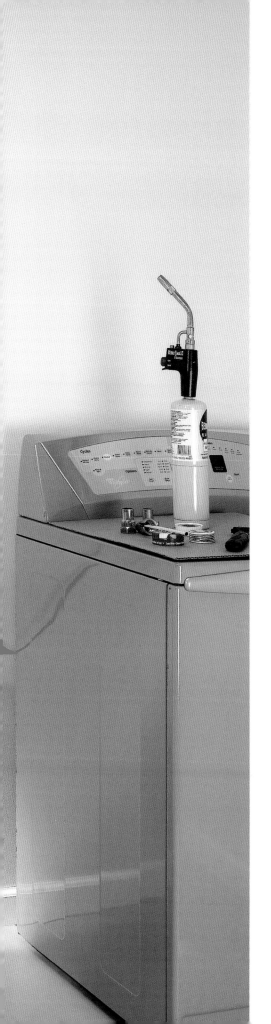

Installing Fixtures & Faucets

Although it might be a bit of a stretch to refer to any aspect of plumbing as glamorous or fun, installing fixtures like sinks and showers is the heart of the plumbing pursuit. It is the aspect of plumbing we naturally think of first, and in many cases the payoff is almost instantaneous.

In this section you will find photos and step-by-step instructions for the plumbing fixture installations you, as a do-it-yourselfer, are most likely to attempt. The section with the most common fixture project by far is Toilets. From removal of the old unit to wrangling the new one into place, making all the hookups and even installing the seat, the entire project is laid out for you in full color photos. From there, you'll find a series of projects that move from kitchen to bath to laundry and back again, all shown in full detail.

In this chapter:
- Toilets
- Kitchen Faucets
- Kitchen Drains & Traps
- Dishwashers
- Food Disposers
- Water Heaters
- Bathroom Faucets
- Shower Kits
- Custom Shower Bases
- Wet Rooms & Curbless Showers
- Alcove Bathtubs
- Sliding Tub Doors
- Jetted Tub
- Bidets
- Urinals
- Water Softeners
- Hot Water Dispenser
- Icemakers
- Pot Filler
- Reverse-Osmosis Water Filters
- Frost-proof Sillcocks
- Pedestal Sinks
- Wall-Hung Vanities
- Vessel Sinks
- Wall-Mounted Sinks
- Plumbing a Double-Bowl Vanity
- Hands-Free Bathroom Faucets
- Kitchen Sinks
- Standpipe Drains

Toilets

You can replace a poorly functioning or inefficient toilet with a high-efficiency, high-quality new toilet in just a single afternoon. All toilets made since 1994 have been required to use 1.6 gallons or less per flush, which has been a huge challenge for the industry. Today, the most evolved water-saving toilets have wide passages behind the bowl and wide (3") flush valve openings—features that facilitate short, powerful flushes. This means fewer second flushes and fewer clogged toilets. These problems were common complaints of the first generation of 1.6-gallon toilets and continue to beleaguer inferior models today. See which toilets are available at your local home center in your price range, then go online and see what other consumers' experiences with those models have been. New toilets often go through a "de-bugging" stage when problems with leaks and malfunctioning parts are more common. Your criteria should include ease of installation, good flush performance, and reliability. With a little research, you should be able to purchase and install a high-functioning, economical toilet that will serve you well for years to come.

TOOLS & MATERIALS

Adjustable wrench
Bucket and sponge
Channel-type pliers
Hacksaw
Penetrating oil
Pliers
Putty knife
Rubber gloves
Screwdriver
Supply tube
Teflon tape
Toilet seat bolts
Toilet seat
Towels
Utility knife
Wax ring without flange or
   wax ring with flange

Replacing a toilet is simple, and the newer models of water-saving toilets have overcome the performance problems of earlier models.

Gravity-assisted toilets are now designed with taller tanks and steeper bowl walls to increase the effects of gravity.

Choosing a New Toilet

Toilets have changed in recent years. There's a toilet to fit every style. You can even buy a square or stainless-steel toilet, among many other new options. The new designs are efficient, durable, and less susceptible to clogs.

A toilet's style is partly affected by the way it's built. You have a number of options from which to choose:

Two-piece toilets have a separate water tank and bowl.

One-piece toilets have a tank and bowl made of one seamless unit.

Elongated bowls are roughly 2" longer than regular bowls.

Elevated toilets have higher seats, generally 18", rather than the standard 15".

You have a choice of two basic types of flush mechanisms: gravity- and pressure-assisted.

Gravity-assisted toilets allow water to rush down from an elevated tank into the toilet bowl. Federal law mandates that new toilets consume no more than 1.6 gallons of water per flush, less than half the volume used by older styles.

Pressure-assisted toilets rely on either compressed air or water pumps to boost flushing power.

Dual-flush systems feature two flush buttons on the top of the tank, allowing you to select either an 8-ounce flush for liquids or a 1.6-gallon flush for solids.

Two-piece toilets with a separate tank and bowl are much more common than one-piece models, and usually a lot less costly. The cheapest models are compact with a seat that is not as high above the floor as a full-size model. This can create access difficulty for some users. Round-bowl models usually cost less than models with a larger, elongated bowl.

Large-diameter flush valve

Narrow trapway

Some high-end toilets are designed to get maximum pressure out of a small amount of water. Many employ narrower trapways (the path water travels through the bowl) in conjunction with large-diameter flush valves. Some models use as little as 1.2 gallons of water.

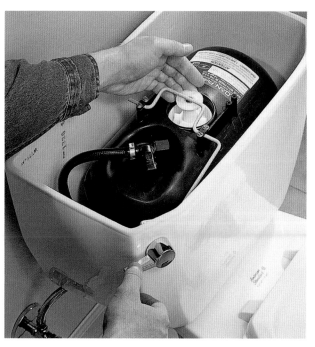

Pressure-assisted toilets are relatively expensive, but they can reduce your water usage significantly by eliminating multiple flushes. The flush mechanism of a pressure-assisted toilet boosts the flushing power by using either compressed air or water pumps.

How to Remove a Toilet

Coupling nut

Stop valve

Remove the old supply tube. First, turn off the water at the stop valve. Flush the toilet, holding the handle down for a long flush, and sponge out the tank. Use a wet/dry vac to clear any remaining water out of the tank and bowl. Unthread the coupling nut for the water supply below the tank using channel-type pliers.

Grip each tank bolt nut with a box wrench or pliers and loosen it as you stabilize each tank bolt from inside the tank with a large slotted screwdriver. If the nuts are stuck, apply penetrating oil to the nut and let it sit before trying to remove them again. You may also cut the tank bolts between the tank and the bowl with an open-ended hacksaw. Remove and discard the tank.

Remove the nuts that hold the bowl to the floor. First, pry off the bolt covers with a screwdriver. Use a socket wrench, locking pliers, or your channel-type pliers to loosen the nuts on the tank bolts. Apply penetrating oil and let it sit if the nuts are stuck, then take them off. As a last resort, cut the bolts off with a hacksaw by first cutting down through one side of the nut. Tilt the toilet bowl over and remove it.

PRYING UP WAX RINGS

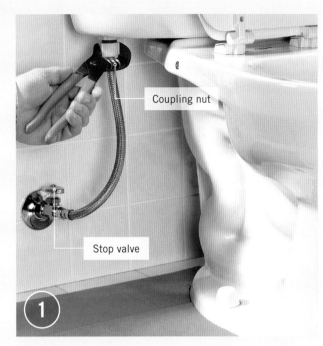

Removing an old wax ring is one of the more disgusting jobs you'll encounter in the plumbing universe (the one you see here is actually in relatively good condition). Work a stiff putty knife underneath the plastic flange of the ring (if you can) and start scraping. In many cases the wax ring will come off in chunks. Discard each chunk right away—they stick to everything. If you're left with a lot of residue, scrub with mineral spirits. Once clean, stuff a rag-in-a-bag in the drain opening to block sewer gas.

How to Install a Toilet

Clean and inspect the old closet flange. Look for breaks or wear. Also inspect the flooring around the flange. If either the flange or floor is worn or damaged, repair the damage. Use a rag and mineral spirits to completely remove residue from the old wax ring. Place a rag-in-a-bag into the opening to block odors.

Insert new tank bolts (don't reuse old ones) into the openings in the closet flange. Make sure the heads of the bolts are oriented to catch the maximum amount of flange material. To firmly hold the bolts upright, slide on the plastic washers and press them down.

If you will be replacing your toilet flange or if your existing flange can be unscrewed and moved, orient the new flange so the slots are parallel to the wall. This allows you to insert bolts under the slotted areas, which are much stronger than the areas at the ends of the curved grooves.

Remove the wax ring and apply it to the underside of the bowl, around the horn. Remove the protective covering. Do not touch the wax ring. It is very sticky. Remove the rag-in-a-bag. If you have an older 4-inch flange, place the ring on the flange rather than the toilet to make sure it is centered.

(continued)

Install the flush valve. Some tanks come with a flush valve and a fill valve preinstalled. For models that do not have this, insert the flush valve through the tank opening and tighten a spud nut over the threaded end of the valve. Place a foam spud washer on top of the spud nut.

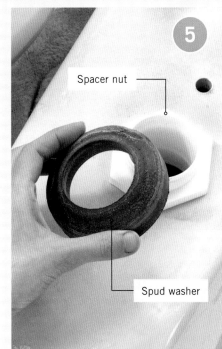

Spacer nut

Spud washer

Lower the bowl onto the flange, taking care not to disturb the wax ring. The holes in the bowl base should align perfectly with the tank bolts. Add a washer and tighten a nut onto each bolt. Hand-tighten each nut and then use channel-type pliers to further tighten the nuts. Alternate tightening the nuts until the bowl is secure. Do not overtighten.

NOTE: Some disagreement exists among plumbers as to whether you should seal the joint between the bowl and the floor. Most codes require that you do. The easiest and least visible way to seal it is to apply a thick bead of clear silicone caulk to the bottom rim of the bowl before you set it on the floor. Another option is to apply a bead of caulk between the bowl and the floor after the toilet is installed.

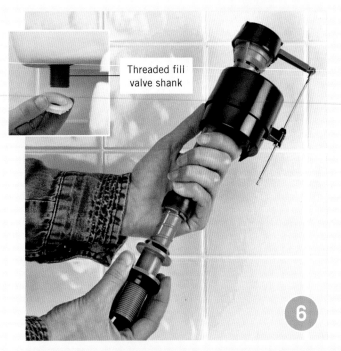

Threaded fill valve shank

Intermediate nut goes between tank and bowl

Adjust the fill valve as directed by the manufacturer to set the correct tank water level height and install the valve inside the tank. Hand tighten the nylon lock nut that secures the valve to the tank (inset photo) and then tighten it further with channel-type pliers.

With the tank lying on its back, thread a rubber washer onto each tank bolt and insert it into the bolt holes from inside the tank. Then, thread a brass washer and hex nut onto the tank bolts from below and tighten them to a quarter turn past hand tight. Do not overtighten.

Position the tank on the bowl, spud washer on opening, bolts through bolt holes. Put a rubber washer, followed by a brass washer and a wing nut, on each bolt and tighten these up evenly.

Intermediate nut

You may stabilize the bolts with a large slotted screwdriver from inside the tank, but tighten the nuts, not the bolts. You may press down a little on a side, the front, or the rear of the tank to level it as you tighten the nuts by hand. Do not overtighten and crack the tank. The tank should be level and stable when you're done.

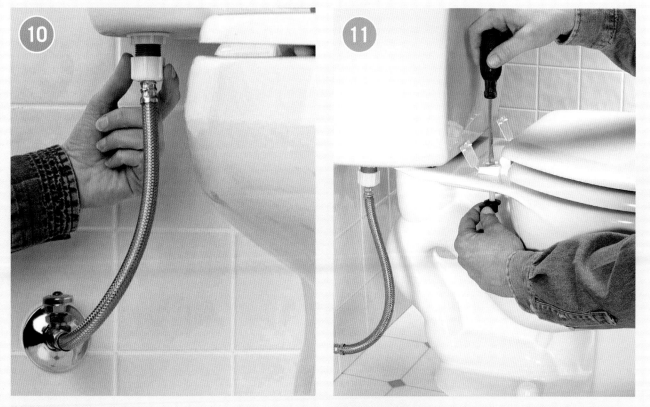

Hook up the water supply by connecting the supply tube to the threaded fill valve with the coupling nut provided. Turn on the water and test for leaks. Do not overtighten.

Attach the toilet seat by threading the plastic or brass bolts provided with the seat through the openings on the back of the rim and attaching nuts.

Kitchen Faucets

M̲ost new kitchen faucets feature single-handle control levers and washerless designs that rarely require maintenance. Additional features include brushed metallic finishes, detachable spray nozzles, or even push-button controls.

Connect the faucet to hot and cold water lines with easy-to-install flexible supply tubes made from vinyl or braided steel. If your faucet has a separate sprayer, install the sprayer first. Pull the sprayer hose through the sink opening and attach to the faucet body before installing the faucet.

Where local codes allow, use plastic tubes for drain hookups. A wide selection of extensions and angle fittings lets you easily plumb any sink configuration. Manufacturers offer kits that contain all the fittings needed for attaching a food disposer or dishwasher to the sink drain system.

TOOLS & MATERIALS

Adjustable wrench

Basin wrench
    or channel-type pliers

Hacksaw

Faucet

Putty knife

Screwdriver

Silicone caulk

Scouring pad

Scouring cleaner

Plumber's putty

Flexible vinyl or braided steel
    supply tubes

Drain components

Penetrating oil

Modern kitchen faucets tend to be single-handle models, often with useful features such as a pull-out head that functions as a sprayer. Most models come with an optional mounting plate that conceals sink holes when mounted on a predrilled sink flange.

Choosing a New Kitchen Faucet

You'll find many options when choosing a new kitchen faucet. The best place to start the process is with your sink. In the past, most faucets were mounted directly to the sink deck, which had three or four predrilled holes to accommodate the faucets, spout, sprayer, and perhaps a liquid soap dispenser or an air gap for your dishwasher. Modern kitchen faucets don't always conform to this setup, with many of them designed to be installed in a single hole in the sink deck or in the countertop. If you plan to keep your old sink, look for a faucet that won't leave empty holes in the deck. Generally, it's best to replace like for like, but unfilled stainless sink holes can be filled with snap-in plugs or a soap dispenser.

The two most basic kitchen faucet categories are single-handle and two-handle. Single-handle models are much more popular now because you can adjust the water temperature easily with just one hand. Another difference is in the faucet body. Some faucets have the taps and the spout mounted onto a faucet body so the spacing between the tailpieces is preset. Others, called widespread faucets, have independent taps and spouts that can be configured however you please, as long as the tubes connecting the taps to the spouts reach. This type is best if you are installing the faucet in the countertop (a common way to go about it with new countertops such as solid surface, quartz, or granite).

In the past, kitchen faucets almost always had a remote pull-out sprayer. The sprayer was attached to the faucet body with a hose directly below the mixing valve. While this type of sprayer is still fairly common, many faucets today have an integral pull-out spout that is very convenient and less prone to failure than the old-style sprayers.

Single-handle faucets may require four holes, as this model does with its side sprayer and matching soap/lotion dispenser.

A single-handle, high arc faucet with traditional remote sprayer. The mounting plate is decorative and optional.

A single-handle faucet with pull-out spray head requires only one hole in your sink deck or countertop—a real benefit if your sink is not predrilled or if it is an undermount model.

Two-handled faucets are less common, but remain popular choices for traditional kitchens. The gooseneck spout also has a certain elegance, but avoid this type if you have a shallow sink that's less than 8" deep.

How to Remove an Old Faucet

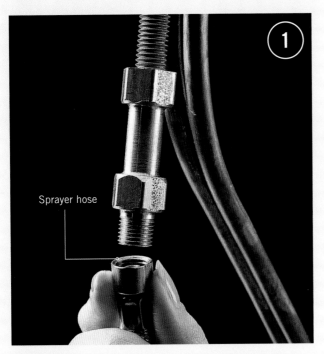

To remove the old faucet, start by clearing out the cabinet under the sink and laying down towels. Turn off the hot and cold stop valves and open the faucet to make sure the water is off. Detach the sprayer hose from the faucet sprayer nipple and unscrew the retaining nut that secures the sprayer base to the sink deck. Pull the sprayer hose out through the sink deck opening.

Spray the mounting nuts that hold the faucet or faucet handles (on the underside of the sink deck) with penetrating oil for easier removal. Let the oil soak in for a few minutes. If the nut is rusted and stubbornly stuck, you may need to drill a hole in its side, then tap the hole with a hammer and screwdriver to loosen it.

Mounting nut

Unhook the supply tubes at the stop valves. Don't reuse old chrome supply tubes. If the stops are missing or unworkable, replace them. Then remove the coupling nuts and the mounting nuts on the tailpieces of the faucet with a basin wrench or channel-type pliers.

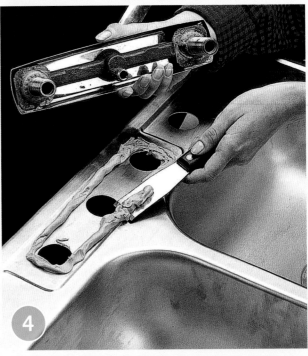

Pull the faucet body from the sink. Remove the sprayer base if you wish to replace it. Scrape off any putty or caulk with a putty knife and clean off the sink with a scouring pad and a nonabrasive cleaner.

How to Install a Pullout Kitchen Sink Faucet

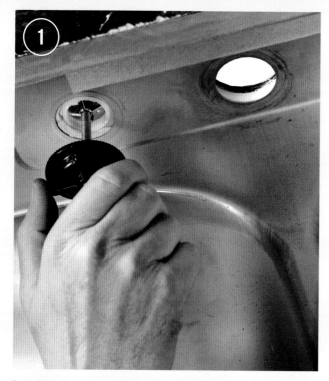

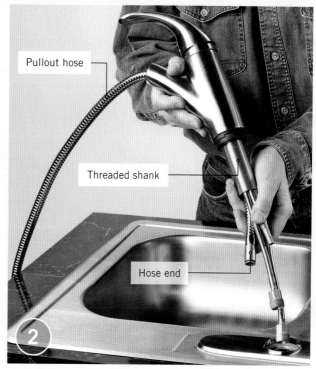

Install the base plate (if your faucet has one) onto the sink flange so it is centered. Have a helper hold it straight from above as you tighten the mounting nuts that secure the base plate from below. Make sure the plastic gasket is centered under the base plate. These nuts can be adequately tightened by hand.

Retract the pullout hose by drawing it out through the faucet body until the fitting at the end of the hose is flush with the bottom of the threaded faucet shank. Insert the shank and the supply tubes down through the top of the deck plate.

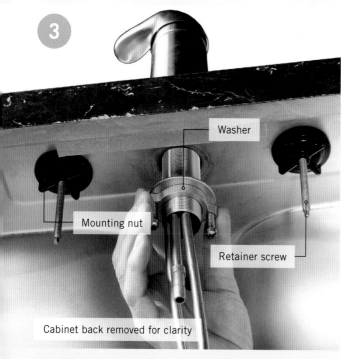

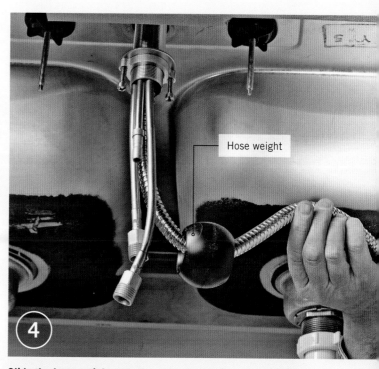

Slip the mounting nut and washer over the free ends of the supply tubes and pullout hose, then thread the nut onto the threaded faucet shank. Hand tighten. Tighten the retainer screws with a screwdriver to secure the faucet.

Slide the hose weight onto the pullout hose (the weight helps keep the hose from tangling and it makes it easier to retract).

(continued)

Connect the end of the pullout hose to the outlet port on the faucet body using a quick connector fitting.

Output port

5

Connect the supply tubes to the supply risers at the stop valves. Make sure to get the hot lines and cold lines attached correctly.

7

Water supply tube

6

Hook up the water supply tubes to the faucet inlets. Make sure the tubes are long enough to reach the supply risers without stretching or kinking.

8

Attach the spray head to the end of the pullout hose and turn the fitting to secure the connection. Turn on the water supply and test.

TIP: Remove the aerator in the tip of the spray head and run hot and cold water to flush out any debris.

Thoroughly clean the area around the sink's holes. Slip the faucet's plastic washer onto the underside of the base plate. Press the faucet in place, and have a helper hold it in place while you work from below.

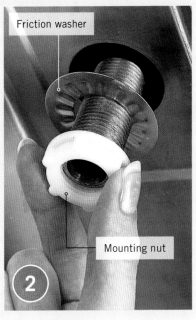

Friction washer

Mounting nut

Slip a friction washer onto each tailpiece and then hand tighten a mounting nut. Tighten the mounting nut with channel-type pliers or a basin wrench. Wipe up any silicone squeeze-out on the sink deck with a wet rag before it sets up.

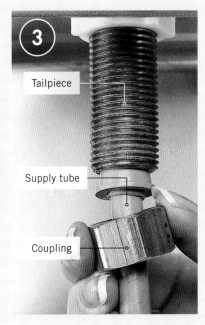

Tailpiece

Supply tube

Coupling

Connect supply tubes to the faucet tailpieces. Make sure the tubes you buy are long enough to reach the stop valves and that the coupling nuts will fit the tubes and tailpieces.

Sprayer tailpiece

Apply a ¼" bead of plumber's putty to the underside of the sprayer base. With the base threaded onto the sprayer hose, insert the tailpiece of the sprayer through the opening in the sink deck.

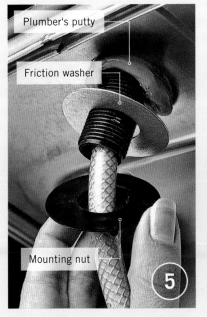

Plumber's putty

Friction washer

Mounting nut

From beneath, slip the friction washer over the sprayer tailpiece and then screw the mounting nut onto the tailpiece. Tighten with channel-type pliers or a basin wrench. Clean up any excess putty or caulk.

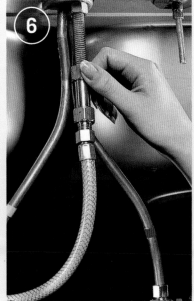

Screw the sprayer hose onto the hose nipple on the bottom of the faucet. Hand tighten and then give the nut one quarter turn with channel-type pliers or a basin wrench. Turn on the water supply at the shutoff, remove the aerator, and flush debris from the faucet.

Kitchen Drains & Traps

Kitchen traps, also called sink drains or trap assemblies, are made of 1½-inch pipes (also called tubes), slip washers, and nuts, so they can be easily assembled and disassembled. Most plastic types can be tightened by hand, with no wrench required. Pipes made of chromed brass will corrode in time, and rubber washers will crumble, meaning they need to be replaced. Plastic pipes and plastic washers last virtually forever. All traps are liable to get bumped out of alignment; when this happens, they should be taken apart and reassembled.

A trap's configuration depends on how many bowls the sink has, whether or not you have a food disposer and/or a dishwasher drain line, and local codes. On this page we show three of the most common assembly types. Tee fittings on these traps often have a baffle, which reduces the water flow somewhat. Check local codes to make sure your trap is compliant.

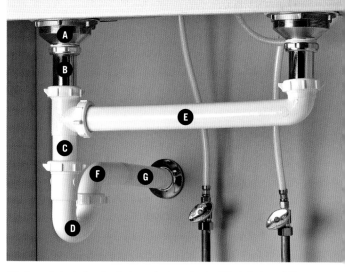

Kitchen sink drains include a strainer body (A), tailpiece (B), waste tee (C), P-trap (D), outlet drain line (E), trap arm (F), and wall stubout with coupling (G).

In this arrangement, the dishwasher drain hose (A) attaches to the food disposer (B), and a trap arm (C) leads from the disposer to the P-trap (D).

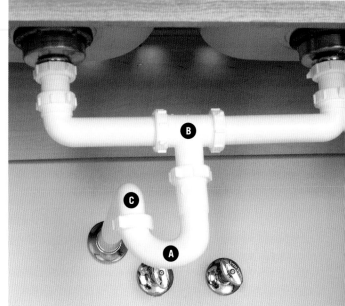

A "center tee" arrangement has a single P-trap (A) that is connected to a waste tee (B) and the trap arm (C).

DRAIN KITS

Kits for installing a new sink drain include all the pipes, slip fittings, and washers you'll need to get from the sink tailpieces (most kits are equipped for a double bowl kitchen sink) to the trap arm that enters the wall or floor. For wall trap arms, you'll need a kit with a P-trap. Both drains normally are plumbed to share a trap. Chromed brass or PVC with slip fittings let you adjust the drain more easily and pull it apart and then reassemble if there is a clog. Some pipes have fittings on their ends that eliminate the need for a washer. Kitchen sink drains and traps should be 1½" o.d. pipe—the 1¼" pipe is for lavatories and doesn't have enough capacity for a kitchen sink.

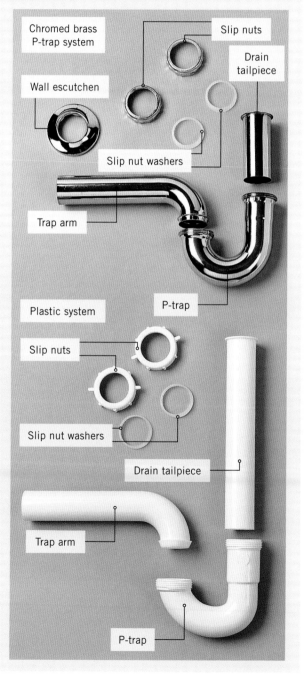

Chromed brass P-trap system

Slip nuts

Drain tailpiece

Wall escutchen

Slip nut washers

Trap arm

P-trap

Plastic system

Slip nuts

Slip nut washers

Drain tailpiece

Trap arm

P-trap

TIPS FOR CHOOSING DRAINS

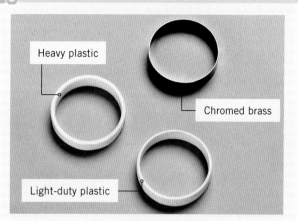

Heavy plastic

Chromed brass

Light-duty plastic

Wall thickness varies in sink drain pipes. The thinner plastic material is cheaper and more difficult to obtain a good seal with than the thicker, more expensive tubing. The thin product is best reserved for lavatory drains, which are far less demanding.

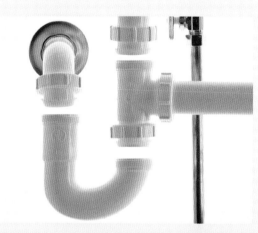

Slip joints are formed by tightening a male-threaded slip nut over a female-threaded fitting, trapping and compressing a beveled nylon washer to seal the joint.

Use a spud wrench to tighten the strainer body against the underside of the sink bowl. Normally, the strainer flange has a layer of plumber's putty to seal beneath it above the sink drain, and a pair of washers (one rubber, one fibrous) to seal below.

How to Hook Up a Kitchen Sink Drain

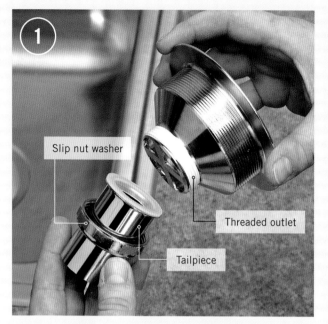

(1)

Slip nut washer

Threaded outlet

Tailpiece

If you are replacing the sink strainer body, remove the old one and clean the top and bottom of the sink deck around the drain opening with mineral spirits. Attach the drain tailpiece to the threaded outlet of the strainer body, inserting a nonbeveled washer between the parts if your strainer kits include one. Lubricate the threads or apply Teflon tape so you can get a good, snug fit.

Apply plumber's putty around the perimeter of the drain opening and seat the strainer assembly into it. Add washers below as directed and tighten the strainer locknut with a spud wrench (see photo, previous page) or by striking the mounting nubs at the top of the body with a flat screwdriver.

(2)

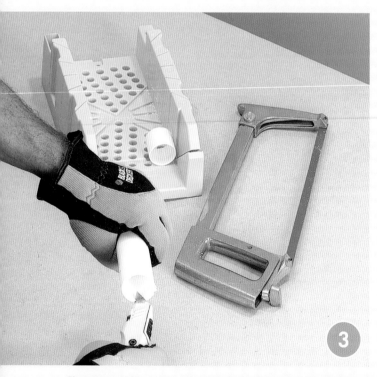

(3)

You may need to cut a trap arm or drain tailpiece to length. Cut metal tubing with a hacksaw. Cut plastic tubing with a handsaw, power miter saw, or a hand miter box and a backsaw or hacksaw. You can use a tubing cutter for any material. Deburr the cut end of plastic tubing with a utility knife.

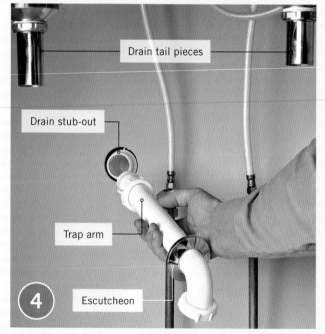

Drain tail pieces

Drain stub-out

Trap arm

(4)

Escutcheon

Attach the trap arm to the male-threaded drain stubout in the wall, using a slip nut and beveled compression washer. The outlet for the trap arm should point downward.

NOTE: The trap arm must be lower on the wall than any of the horizontal lines in the set-up, including lines to dishwasher, disposer, or the outlet line to the second sink bowl.

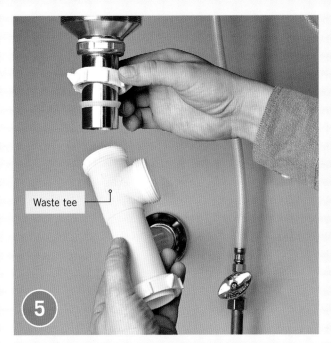

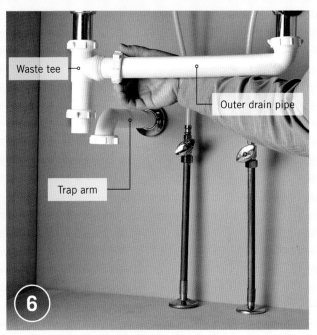

Attach a waste tee fitting to the drain tailpiece, orienting the opening in the fitting side so it will accept the outlet drain line from the other sink bowl. If the waste tee is higher than the top of the trap arm, remove it and trim the drain tailpiece.

Join the short end of the outlet drain pipe to the tailpiece for the other sink bowl and then attach the end of the long run to the opening in the waste tee. The outlet tube should extend into the tee ½"—make sure it does not extend in far enough to block water flow from above.

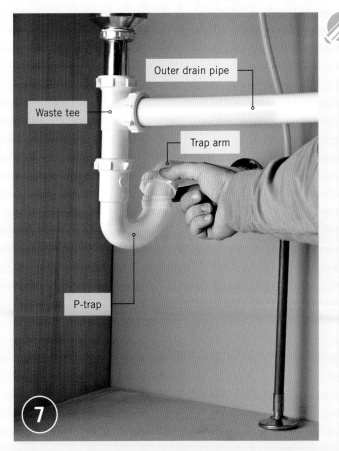

Attach the long leg of a P-trap to the waste tee and attach the shorter leg to the downward-facing opening of the trap arm. Adjust as necessary and test all joints to make sure they are still tight, and then test the system.

VARIATION: DRAIN IN FLOOR

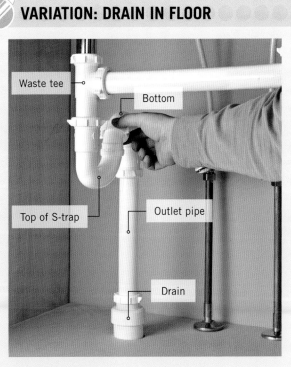

If your drain stubout comes up out of the floor or cabinet base instead of the wall, you probably have a two-part S-trap instead of a P-trap in your drain line. This arrangement is illegal in some areas, because a heavy surge of waterflow from a nearby fixture can siphon the trap dry, rendering it unable to block gases. Check with your local plumbing inspector to learn if S-traps are allowed in your area.

Dishwashers

A dishwasher that's past its prime may be inefficient in more ways than one. If it's an old model, it probably wasn't designed to be very efficient to begin with. But more significantly, if it no longer cleans effectively, you're probably spending a lot of time and hot water pre-rinsing the dishes. This alone can consume more energy and water than a complete wash cycle on a newer machine. So even if your old dishwasher still runs, replacing it with an efficient new model can be a good green upgrade.

In terms of sizing and utility hookups, dishwashers are generally quite standard. If your old machine is a built-in and your countertops and cabinets are standard sizes, most full-size dishwashers will fit right in. Of course, you should always measure the dimensions of the old unit before shopping for a new one to avoid an unpleasant surprise at installation time. Also be sure to review the manufacturer's instructions before starting any work.

TOOLS & MATERIALS

Screwdrivers
Adjustable wrench
2-ft. level
¾" discharge tube
½" flexible supply tubing
Cable connector
Teflon tape
Hose clamps
Wire connectors
Carpet scrap
Bowl

Replacing an old, inefficient dishwasher is a straightforward project that usually takes just a few hours. The energy and water savings start with the first load of dishes and continue with every load thereafter.

How to Replace a Dishwasher

Disconnect old plumbing connections. First unscrew the front access panel. Once the access panel is removed, disconnect the water supply line from the L-fitting on the bottom of the unit. This is usually a brass compression fitting, so just turning the compression nut counterclockwise with an adjustable wrench should do the trick. Use a bowl to catch any water that might leak out when the nut is removed.

Start by shutting off the electrical power to the circuit at the main service panel. Also, turn off the water supply at the shutoff valve, usually located directly under the floor or in the cabinet beneath the kitchen sink.

NOTE: Most local codes now require that dishwashers be on a GFCI-protected circuit. If yours is not, it's always a good idea to replace the regular receptacle with a GFCI-protected model, or to replace the circuit breaker at the main panel with a GFCI breaker.

L-fitting

Disconnect old wiring connections. The dishwasher has an integral electrical box at the front of the unit where the power cable is attached to the dishwasher's fixture wires. Take off the box cover and remove the wire connectors that join the wires together.

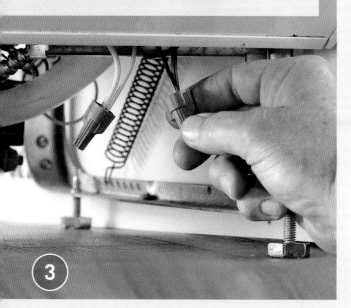

Disconnect the discharge hose, which is usually connected to the dishwasher port on the side of the garbage disposer. To remove it, just loosen the screw on the hose clamp and pull it off. You may need to push this hose back through a hole in the cabinet wall and into the dishwasher compartment so it won't get caught when you pull the dishwasher out.

(continued)

Detach the unit from the cabinets before you pull it out. Remove the screws that hold the brackets to the underside of the countertop. Then put a piece of cardboard or old carpet under the front legs to protect the floor from getting scratched, and pull the dishwasher out.

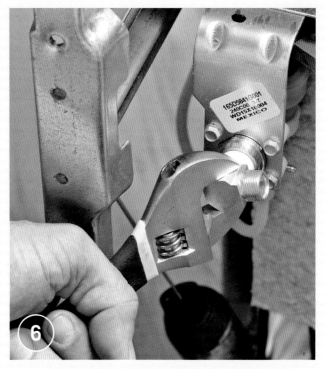

First, read the appliance's installation instructions carefully and then prepare the new dishwasher to be installed. Tip it on its back and attach the new L-fitting into the threaded port on the solenoid. Apply some Teflon tape to the fitting threads before tightening to allow the coupling to be tightened fully.

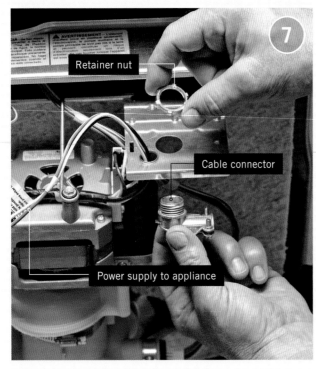

Retainer nut

Cable connector

Power supply to appliance

Prepare for the wiring connections. Like the old dishwasher, the new one will have an integral electrical box for making the wiring connections. To gain access to the box, just remove the box cover. Then install a cable connector on the back of the box and bring the power cable from the service panel through this connector. Power should be shut off at the main service panel at all times.

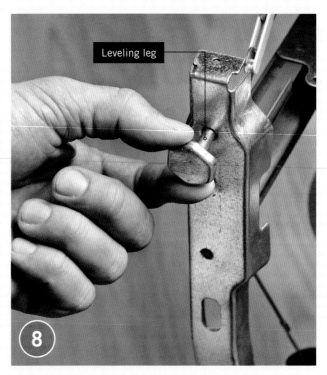

Leveling leg

Install a leveling leg at each of the four corners while the new dishwasher is still on its back. Just turn the legs into the threaded holes designed for them. Leave about ½" of each leg projecting from the bottom of the unit. These will have to be adjusted later to level the appliance. Tip the appliance up onto the feet and slide it into the opening. Check for level in both directions and adjust the feet as required.

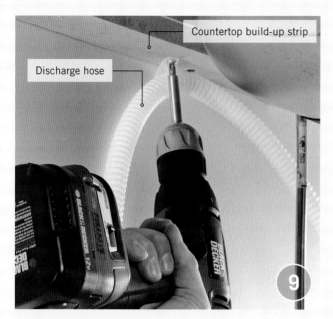

Countertop build-up strip

Discharge hose

(9)

Push an adapter over the disposer's discharge nipple and tighten it in place with a hose clamp. If you don't have a disposer, replace one of the drain tailpieces with a dishwasher tailpiece, and clamp the discharge tube to its fitting.

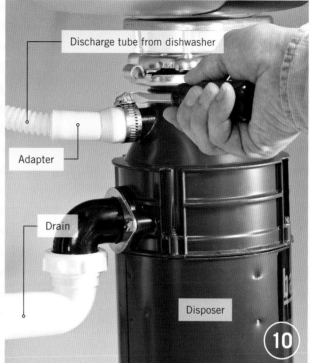

Discharge tube from dishwasher

Adapter

Drain

Disposer

(10)

Once the dishwasher is level, attach the brackets to the underside of the countertop to keep the appliance from moving. Then pull the discharge hose into the sink cabinet and install it so there's a loop that is attached with a bracket to the underside of the countertop. This loop prevents waste water from flowing from the disposer back into the dishwasher.

NOTE: Some codes require that you install an air gap fitting for this purpose. Check with your local plumbing inspector.

TUBE CHOICES

Codes still allow flexible copper supply tubes like the one shown in the next step, but a flexible dishwasher supply tube, such as reinforced, braided stainless steel, is a better choice in just about any situation. Copper tubes may crimp and either burst or restrict water flow when you move the dishwasher.

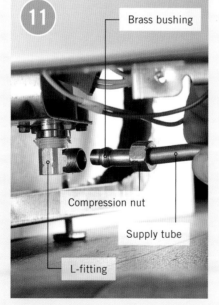

(11)

Brass bushing

Compression nut

Supply tube

L-fitting

Adjust the L-fitting on the dishwasher's water inlet valve until it points directly toward the water supply tubing. Then lubricate the threads slightly with a drop of dishwashing liquid and tighten the tubing's compression nut onto the fitting, keeping the brass bushing between the nut and the L-fitting. Use an adjustable wrench and turn the nut clockwise.

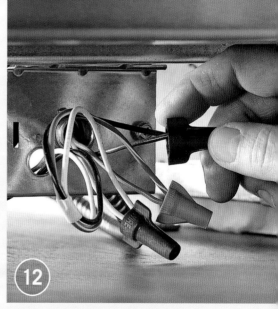

(12)

Complete the electrical connections by clamping the cable and joining the wires with wire nuts, following manufacturer's instructions. Replace the electrical cover, usually by hooking it onto a couple of prongs and driving a screw. Restore power and water, and test. Replace the toe-kick.

Food Disposers

Food disposers are standard equipment in the modern home, and most of us have come to depend on them to macerate our plate leavings and crumbs so they can exit the house along with waste water from the sink drain. If your existing disposer needs replacing, you'll find that the job is relatively simple, especially if you select a replacement appliance that is the same model as the old one. In that case, you can probably reuse the existing mounting assembly, drain sleeve, and drain plumbing.

Disposers are available with power ratings between $\frac{1}{3}$ and 1 HP (horsepower). More powerful models bog down less under load and the motors last longer because they don't have to work as hard. They are also costlier.

TOOLS & MATERIALS

Screwdriver	Putty knife
Channel-type pliers	Mineral spirits
Spud wrench (optional)	Plumber's putty
Hammer	Wire caps
Hacksaw or tubing cutter	Hose clamps
Kitchen drain supplies	Threaded wye fitting
Drain auger	Electrical tape

Choose a switch option that meets your family's safety needs. A "continuous feed" disposer may be controlled by a standard on-off switch on the wall. Another option is a disposer that stays on only when the switch is actively pressed. A "batch feed" disposer can turn on only when a lid is locked onto it, eliminating the possibility of harming fingers. Some models are controlled at the lid, without a wall switch. Continuous food disposers are the most common.

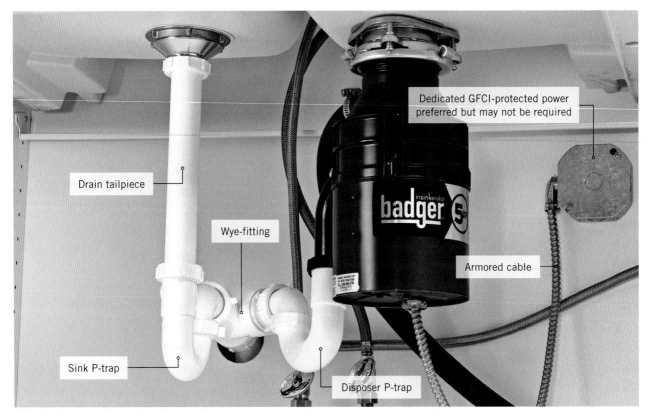

A properly functioning food disposer that's used correctly can help reduce clogs. Some plumbers use separate P-traps for the disposer and the drain outlet tube as shown here. Others contend that configuring the drain line with a single P-trap minimizes the chance that a trap will have its water seal broken by suction from the second trap.

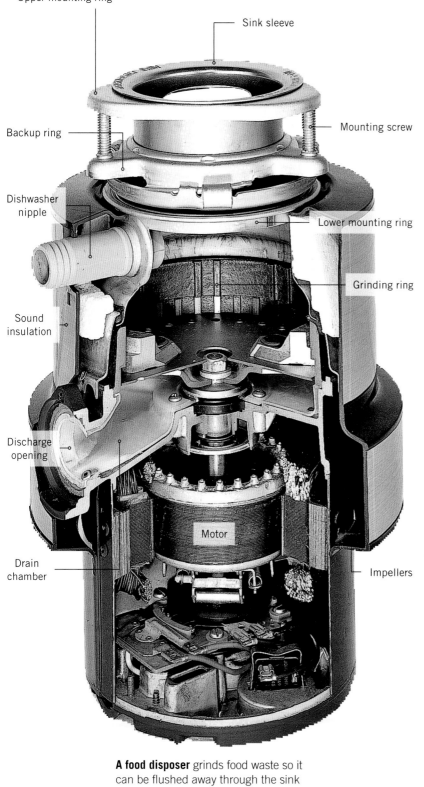

Upper mounting ring

Sink sleeve

Backup ring

Mounting screw

Dishwasher nipple

Lower mounting ring

Grinding ring

Sound insulation

Discharge opening

Motor

Drain chamber

Impellers

A food disposer grinds food waste so it can be flushed away through the sink drain system. A quality disposer has a ½–horsepower, or larger, self-reversing motor. Other features to look for include foam sound insulation, a grinding ring, and overload protection that allows the motor to be reset if it overheats. Better food disposers have a 5-year manufacturer's warranty.

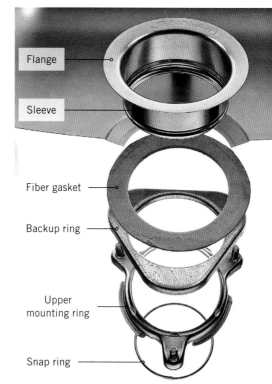

Flange

Sleeve

Fiber gasket

Backup ring

Upper mounting ring

Snap ring

The disposer is attached directly to the sink sleeve, which comes with the disposer and replaces the standard sink strainer. A snap ring fits into a groove around the sleeve of the strainer body to prevent the upper mounting ring and backup ring from sliding down while the upper mounting ring is tightened against the backup ring with mounting screws. Use a fiber gasket compressor when the mounting screws are tightened to create a better seal under the flange.

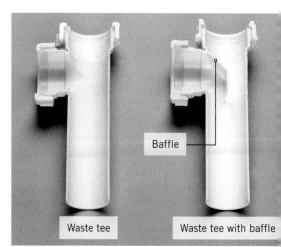

Baffle

Waste tee

Waste tee with baffle

Kitchen and drain tees are required to have a baffle if the tee is connected to a dishwasher or disposer. The baffle is intended to prevent discharge from finding its way up the drain and into the sink.

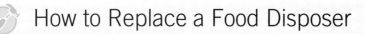

How to Replace a Food Disposer

Remove the old disposer if you have one. You'll need to disconnect the drain pipes and traps first. If your old disposer has a special wrench for the mounting lugs, use it to loosen the lugs. Otherwise, use a screwdriver. If you do not have a helper, place a solid object directly beneath the disposer to support it before you begin removal. **Important: Shut off electrical power at the main service panel before you begin removal.** Disconnect the wire leads, cap them, and stuff them into the electrical box.

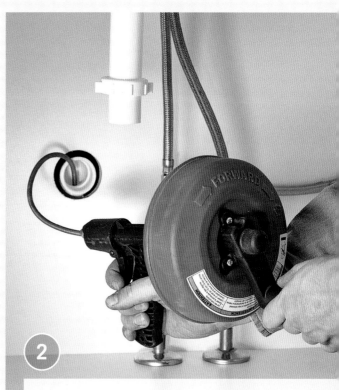

Clear the drain lines all the way to the branch drain before you begin the new installation. Remove the trap and trap arm first.

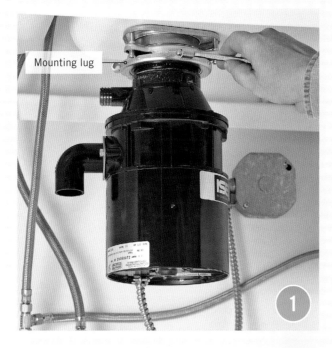

Mounting lug

Upper mounting ring

Lower mounting ring

Snap ring

Sink sleeve

Disassemble the mounting assembly and then separate the upper and lower mounting rings and the backup ring. Also remove the snap ring from the sink sleeve. See photo, previous page.

Press the flange of the sink sleeve for your new disposer into a thin coil of plumber's putty that you have laid around the perimeter of the drain opening. The sleeve should be well-seated in the coil.

Slip the fiber gasket and then the backup ring onto the sink sleeve, working from inside the sink base cabinet. Make sure the backup ring is oriented the same way it was before you disassembled the mounting assembly.

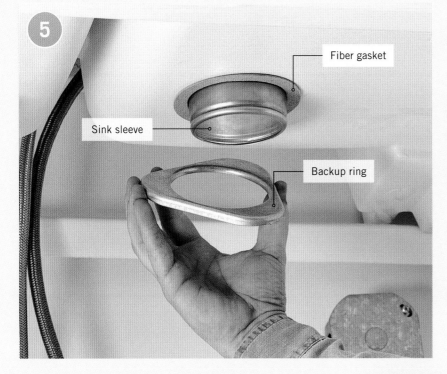

Fiber gasket

Sink sleeve

Backup ring

Insert the upper mounting ring onto the sleeve with the slotted ends of the screws facing away from the backup ring so you can access them. Then, holding all three parts at the top of the sleeve, slide the snap ring onto the sleeve until it snaps into the groove.

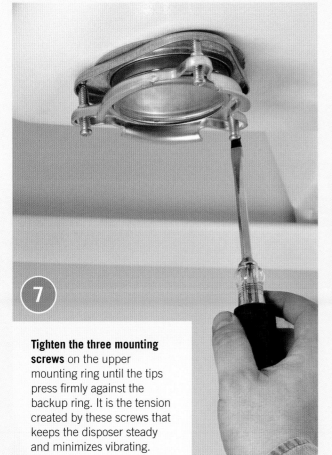

Tighten the three mounting screws on the upper mounting ring until the tips press firmly against the backup ring. It is the tension created by these screws that keeps the disposer steady and minimizes vibrating.

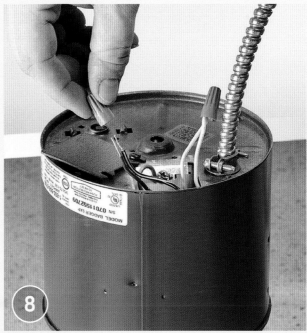

Make electrical connections before you mount the disposer unit on the mounting assembly. Shut off the power at the service panel if you have turned it back on. Remove the access plate from the disposer. Attach the white and black branch circuit wires from the electrical box to the white and black wires (respectively) inside the disposer. Twist a small wire cap onto each connection and wrap it with electrical tape for good measure. Also attach the green ground wire from the box to the grounding terminal on your disposer.

(continued)

Knock out the plug in the disposer port if you will be connecting your dishwasher to the disposer. If you have no dishwasher, leave the plug in. Insert a large flathead screwdriver into the port opening and rap it with a mallet. Retrieve the knock-out plug from inside the disposer canister.

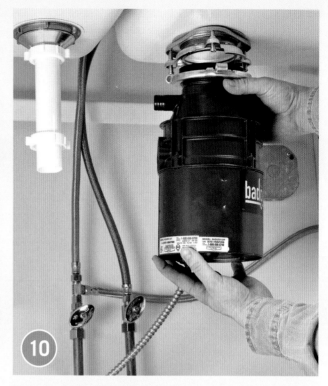

Hang the disposer from the mounting ring attached to the sink sleeve. To hang it, simply lift it up and position the unit so the three mounting ears are underneath the three mounting screws and then spin the unit so all three ears fit into the mounting assembly. Wait until after the plumbing hookups have been made to lock the unit in place.

Attach the discharge tube to the disposer according to the manufacturer's instructions. It is important to get a very good seal here, or the disposer will leak. Go ahead and spin the disposer if it helps you access the discharge port.

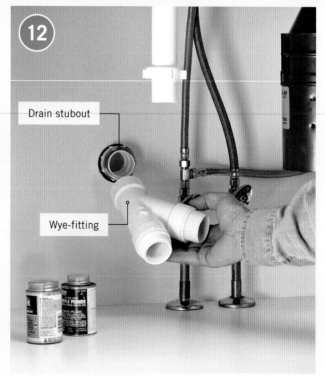

Drain stubout

Wye-fitting

Attach a Wye-fitting at the drain stubout. The Wye-fitting should be sized to accept a drain line from the disposer and another from the sink. Adjust the sink drain plumbing as needed to get from the sink P-trap to one opening of the Wye.

Install a trap arm for the disposer in the open port of the Wye-fitting at the wall stubout. Then, attach a P-trap or a combination of a tube extension and a P-trap so the trap will align with the bottom of the disposer discharge tube.

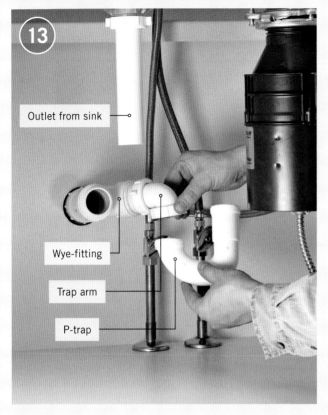

Outlet from sink

Wye-fitting

Trap arm

P-trap

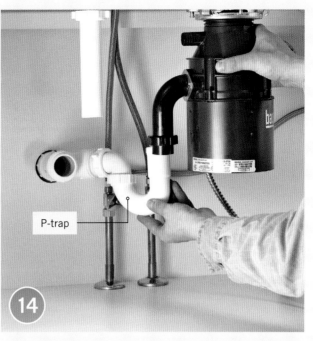

P-trap

Spin the disposer so the end of the discharge tube is lined up over the open end of the P-trap and confirm that they will fit together correctly. If the discharge tube extends down too far, mark a line on it at the top of the P-trap and cut at the line with a hacksaw. If the tube is too short, attach an extension with a slip joint. You may need to further shorten the discharge tube first to create enough room for the slip joint on the extension. Slide a slip nut and beveled compression washer onto the discharge tube and attach the tube to the P-trap.

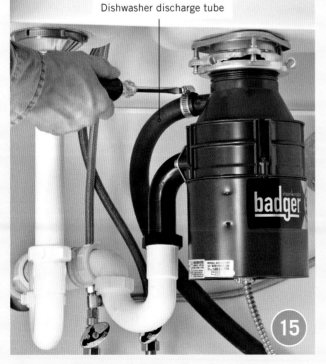

Dishwasher discharge tube

Connect the dishwasher discharge tube to the inlet port located at the top of the disposer unit. This may require a dishwasher hookup kit. Typically, a hose clamp is used to secure the connection.

Lock the disposer into position on the mounting ring assembly once you have tested to make sure it is functioning correctly and without leaks. Lock it by turning one of the mounting lugs until it makes contact with the locking notch.

Water Heaters

Water heaters typically last for at least 10 years, but once they start to show signs of aging, it's a good idea to replace them with a new, more efficient appliance.

Replacing a water heater is a relatively easy DIY plumbing task, as long as it is a like-for-like replacement. In an ideal situation, you'd replace the old unit with one of the exact same size and make, and thereby avoid having to move any gas, water, or electrical lines. But if you choose to upgrade or downgrade in size, you'll find that relocating the necessary lines isn't that difficult. Although you can usually realize some energy cost savings in the long run, be aware that replacing an electric water heater with a gas-fueled model requires installing a vent and an approved combustion air source (and usually a permit).

It is a commonly held belief that a water heater should last around 10 years. The longevity depends on many factors, including initial quality, usage levels, maintenance diligence, and other miscellaneous factors such as hardness of water. While it is everyone's goal to get as much use out of our major appliances as possible, it is also undeniable that the best time to replace a water heater is before it leaks and fills your basement with water. It's a bit of a gamble, but once your old heater starts showing signs of wear and perhaps even acting up a bit, go ahead and make the change.

Water heaters for primary duty in residences range in size from 30 gallons to 65 gallons. For a family of four, a 40- or 50-gallon model should be adequate. While you don't want to run out of hot water every morning, you also don't want to pay to heat more water than you use. Base your choice on how well your current water heater is meeting your demand.

Follow local codes when choosing the pipe and fittings for both gas and water. Make sure there is a gas shutoff within 5 feet of the water heater. Also, there should be a union between the shutoff and the water heater, so pipes can be easily dismantled for service.

TOOLS & MATERIALS

Tubing cutter	Screwdriver	Discharge tube	Gas supply pipe and fittings
Hacksaw	MAPP torch kit	Garden hose	Copper soldering supplies
Pipe wrenches (2)	Appliance dolly	Drain pan	Leak detector solution
Adjustable wrench	Water heater	Pipe thread lubricant	Ball-type water shutoff valve
Channel-type pliers	T & P relief valve	Vent pipe elbow	

The nameplate on the side of a water heater lists tank capacity, insulation R-value, and working pressure (pounds per square inch). More efficient water heaters have an insulation R-value of 7 or higher. The nameplate for an electric water heater includes the voltage and the wattage capacity of the heating elements and thermostats. Water heaters also have a yellow energy guide label that lists typical yearly operating costs.

Use armored cable or wires housed in metal conduit to bring electrical power to electric water heaters. The armored cable or conduit should enter the top of the unit through a conduit clamp.

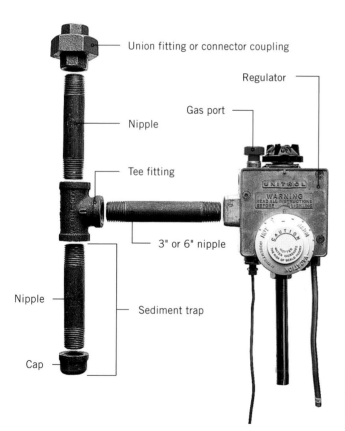

- Union fitting or connector coupling
- Regulator
- Gas port
- Nipple
- Tee fitting
- 3" or 6" nipple
- Nipple
- Sediment trap
- Cap

Install a sediment trap between the gascock and the gas port on your gas water heater. A sediment trap is simply a vertical pipe nipple that is installed at the base of the union to allow any impurities in the fuel to collect rather than being drawn into the combustion chamber through the port. In most cases it is easier to locate the sediment trap at the water heater connection point, not the gascock fitting on the supply pipe.

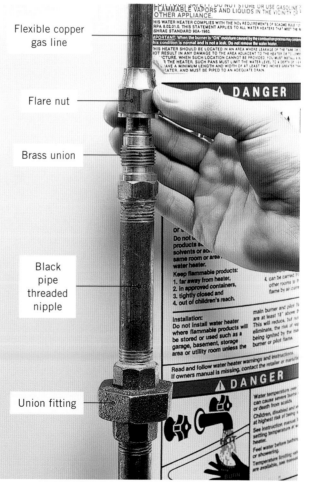

- Flexible copper gas line
- Flare nut
- Brass union
- Black pipe threaded nipple
- Union fitting

If your house has soft copper gas supply lines, use a flare fitting to connect an additional threaded nipple from the black pipe assembly that connects to the water heater regulator. If you have black pipe supply lines, use a union fitting.

Gas Water Heater

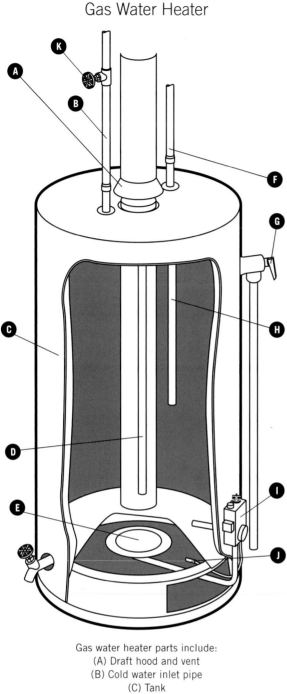

Electric Water Heater

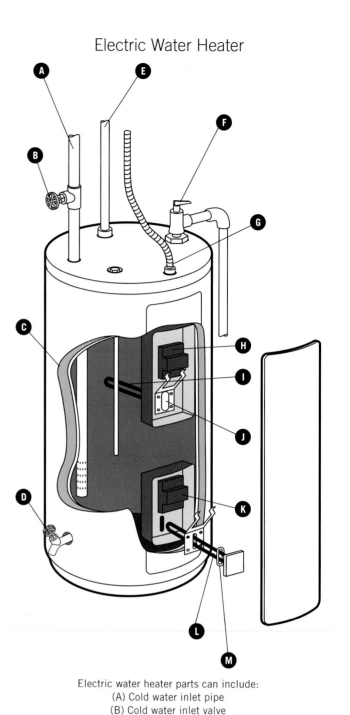

Gas water heater parts include:
(A) Draft hood and vent
(B) Cold water inlet pipe
(C) Tank
(D) Dip tube
(E) Gas burner
(F) Hot water outlet
(G) Temperature/pressure relief valve
(H) Anode rod
(I) Thermostat
(J) Thermocouple
(K) Cold water inlet valve

Electric water heater parts can include:
(A) Cold water inlet pipe
(B) Cold water inlet valve
(C) Insulation
(D) Draincock
(E) Hot water outlet pipe
(F) Temperature/pressure relief valve
(G) Power cable
(H) Upper heating element thermostat
(I) Upper heating element
(J) Bracket
(K) Lower heating thermostat
(L) Lower heating element
(M) Gasket

Gas water heaters operate on either propane or natural gas and are generally very economical to run. They do cost a bit more than electric heaters up front. The following installation features a gas water heater. Check with your local building department to find out if homeowners are allowed to install gas appliances in your municipality.

Electric water heaters require 240-volt service, which might overload your service panel if you are replacing a gas heater with an electric model. Their primary advantage is that they are cheaper to purchase (but not to operate) and they do not require that you make gas connections.

How to Remove a Water Heater

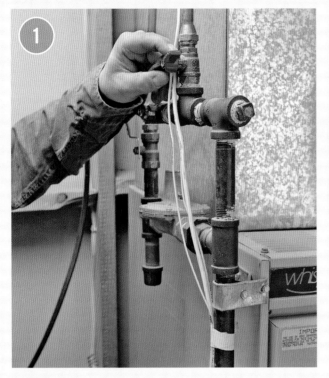

Shut off the gas supply at the stopcock installed in the gas line closest to the water heater. The handle of the stopcock should be perpendicular to the gas supply pipe. Also shut off the water supply.

Drain the water from the old heater by hooking a garden hose up to the sillcock drain and running it to a floor drain. If you don't have a floor drain, drain the water into buckets. For your personal safety, wait until the water heater has been shut off for a couple of hours before draining it.

Disconnect the gas supply from the water heater. To do so, loosen the flare fitting with two wrenches or pliers in a soft copper supply line or loosen the union fitting with two pipe wrenches for black pipe supply lines (right photo).

(continued)

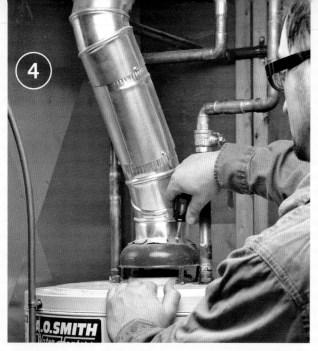

Disconnect the vent pipe from the draft hood by withdrawing the sheet metal screws connecting the parts. Also remove vent pipes up to and including the elbow so you may inspect them for corrosion buildup and replace if needed.

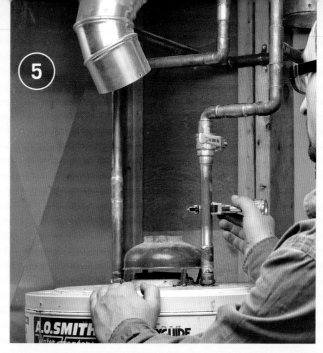

Cut the water supply lines. Prior to cutting, shut off the cold water supply either at the stop valve downline from the heater or at the water meter. Replace the shutoff valve with a new ball-type shutoff valve.

INSTALL A RELIEF VALVE

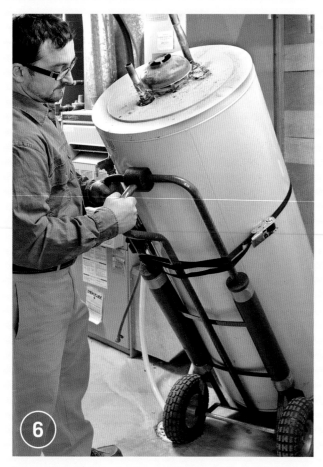

Remove the old water heater and dispose of it properly. Most trash collection companies will haul it away for $20 or $30. Don't simply leave it out at the curb unless you know that is allowed by your municipal waste collection department. A two-wheel truck or appliance dolly is a big help here. Water heaters usually weigh around 150 pounds.

Prepare the new water heater for installation. Before you put the water heater in place, add a T & P relief valve at the valve opening. Make sure to read the manufacturer's instructions and purchase the recommended valve type. Lubricate the threads and tighten the valve into the valve opening with a pipe wrench.

How to Install a Gas Water Heater

Remove the old unit (see previous pages) and position the new unit in the installation area. A drip pan is required if the water heater is installed where a leak could cause damage. This usually means anywhere except a crawlspace or an unfinished basement. If the water heater is not level, level it by shimming under the bottom with a metal or composite shim.

Hose bib

Drip pan

Attach a discharge tube to the T & P relief valve. You may use either copper pipe or CPVC drain pipe. Cut the tube so the free end is between 1½ and 6" above the floor. If you have floorcoverings you wish to protect, add a 90-degree elbow and a copper drain tube that leads from the discharge tube to a floor drain.

Attach the draft hood for the flue to the top of the unit with the provided hardware. Attach any other connector parts that are not preattached according to the manufacturer's instructions.

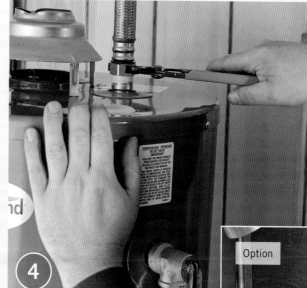

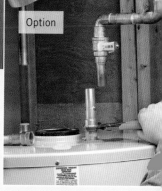

Option

Attach approved supply connectors to the inlet and outlet ports at the top of the appliance. Flexible connectors are much easier to work with, but you may use copper tubing if you prefer. If using copper, you'll need a red-coded copper nipple for the outlet port and a blue-coded copper nipple for the inlet port (inset photo).

(continued)

Assemble the vent and attach the end to the draft hood for the flue.

Join the supply connectors to the supply tubing with approved couplings. If the supply line feeding the water heater has no shutoff valve nearby, it is recommended that you add one. As long as there is a shutoff on the incoming supply side you do not need one on the outgoing (hot water) line.

Begin making the gas connections. Working with gas pipes and tubing is dangerous and you should only attempt it if you have considerable experience in this skill area. If you are not comfortable working with gas pipe, hire a plumber to take on this part of the job. You'll still save plenty of money by doing the rest of the work yourself. Begin by screwing the male-threaded union securely into the gas regulator port. Wrap gas-approved lubricating tape around the threads first. Tighten with channel-type pliers, taking care not to overtighten or cause undue pressure on the regulator.

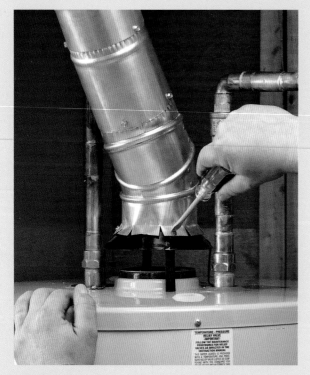

OPTION: If you are running a new vent, you will most likely need to use an elbow fitting and adjustable fittings to achieve the configuration you need. The new vent should be inspected and approved by your local building department.

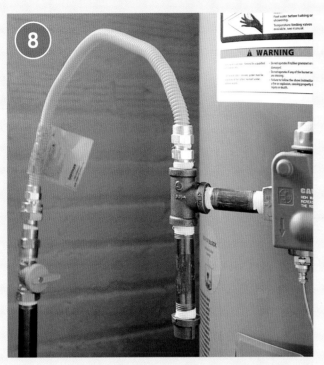

Connect a flexible gas supply tube to the port on a shutoff valve on the gas supply line. The shutoff must be within six feet of the appliance. Connect the other end to the union at the regulator. Wrap the threads in each threaded connection with three or four tight courses of gas-rated lubricating tape first. Include a sediment trap in the hook-up (see page 43).

Turn on the gas supply and test the gas connections with testing solution (inset photo) to make sure there are no leaks—do not use dish soap or any other products that may contain chlorides. Make sure the tank drain valve is closed, then turn on the water supply and check for water leaks. Once you have determined there are no plumbing leaks, light the pilot light (the instructions are always printed on a label near the pilot light).

HOOKING UP ELECTRIC WATER HEATERS

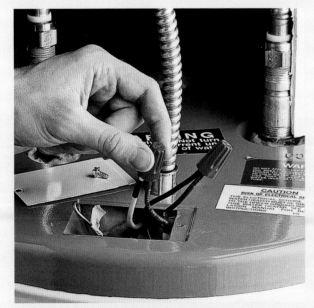

The fuel supply connection is the only part of installing an electric water heater that differs from installing a gas heater, except that electric heaters do not require a vent. The branch circuit wires (240 volts) are twisted together with mating wires in the access panel located at the top of the unit.

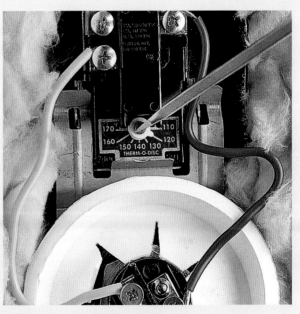

Temperature adjustments on electric water heaters are made by tightening or loosening a thermostat adjustment screw located near the heating element. Always shut off power to the unit before making an adjustment. In this photo you can see how close the live terminals for the heating element are to the thermostat.

Tankless Water Heater

A tankless water heater, as its name indicates, does not keep a tankful of hot water at all times. It heats water only when a hot-water faucet is opened, and so is also called an "on-demand" water heater. A tankless unit can cost a good deal more initially than a standard tank unit, but it typically saves enough in energy costs to pay back the investment within three to five years. Another advantage: you'll never run out of hot water.

Consult with your salesperson to choose a unit large enough to supply all the hot water you may simultaneously need. The model shown, for instance, is rated at nearly 200,000 BTUs and can supply up to 9.5 gallons per minute (GPM), supplying enough hot water for two or three faucets (including shower faucets) or appliances at a time. In addition to a whole-house unit like this, you may also purchase a smaller "point-of-use" unit to supply hot water for, say, a single bathroom. Many of these units are small enough to fit inside a cabinet.

The following pages show installing a gas-fired condensing tankless water heater, which is more efficient than non-condensing units. It requires running two PVC vent pipes out the wall or roof.

This is a pretty ambitious project but within reach of a do-it-yourselfer with good plumbing skills. Consult with your local building department and get a permit before starting work. You will likely need to have the project inspected.

Select a suitable location, perhaps right where the old tank unit was. Always read and follow the manufacturer's installation instructions. It should be near the main cold-water supply pipe and a hot-water pipe leading to the house's faucets and appliances. You will need an electrical receptacle and gas supply line to run vent pipes out the wall or up through the roof.

A tankless water heater can be installed near the old water heater's location to minimize new water and gas pipe runs. It takes up far less space than a standard tank heater. The unit shown on the following pages is a gas-fired condensing unit, which requires two vent pipes; non-condensing units have only one vent pipe. Vent pipes run outside the house at a downward slope. There are connections and valves for a gas supply, a cold-water supply, and a hot-water line to the house, and the unit can simply be plugged into a 120-volt electrical receptacle.

TOOLS & MATERIALS

Tankless water heater with thermostat	Tubing cutter	Pipe straps	Solder and flux
Drill with screwdriver bit and hole saw	Saw for cutting PVC pipe	Screws	Black gas pipe with pipe dope
Channel-type pliers	Propane torch	PVC pipe	Shutoff valves for water and gas
Pipe wrench	Level	PVC primer and cement	T & P valve
	Electrical tools	Copper supply pipe	

How to Install a Tankless Water Heater

Position the water heater away from combustible materials and where it can be easily accessed for servicing. Mount the unit securely to a wall using the brackets provided, driving screws into studs. If the wall is masonry, use masonry screws or lag screws with shields.

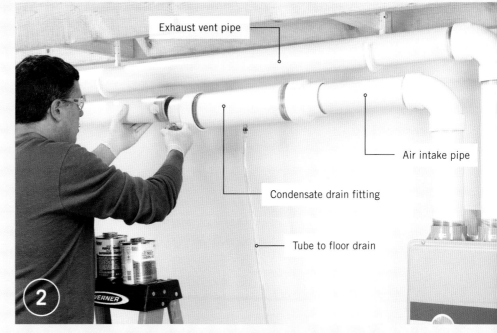

Exhaust vent pipe

Air intake pipe

Condensate drain fitting

Tube to floor drain

Plan the path for the exhaust vent pipe and the air intake pipes, which must exit the house at a recommended location (if the exit location is a house wall, the distance from windows and eaves must meet manufacturers' requirements). Cut PVC pipe and assemble with fittings, using primer and cement. If you live in a cold climate, on the air intake pipe, install a condensate drain fitting at a convenient point for running the drain tube to a floor drain.

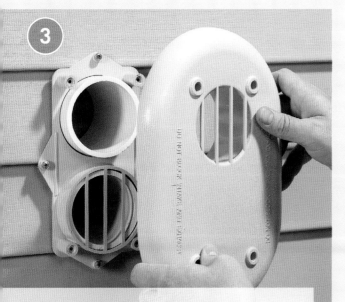

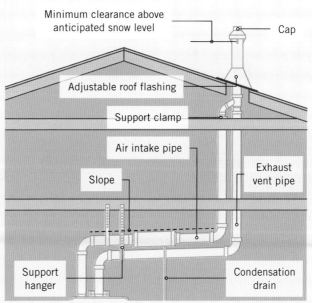

Minimum clearance above anticipated snow level

Cap

Adjustable roof flashing

Support clamp

Air intake pipe

Slope

Exhaust vent pipe

Support hanger

Condensation drain

Run the pipes out of the house. Make sure all horizontally run pipes slope slightly downward, and support pipes with straps. Using the parts from a "termination kit," cut two holes for the pipes, slip on interior flanges, and run the pipes through the flanges and out the wall. On the outside, attach a termination cap with screws, and caulk the edges.

If venting out a wall is not feasible, you may need to run the pipes up and out the roof. In this case, all horizontal runs should be sloped upward, so condensed water runs back into the water heater. In the attic, join the two pipes together with a wye fitting. Run the pipe out the roof, slip on adjustable roof flashing, cut the pipe to the approved height above the roof, and add an approved cap to the top of the pipe.

(continued)

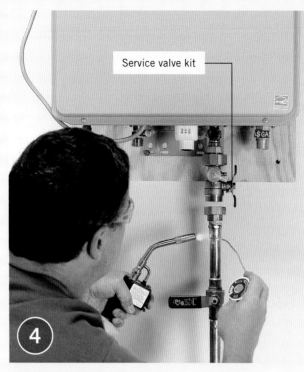

Service valve kit

Turn on the valves to run cold water briefly through the unit, to be sure water flows freely. Close the unit's shutoff valve, then remove and clean the water heater's internal filter (inset). If there is a good deal of debris, repeat this process until the debris is gone.

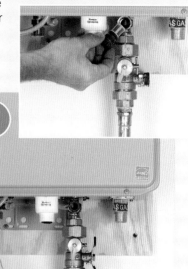

5

4

Hook up the cold-water connections. If your house has copper piping, do not use heat to sweat pipes or fittings that are connected to the tankless heater, or you could damage internal parts. Buy the service valve kit made for your unit. Install a cold-water shutoff valve prior to the connection parts. Connect the cold-water parts. Allow them to cool (if you sweated copper), then connect to the unit's valve.

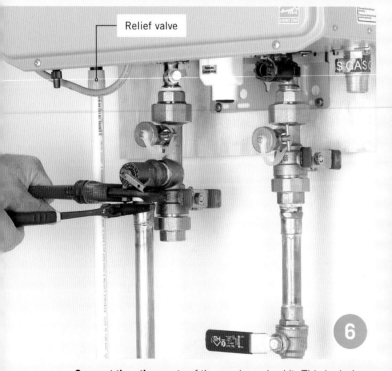

Relief valve

6

7

Drain valve

Connect the other parts of the service valve kit. This includes another valve for the hot water, as well as a relief valve. Extend the relief valve's pipe down to a point near where it can run to a floor drain. Also run a drain tube from the unit to a floor drain or utility sink.

Connect to the house's hot-water line. Provide for a drain valve as shown, so you can drain the tank for service. As with the cold-water line (step 4), if the pipes are copper, do not heat any pipes or fittings while they are connected to the heater.

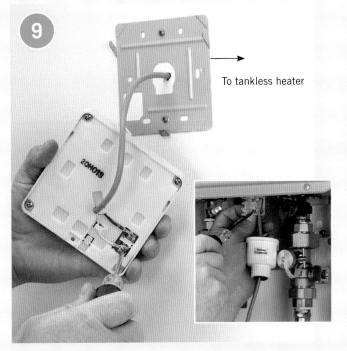

To tankless heater

Hook up the gas connection. Working with black gas pipe, install a gas shutoff valve just below the unit, then install a union so you can easily disconnect the pipes for servicing. Connect the other pipes as shown; make sure to include a vertical sediment trap. Turn on the gas, and test with leak detector solution to make sure there are no leaks.

Connect the thermostat. Connect two-wire thermostat cable to the unit (inset), and run it to a convenient location for controlling the water heater. Attach the thermostat's plate to the wall and run the cable through it. Attach the wires to the back of the thermostat's cover, and snap on the cover.

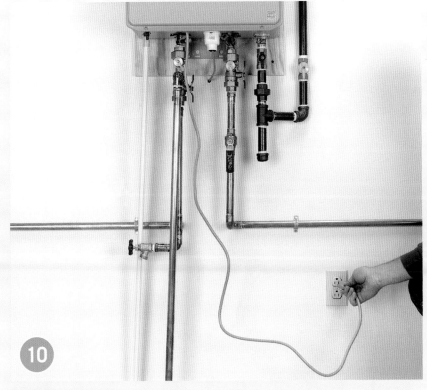

Test the water heater. Turn on the water supply and plug the unit into an electrical receptacle. Make sure you know which circuit breaker controls the water heater. When there is a demand for hot water (from a faucet or appliance), the water heater will turn on automatically and an electric spark will ignite the gas.

Program the thermostat. Turn off the gas and water to the water heater by closing the shutoff valves, and follow the manufacturer's instructions for setting the water temperature.

Bathroom Faucets

One-piece faucets, with either one or two handles, are the most popular fixtures for bathroom installations.

"Widespread" faucets with separate spout and handles are being installed with increasing frequency, however. Because the handles are connected to the spout with flex tubes that can be 18" or longer, widespread faucets can be arranged in many ways.

TOOLS & MATERIALS

Hacksaw or tin snips
Channel-type pliers
Pliers
Basin wrench
Adjustable wrench
Screwdriver
Plumber's putty

Teflon tape
Faucet kit
Pipe joint compound
Flexible supply tubes
Heat-proof grease
Loctite basin

Bathroom sink faucets come in two basic styles: the widespread with independent handles and spout (top); and the single-body, deck-mounted version (bottom).

Bathroom Faucet & Drain Hookups

Widespread lavatory faucets have valves that are independent from the spout so they can be configured however you choose, provided that your flex tube connectors are long enough to span the distance.

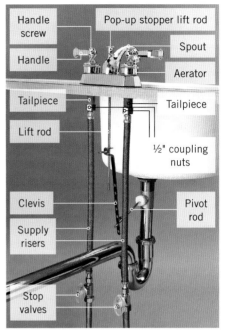

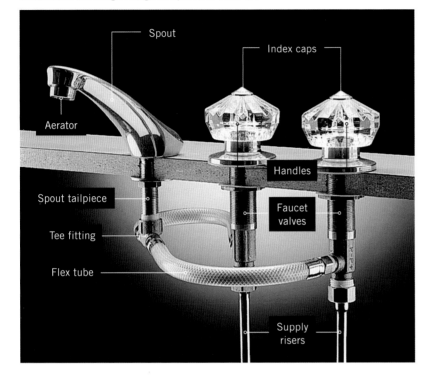

Single-body lavatory faucets have both valves and the spout permanently affixed to the faucet body. They do not offer flexibility in configurations, but they are very simple to install.

The pop-up stopper fits into the drain opening so the stopper will close tightly against the drain flange when the pop-up handle is lifted up.

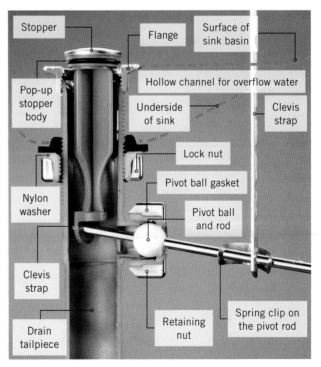

The linkage that connects the pop-up stopper to the pop-up handle fits into a male-threaded port in the drain tailpiece. Occasionally the linkage will require adjustment or replacement.

How to Install a Widespread Faucet

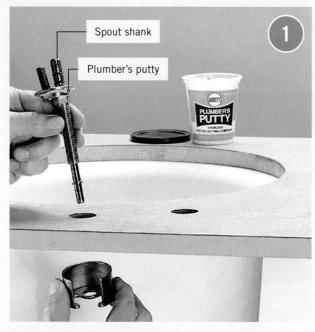

Spout shank

Plumber's putty

(1)

Insert the shank of the faucet spout through one of the holes in the sink deck (usually the center hole, but you can offset it in one of the end holes if you prefer). If the faucet is not equipped with seals or O-rings for the spout and handles, pack plumber's putty on the undersides before inserting the valves into the deck.

NOTE: If you are installing the widespread faucet in a new sink deck, drill three holes of the size suggested by the faucet manufacturer.

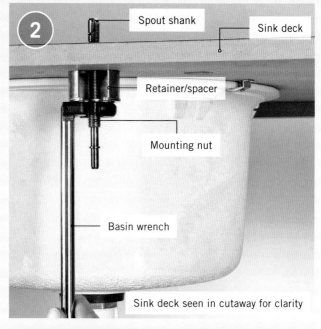

(2)

Spout shank

Sink deck

Retainer/spacer

Mounting nut

Basin wrench

Sink deck seen in cutaway for clarity

In addition to mounting nuts, many spout valves for widespread faucets have an open-retainer fitting that goes between the underside of the deck and the mounting nut. Others have only a mounting nut. In either case, tighten the mounting nut with pliers or a basin wrench to secure the spout valve. You may need a helper to keep the spout centered and facing forward.

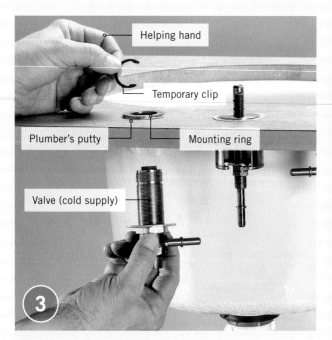

Helping hand

Temporary clip

Plumber's putty

Mounting ring

Valve (cold supply)

(3)

Mount the valves to the deck using whichever method the manufacturer specifies (it varies quite a bit). In the model seen here, a mounting ring is positioned over the deck hole (with plumber's putty seal) and the valve is inserted from below. A clip snaps onto the valve from above to hold it in place temporarily (you'll want a helper for this).

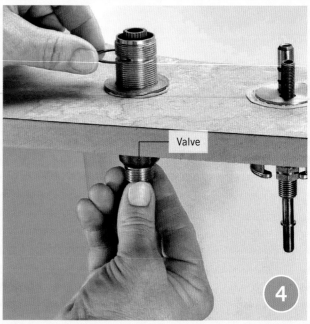

Valve

(4)

From below, thread the mounting nuts that secure the valves to the sink deck. Make sure the cold water valve (usually has a blue cartridge inside) is in the right-side hole (from the front) and the hot water valve (red cartridge) is in the left hole. Install both valves.

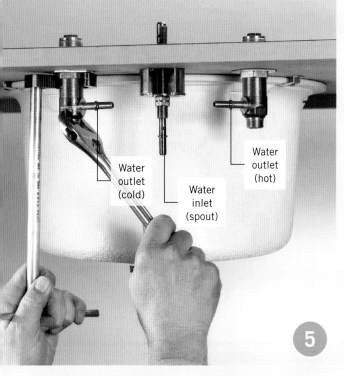

Water outlet (cold)

Water inlet (spout)

Water outlet (hot)

5

Once you've started the nut on the threaded valve shank, secure the valve with a basin wrench, squeezing the lugs where the valve fits against the deck. Use an adjustable wrench to finish tightening the lock nut onto the valve. The valves should be oriented so the water outlets are aimed at the inlet on the spout shank.

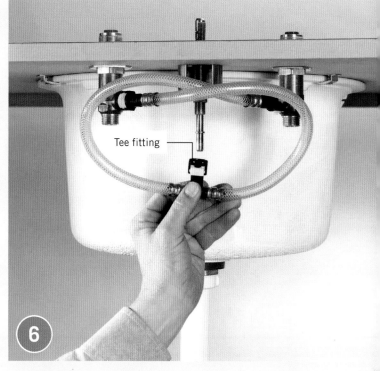

Tee fitting

6

Attach the flexible supply tubes (supplied with the faucet) to the water outlets on the valves. Some twist onto the outlets, but others (like the ones above) click into place. The supply hoses meet in a tee fitting that is attached to the water inlet on the spout.

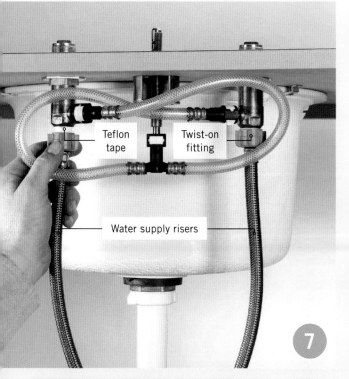

Teflon tape

Twist-on fitting

Water supply risers

7

Attach flexible braided-metal supply risers to the water stop valves and then attach the tubes to the inlet port on each valve (usually with Teflon tape and a twist-on fitting at the valve end of the supply riser).

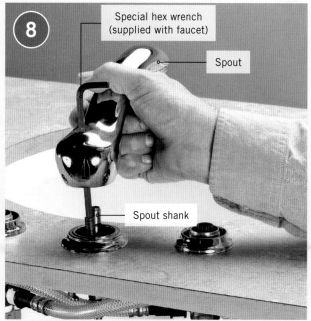

8

Special hex wrench (supplied with faucet)

Spout

Spout shank

Attach the spout. The model shown here comes with a special hex wrench that is threaded through the hole in the spout where the lift rod for the pop-up drain will be located. Once the spout is seated cleanly on the spout shank, you tighten the hex wrench to secure the spout. Different faucets will use other methods to secure the spout to the shank.

(continued)

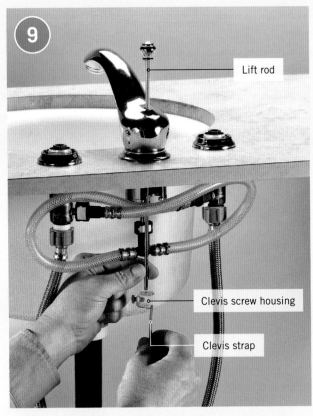

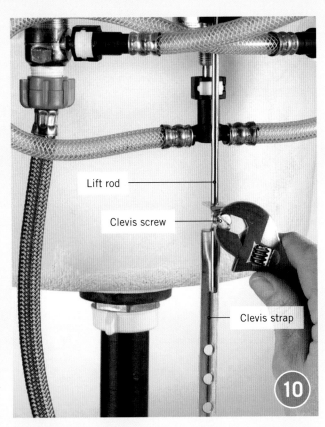

If your sink did not have a pop-up stopper, you'll need to replace the sink drain tailpiece with a pop-up stopper body (often supplied with the faucet). See page 55. Insert the lift rod through the hole in the back of the spout and, from below, thread the pivot rod through the housing for the clevis screw.

Attach the clevis strap to the pivot rod that enters the pop-up drain body, and adjust the position of the strap so it raises and lowers properly when the lift rod is pulled up. Tighten the clevis screw at this point. It's hard to fit a screwdriver in here, so you may need to use a wrench or pliers.

Attach the faucet handles to the valves using whichever method is required by the faucet manufacturer. Most faucets are designed with registration methods to ensure that the handles are symmetrical and oriented in an ergonomic way once you secure them to the valves.

Turn on the water supply and test the faucet. Remove the faucet aerator and run the water for 10 to 20 seconds so any debris in the lines can clear the spout. Replace the aerator.

1

High-quality faucets come with flexible plastic gaskets that create a durable watertight seal at the bottom of the faucet, where it meets the sink deck. However, an inexpensive faucet may have a flimsy-looking foam seal that doesn't do a good job of sealing and disintegrates after a few years. If that is the case with your faucet, discard the seal and press a ring of plumber's putty into the sealant groove on the underside of the faucet body.

Insert the faucet tailpieces through the holes in the sink. From below, thread washers and mounting nuts over the tailpieces, then tighten the mounting nuts with a basin wrench until snug. Put a dab of pipe joint compound on the threads of the stop valves and thread the metal nuts of the flexible supply risers to these. Wrench tighten about a half-turn past hand tight. Overtightening these nuts will strip the threads. Now tighten the coupling nuts to the faucet tailpieces with a basin wrench.

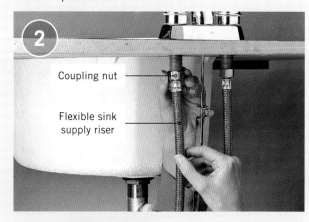

2

Coupling nut

Flexible sink supply riser

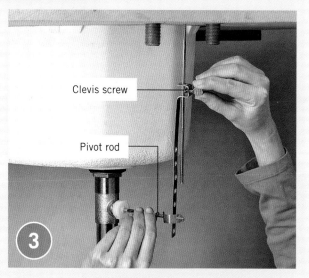

Clevis screw

Pivot rod

3

Slide the lift rod of the new faucet into its hole behind the spout. Thread it into the clevis past the clevis screw. Push the pivot rod all the way down so the stopper is open. With the lift rod also all the way down, tighten the clevis to the lift rod.

4

Grease the fluted valve stems with faucet grease, then put the handles in place. Tighten the handle screws firmly, so they won't come loose during operation. Cover each handle screw with the appropriate index cap—Hot or Cold.

5

Unscrew the aerator from the end of the spout. Turn the hot and cold water taps on full. Turn the water back on at the stop valves and flush out the faucet for a couple of minutes before turning off the water at the faucet. Check the riser connections for drips. Tighten a compression nut only until the drip stops. Replace the aerator.

How to Install a Pop-up Drain

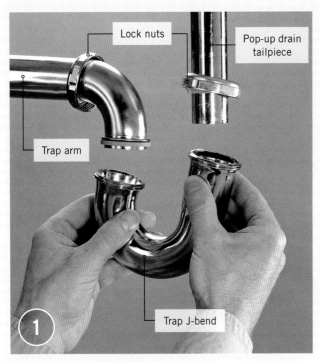

Lock nuts

Pop-up drain tailpiece

Trap arm

Trap J-bend

1

Put a basin under the trap to catch water. Loosen the nuts at the outlet and inlet to the trap J-bend by hand or with channel-type pliers and remove the bend. The trap will slide off the pop-up body tailpiece when the nuts are loose. Keep track of washers and nuts and their up/down orientation by leaving them on the tubes.

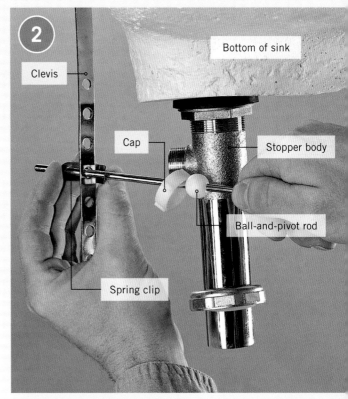

Unscrew the cap holding the ball-and-pivot rod in the pop-up body and withdraw the ball. Compress the spring clip on the clevis and withdraw the pivot rod from the clevis.

2

Clevis

Bottom of sink

Cap

Stopper body

Ball-and-pivot rod

Spring clip

Stopper

Flange

3

Remove the pop-up stopper. Then, from below, remove the lock nut on the stopper body. If needed, keep the flange from turning by inserting a large screwdriver in the drain from the top. Thrust the stopper body up through the hole to free the flange from the basin, and then remove the flange and the stopper body.

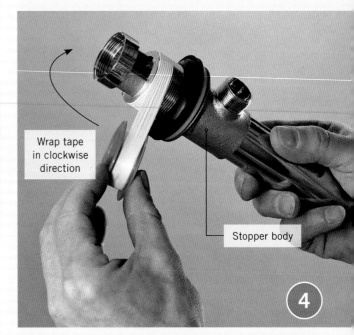

Wrap tape in clockwise direction

Stopper body

4

Clean the drain opening above and below, and then thread the locknut all the way down the new pop-up body, followed by the flat washer and the rubber gasket (beveled side up). Wrap three layers of Teflon tape clockwise onto the top of the threaded body. Make a ½"-dia. snake from plumber's putty, form it into a ring, and stick the ring underneath the drain flange.

Plumber's putty

5

From below, face the pivot rod opening directly back toward the middle of the faucet and pull the body straight down to seat the flange. Thread the locknut/washer assembly up under the sink, then fully tighten the locknut with channel-type pliers. Do not twist the flange in the process, as this can break the putty seal. Clean off the squeezeout of plumber's putty from around the flange.

Drop the pop-up stopper into the drain hole so the hole at the bottom of its post is closest to the back of the sink. Put the beveled nylon washer into the opening in the back of the pop-up body with the bevel facing back.

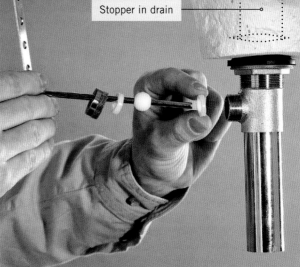

6

Stopper in drain

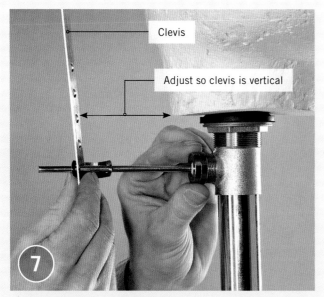

Clevis

Adjust so clevis is vertical

7

Put the cap behind the ball on the pivot rod as shown. Sandwich a hole in the clevis with the spring clip and thread the long end of the pivot rod through the clip and clevis. Put the ball end of the pivot rod into the pop-up body opening and into the hole in the the stopper stem. Screw the cap on to the pop-up body over the ball.

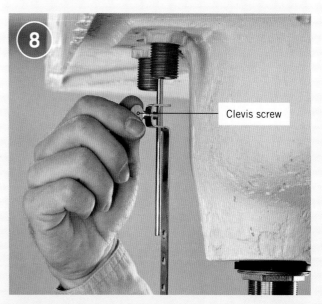

8

Clevis screw

Loosen the clevis screw holding the clevis to the lift rod. Push the pivot rod all the way down (which fully opens the pop-up stopper). With the lift rod also all the way down, tighten the clevis screw to the rod. If the clevis runs into the top of the trap, cut it short with your hacksaw or tin snips. Reassemble the J-bend trap.

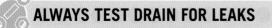

ALWAYS TEST DRAIN FOR LEAKS

To make sure the sink will not leak, do a thorough test. Close the stopper and turn on the faucet to fill the bowl. Once full, open the stopper and look carefully beneath the sink. Feel the trap parts; they should be dry. If there is any indication of moisture, tighten trap parts as needed.

Shower Kits

The fastest and easiest way to create a new shower in your bathroom is to frame in the stall area with lumber and drywall and then install a shower enclosure kit. Typically consisting of three fiberglass or plastic walls, these enclosure kits snap together at the corners and nestle inside the flanges of the shower pan (also called the receptor) to create nearly foolproof mechanical seals. Often, the walls are formed with shelves, soap holders, and other conveniences.

If you are on a tight budget, you can find extremely inexpensive enclosure kits to keep costs down. You can even create your own custom enclosure using waterproof beadboard panels and snap-together connectors. Or, you can invest in a higher grade kit made from thicker material that will last much longer. Some kits are sold with the receptor (and perhaps even the door) included. The kit shown here is designed to be attached directly to wall studs, but others require a backer wall for support. The panels are attached to the backer with high-tack panel adhesive.

A paneled shower surround is inexpensive and easy to install. Designed for alcove installations, they often are sold with matching shower pans (called receptors). A shower surround requires a minimum of 80 inches of clear ceiling height and 24 inches of clear opening area in front of the shower.

TOOLS & MATERIALS

Tape measure	Level	File	Shower enclosure kit	Panel adhesive
Pencil	Strap wrench	Utility knife	Pan (receptor)	Spud wrench
Hammer	Adjustable wrench	Hacksaw	Shower door	Large-head roofing nails
Carpenter's square	Pliers	Masking tape	Showerhead	Jigsaw
Screwdrivers	Drill/driver	Silicone caulk	Faucet	Duct tape
Pipe wrench	Center punch	and caulk gun	Plumbing supplies	Miter box

How to Install a Shower Enclosure

Mark out the location of the shower, including any new walls, on the floor and walls. Most kits can be installed over cementboard, but you can usually achieve a more professional-looking wall finish if you remove the wallcovering and floor covering in the installation area. Dispose of the materials immediately and thoroughly clean the area.

If you are adding a wall to create the alcove, lay out the locations for the studs and plumbing on the new wood sill plate. Also lay out the stud locations on the cap plate that will be attached to the ceiling. Refer to the enclosure kit instructions for exact locations and dimensions of studs. Attach the sill plate to the floor with deck screws and panel adhesive, making sure it is square to the back wall and the correct distance from the side wall.

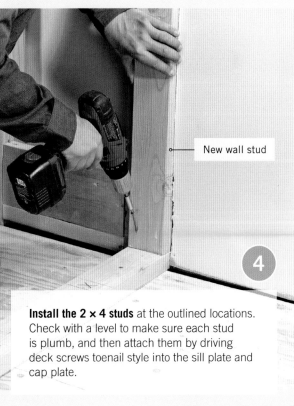

Install the 2 × 4 studs at the outlined locations. Check with a level to make sure each stud is plumb, and then attach them by driving deck screws toenail style into the sill plate and cap plate.

Align a straight 2 × 4 right next to the sill plate and make a mark on the ceiling. Use a level to extend that line directly above the sill plate. Attach the cap plate at that point.

(continued)

Cut an access hole in the floor for the drain, according to the installation manual instructions. Drill openings in the sill plate of the wet wall (the new wall in this project) for the supply pipes, also according to the instructions.

Install a drain pipe and branch line and then trim the drain pipe flush with the floor. If you are not experienced with plumbing, hire a plumber to install the new drain line.

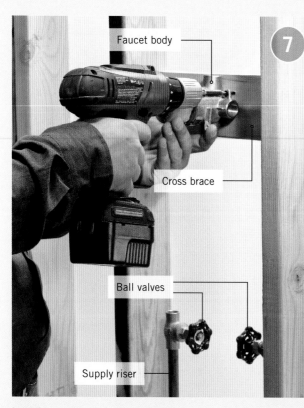

Install new supply risers as directed in the instruction manual (again, have a plumber do this if necessary). Also install cross braces between the studs in the wet wall for mounting the faucet body and shower arm.

If the supply plumbing is located in a wall (old or new) that is accessible from the non-shower side, install framing for a removable access panel.

9 Attach the drain tailpiece that came with your receptor to the underside of the unit, following the manufacturer's instructions precisely. Here, an adjustable spud wrench is being used to tighten the tailpiece.

OPTION: To stabilize the receptor, especially if the floor is uneven, pour or trowel a layer of thinset mortar into the installation area, taking care to keep the mortar out of the drain access hole. Do not apply mortar in areas where the receptor has feet that are intended to make full contact with the floor.

Lay out the locations for the valve hole or holes in the end wall panel that will be installed on the wet wall. Check your installation instructions. Some kits come with a template marked on the packaging carton. Cut the access hole with a hole saw and drill or with a jigsaw and fine-tooth blade. If using a jigsaw, orient the panel so the good surface is facing down.

11

10 Set the receptor in place, check to make sure it is level, and shim it if necessary. Secure the receptor with large-head roofing nails driven into the wall stud so the heads pin the flange against the stud. Do not overdrive the nails.

(continued)

Remove the end wall so you can prepare the installation area for them. If your kit recommends panel adhesive, apply it to the wall or studs. In the kit shown here, only a small bead of silicone sealant on the receptor flange is required.

Clip connectors

Position the back wall so there is a slight gap (about ⅟₃₂") between the bottom of the panel and the rim of the receptor—set a few small spacers on the rim if need be. Tack a pair of roofing nails above the top of the back panel to hold it in place (or, use duct tape). Position both end walls and test the fits. Make clip connections between panels (inset) if your kit uses them.

Reinstall the end panels, permanently clipping them to the back panel according to the kit manufacturer's instructions. Make sure the front edges of the end panels are flush with the front of the receptor.

Once the panels are positioned correctly and snapped together, fasten them to the wall studs. If the panels have predrilled nail holes, drive roofing nails through them at each stud at the panel tops and every 4" to 6" along vertical studs.

Install wallcovering material above the enclosure panels and anywhere else it is needed. Use cementboard, and maintain a gap of ¼" between the shoulders of the top panel flanges and the wallcovering.

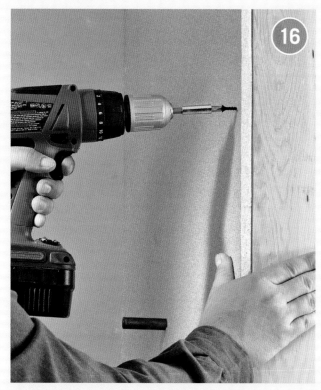

Finish the walls and then caulk between the enclosure panels and the wallcoverings with tub-and-tile caulk.

Access panel

Install the faucet handles and escutcheon and caulk around the escutcheon plate. Install the shower arm escutcheon and showerhead.

You can make an access panel out of plywood framed with mitered case molding, or buy a ready-made plumbing panel. Attach the panel to the opening created in step 8.

How to Install a Hinged Shower Door

Measure the width of the shower opening. If the walls of the shower slope inward slightly before meeting the base, take your measurement from a higher point at the full width of the opening so you don't cut the door base too short. Cut the base piece to fit using a hacksaw and a miter box. File the cut ends if necessary to deburr them.

Place the base jamb on the curb of the shower base. If the joint where the wall meets the curb is sloped, you'll need to trim the corners of the base piece to follow the profile. Place a jamb carefully onto the base and plumb it with a level. Then, mark a drilling point by tapping a centerpunch in the middle of each nail hole in each jamb. Remove the jambs, drill pilot holes, and then attach the jambs with the provided screws.

Identify which side jamb will be the hinge jamb and which will be the strike jamb according to the direction you want your hinged door to swing. Prepare the jambs for installation as directed in your instructions.

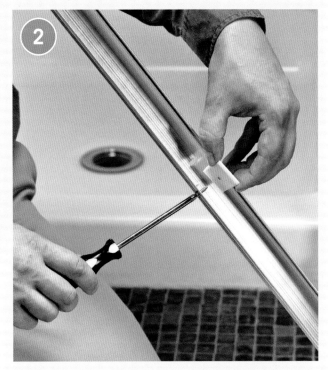

Remove the bottom track and prepare the shower base curb for installation of the base track, following the manufacturer's directions. Permanently install the bottom track. Bottom tracks (not all doors have them) are usually attached to the side jambs or held in place with adhesive. Never use fasteners to secure them to curb.

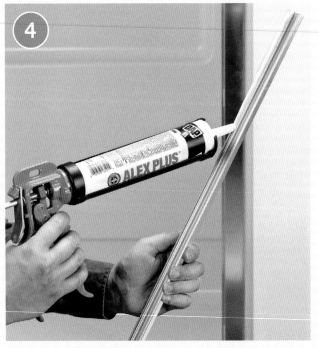

5 Working on the floor or another flat surface, attach the door hinge to the hinge jamb, if required. In most systems, the hinge is fitted over the hinge jamb after you attach it to the wall.

6 Attach the hinge to the door panel, according to the manufacturer's instructions. Attach any cap fitting that keeps water out of the jamb.

7 Fit the hinge jamb over the side jamb and adjust it as directed in your instruction manual. Once the clearances are correct, fasten the jambs to hang the door.

Sweep

8 Install the magnetic strike plate and any remaining caps or accessories such as towel rods. Also attach the sweep that seals the passage, if provided.

Custom Shower Bases

TOOLS & MATERIALS

Tape measure	Thinset mortar
Circular saw	16d galvanized common nails
Hammer	
Utility knife	15# building paper
Stapler	3-piece shower drain
2-ft. level	PVC primer & cement
Mortar mixing box	Galvanized finish nails
Trowel	Galvanized metal lath
Wood float	Thick-bed floor mortar
Felt-tip marker	Latex mortar additive
Ratchet wrench	CPE waterproof membrane & preformed dam corners
Expandable stopper	
Drill	CPE membrane solvent glue
Tin snips	
Torpedo level	CPE membrane sealant
Tools & materials for installing tile	Cementboard & materials
	Utility knife
2 × 4 and 2 × 10 framing lumber	Straightedge

Building a custom-tiled shower base lets you choose the shape and size of your shower rather than having its dimensions dictated by available products. Building the base is quite simple, though it does require time and some knowledge of basic masonry techniques because the base is formed primarily using mortar. What you get for your time and trouble can be spectacular.

Before designing a shower base, contact your local building department regarding code restrictions and to secure the necessary permits. Code requirement will have a major influence on the size and position of the base.

Custom shower bases are designed to be surfaced with tile: usually ceramic, porcelain, or glass. Choose your tile before finalizing the design of the base so you can minimize cutting where possible. Consider that larger floor tile (six by six inch and up) is less likely to develop leaks in the grout lines because there are fewer, and it also requires less cleaning and maintenance than smaller

tiles, such as mosaic. At the same time, however, the existence of more grout lines makes the surface less slippery when wet. Which tile you select is a matter of whether you place higher value on safety or convenience.

Making a custom shower base gives you many options for the shape and size of your shower.

Cross-Section of a Shower Pan

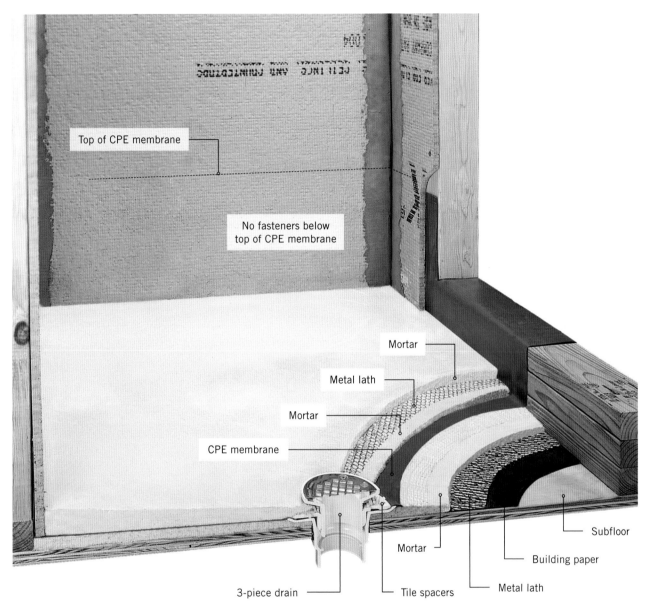

Top of CPE membrane

No fasteners below top of CPE membrane

Mortar

Metal lath

Mortar

CPE membrane

Subfloor

Building paper

Mortar

Metal lath

3-piece drain

Tile spacers

A custom shower pan is a fairly intricate, multi-layered construction, but choosing to build one gives you the ultimate design flexibility.

TIPS FOR BUILDING A CUSTOM SHOWER BASE

A custom-tiled shower base is built in three layers to ensure proper water drainage: the pre-pan, the shower pan, and the shower floor. A mortar pre-pan is first built on top of the subfloor, establishing a slope toward the drain of ¼" for every 12" of shower floor. Next, a waterproof chlorinated polyethylene (CPE) membrane forms the shower pan, providing a watertight seal for the shower base. Finally, a second mortar bed reinforced with wire mesh is installed for the shower floor, providing a surface for tile installation. If water penetrates the tiled shower floor, the shower pan and sloped pre-pan will direct it to the weep holes of the 3-piece drain.

One of the most important steps in building a custom-tiled shower base is testing the shower pan after the CPE membrane has been installed. This allows you to locate and fix any leaks to prevent costly damage.

How to Build a Custom-tiled Shower Base

Remove building materials to expose subfloor and stud walls. Cut three 2 × 4s for the curb and fasten them to the floor joists and the studs at the shower threshold with 16d galvanized common nails. Also cut 2 × 10 lumber to size and install in the stud bays around the perimeter of the shower base. Install (or have installed) drain and supply plumbing.

Staple 15# building paper to the subfloor of the shower base. Disassemble the 3-piece shower drain and glue the bottom piece to the drain pipe with PVC cement. Partially screw the drain bolts into the drain piece, and stuff a rag into the drain pipe to prevent mortar from falling into the drain.

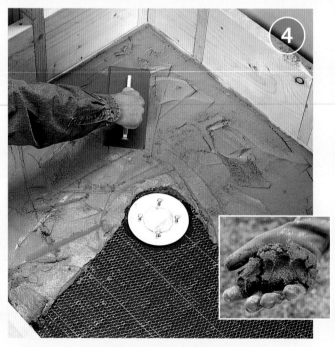

Mark the height of the bottom drain piece on the wall farthest from the center of the drain. Measure from the center of the drain straight across to that wall, then raise the height mark ¼" for every 12" of shower floor to slope the pre pan toward the drain. Trace a reference line at the height mark around the perimeter of the entire alcove, using a level.

Staple galvanized metal lath over the building paper; cut a hole in the lath ½" from the drain. Mix thinset mortar to a fairly dry consistency, using a latex additive for strength; mortar should hold its shape when squeezed (inset). Trowel the mortar onto the subfloor, building the pre-pan from the flange of the drain piece to the height line on the perimeter of the walls.

Continue using the trowel to form the pre-pan, checking the slope using a level and filling any low spots with mortar. Finish the surface of the pre-pan with a wood float until it is even and smooth. Allow the mortar to cure overnight.

Measure the dimensions of the shower floor, and mark it out on a sheet of CPE waterproof membrane, using a felt-tipped marker (be sure to use a high-quality CPE shower liner; less-expensive PVC liners become brittle in time and can develop leaks). From the floor outline, measure out and mark an additional 8" for each wall and 16" for the curb end. Cut the membrane to size, using a utility knife and straightedge. Be careful to cut on a clean, smooth surface to prevent puncturing the membrane. Lay the membrane onto the shower pan.

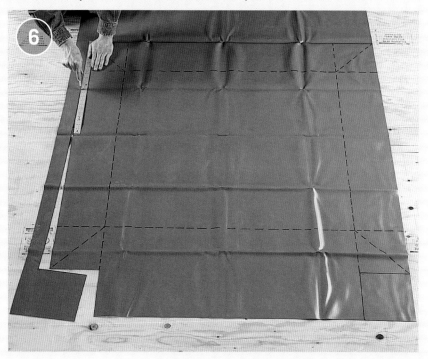

Measure to find the exact location of the drain and mark it on the membrane, outlining the outer diameter of the drain flange. Cut a circular piece of CPE membrane roughly 2" larger than the drain flange, then use CPE membrane solvent glue to weld it into place and reinforce the seal at the drain.

Apply CPE sealant around the drain. Fold the membrane along the floor outline. Set the membrane over the pre-pan so the reinforced drain seal is centered over the drain bolts. Working from the drain to the walls, carefully tuck the membrane tight into each corner, folding the extra material into triangular flaps.

(continued)

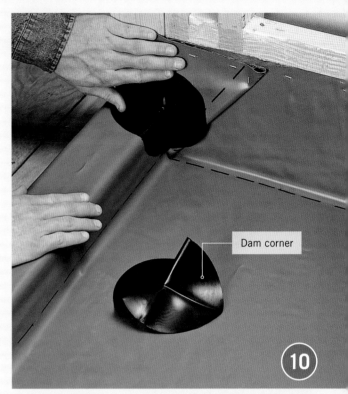

Apply CPE solvent glue to one side, press the flap flat, then staple it in place. Staple only the top edge of the membrane to the blocking; do not staple below the top of the curb, or on the curb itself.

At the shower curb, cut the membrane along the studs so it can be folded over the curb. Solvent glue a dam corner at each inside corner of the curb. Do not fasten the dam corners with staples.

Dam corner

At the reinforced drain seal on the membrane, locate and mark the drain bolts. Press the membrane down around the bolts, then use a utility knife to carefully cut a slit just large enough for the bolts to poke through. Push the membrane down over the bolts.

Use a utility knife to carefully cut away only enough of the membrane to expose the drain and allow the middle drain piece to fit in place. Remove the drain bolts, then position the middle drain piece over the bolt holes. Reinstall the bolts, tightening them evenly and firmly to create a watertight seal.

Test the shower pan for leaks overnight. Plug the drain and fill the shower pan with water, to 1" below the top of the curb. Mark the water level and let the water sit overnight. If the water level remains the same, the pan holds water. If the level is lower, locate and fix leaks in the pan using patches of membrane and CPE solvent.

Install cementboard on the alcove walls, using ¼" wood shims to lift the bottom edge off the CPE membrane. To prevent puncturing the membrane, do not use fasteners in the lower 8" of the cementboard. Cut a piece of metal lath to fit around the three sides of the curb. Bend the lath so it tightly conforms to the curb. Pressing the lath against the top of the curb, staple it to the outside face of the curb. Mix enough mortar for the two sides of the curb.

Apply thinset mortar to the edges of the curb, using a straight board as a guide. When the mortar has set, remove the board and apply thinset to the top of the curb.

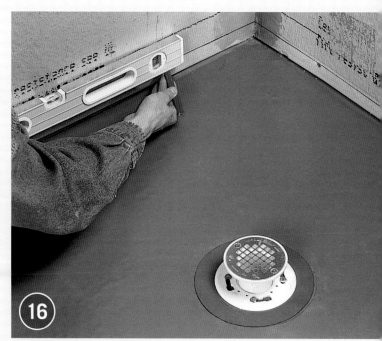

Attach the drain strainer piece to the drain, adjusting it to a minimum of 1½" above the shower pan. On one wall, mark 1½" up from the shower pan, then use a level to draw a reference line around the perimeter of the shower base. Because the pre-pan establishes the ¼" per foot slope, this measurement will maintain that slope.

(continued)

(17)

(18)

Spread tile spacers over the weep holes of the drain to prevent mortar from plugging the holes. Mix the floor mortar, then build up the shower floor to roughly half the planned thickness of this layer. Cut metal lath to cover the mortar bed, keeping it ½" from the drain (see photo in step 18).

Continue to add mortar, building the floor to the reference line on the walls. Use a level to check the slope, and pack mortar into low spots with a trowel. Leave space around the drain flange for the thickness of the tile. Float the surface until it is smooth and slopes evenly to the drain. When finished, allow the mortar to cure overnight before installing the tiles.

(19)

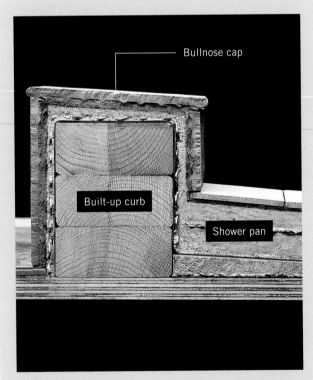

Bullnose cap

Built-up curb

Shower pan

Install the tile. At the curb, cut the tiles for the inside to protrude ½" above the unfinished top of the curb, and the tiles for the outside to protrude ⅝" above the top, establishing a ⅛" slope so water drains back into the shower. Use a level to check the tops of the tiles for level as you work.

OPTION: Apply bullnose cap tiles to the top of the curb, sloping them toward the shower slightly. Make sure cap tiles overhang wall tiles.

Textured surfaces improve the safety of tile floors, especially in wet areas such as this open shower. The shower area is defined by a simple shift in color and size.

Mosaic tile, with its mesh backing and small shapes, works well on walls as well as curved accents around this shower.

The raised curb on this open shower keeps most of the water headed toward the drain. But no matter, the entire bathroom is tiled, so stray droplets are no problem.

Wet Rooms
& Curbless Showers

Wet rooms—a bathroom in which all surfaces are waterproof—have long been a popular choice for upscale remodeling projects and new construction in the UK. But now, thanks to the increasing focus on Universal Design and an ongoing desire for sophisticated bathroom looks, wet rooms are becoming a popular option for American homeowners.

The idea behind a wet room is that moisture doesn't need to be contained in any single area of the room because the whole room is as waterproof as a shower stall. This alleviates the need for divider walls and enclosures, freeing up space and giving a wet room a seamless, streamlined look. Because of the space-saving aspects, wet rooms are particularly well suited for smaller bathrooms.

Installing a wet room involves laying down layers that work together to provide an impermeable barrier to water, in a process called "tanking." That process is made easy with the use of special rubberized waterproof tape and waterproofing compound that is simply rolled onto wall and floor surfaces. Some companies even provide complete wet room kits (see Resources, page 298). The finished surface can be traditional tile (the most common choice), solid panels like the quartz composite surfaces used in contemporary vanity countertops, or sheet flooring, such as vinyl or linoleum.

In practice, the preliminary work is a lot like taping and skim coating a newly drywalled room. The more challenging aspects of wet room installation are making sure all the openings—from drains to water-supply inlets—are properly sealed with special membranes, and correctly sloping the floor to a central drain. Normally, a wet room floor is sloped from all four corners for this purpose, but you can opt for a sleeker look with the use of a concealed linear "trench" drain along one edge of the room. This type of drain requires that the floor be sloped in one direction only.

A curbless shower is a natural part of a wet room. A single wall surface material is commonly used on all walls for ease of installation and to unify the look.

Regardless of the drain used, wet rooms normally include a curbless shower, because there is no need to contain runoff water. Curbless showers present a sleek and sophisticated look, which is why homeowners are choosing to include them in many different bathrooms—including those that are not true wet rooms. Properly installed within an enclosure, a curbless shower can serve a traditional bathroom every bit as well as a raised-pan shower would.

Installing a curbless shower has become a feasible project for even modestly skilled home DIYers thanks to well-thought-out kits that include all the materials you'll need (see page 80). Wet rooms, on the other hand, usually require professional installation to ensure the leaks never become a problem and that all applicable building codes are met.

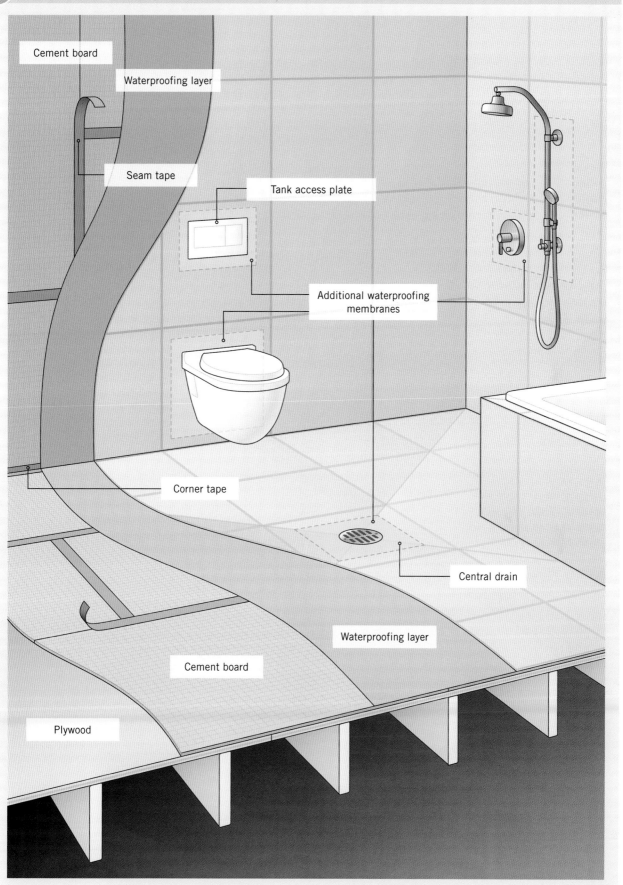

Cement board

Waterproofing layer

Seam tape

Tank access plate

Additional waterproofing membranes

Corner tape

Central drain

Waterproofing layer

Cement board

Plywood

Installing a Curbless Shower

Whether it's part of a complete "wet room," or installed as a standalone feature, a curbless shower combines easy access for those with limited mobility, convenience for other users, and a look that is trendy, sophisticated, and attractive. The trick to installing one of these water features is to ensure the moisture stays inside the shower.

Once upon a time, creating a reliably waterproof enclosure for a curbless shower was no small chore. It meant putting a lot of work into creating a custom shower pan. This kind of project was usually above the skill level or desire of the weekend DIYer, and it generally meant hiring a contractor.

Now you can buy curbless shower pan kits that make installation a breeze. The manufacturers have thought through all the issues that can arise and have developed the kits and shower pans to be as foolproof as possible, while also meeting prevailing codes and best standards and practices. Installing a curbless shower using one of these kits is a realistic project for any home handyperson with even moderate DIY skills and a weekend to spare.

These pans come with preconfigured slopes to ensure optimal drainage away from the shower's edges. The product we used for this project, the Tuff Form kit from Access Reliability Center (See Resources, page 298), includes an offset drain hole that offers the option of rotating the pan in the event of a joist or mechanicals that are in the way. This product is offered in nine different sizes and can be cut with a circular saw to just about any shape—including more unusual, curvy shapes for a truly custom look.

Curbless shower pan manufacturers also sell pans with trench drains for an even sleeker look. The pan we used for this project is typical of the prefab curbless pan construction; it can support 1,100 pounds even though the pan itself weighs less than 70 pounds. It sits right on floor joists, with the addition of blocking to support the area around the drain, and to provide nailing surfaces around the edges.

Kits like these offer advantages beyond the ease of installation and a thoughtful configuration of parts. Usually, the plumbing can be completely adjusted and connected from above, so you won't need to work in the basement or a crawl space, or open up a first-floor ceiling to install a second-floor shower. The kits themselves generally include almost everything you'll need for the installation.

TOOLS & MATERIALS

Circular saw	Putty knife
Caulking gun	Palm sander
Torpedo level	and 120-grit pad
Cordless drill and bits	Scissors
PVC cement and brush	Rubber gloves
Screwdriver	Synthetic paintbrush
Speed square	Roller and roller handle

A curbless shower kit includes almost everything you need. All you have to supply are some basic tools, the tile, and a little elbow grease.

Because a wet room allows the bathroom to be designed with fewer barriers and a single-level floor surface, these rooms are natural partners to a Universal Design approach. If you're thinking about converting a bathroom to a wet room, it's worthwhile to consider a little extra effort to make the space as accessible as possible for the maximum number of users.

Walls. Where codes allow it, consider using thick plywood rather than cementboard for the wall sub-surfaces. Plywood allows for direct installation of grab bars without the need for blocking or locating studs. If you're set on using cementboard, plan out locations for grab bars near toilets, behind and alongside bathtubs, and in showers. Most codes specify that grab bars must be able to support up to 200 pounds—which usually means adding blocking in the walls behind the grab bars.

Shower stall. One of the benefits to adding a curbless shower is easy wheelchair (or walker) access. For maximum accessibility, the shower area should be at least 60 inches wide by at least 36 inches deep (60 inches by 60 inches is preferable). This allows a wheelchair-bound user to occupy the stall with a helper. And, although the idea is a wide-open shower space, it's always a good idea to add a fold down seat. This allows for transfer from a wheelchair, or a place for someone with limited leg strength and endurance to sit.

How to Install a Waterproof Subbase for a Curbless Shower

Remove the existing flooring material in the area of the shower pan (if you're remodeling an existing bathroom). Use a circular saw to cut out and remove the subfloor in the exact dimensions of the shower pan. Finish the cuts with a jigsaw or handsaw.

Reinforce the floor with blocking between joists as necessary. Toenail bridge blocking in on either side of the drain waste pipe location, and between joists anywhere you'll need a nailing surface along the edges of the shower pan. If trusses or joists are spaced more than 16" O.C., add bridge blocking to adequately support the pan.

(continued)

Set the pan in the opening to make sure it fits and is level. If it is not level, screw shims to the tops of any low joists and check again: repeat if necessary until the pan is perfectly level in all directions.

Install or relocate drain pipes as needed. Check with your local building department: if the drain and trap are not accessible from below you may need to have an on-site inspection before you cover up the plumbing.

Check the height of the drainpipe—its top should be exactly 2⅜" from the bottom of the pan—measure down from the top of the joist. If the drainpipe is too high, remove it and trim with a tubing cutter. If it is too low, replace the assembly with a new assembly that has a longer tailpiece.

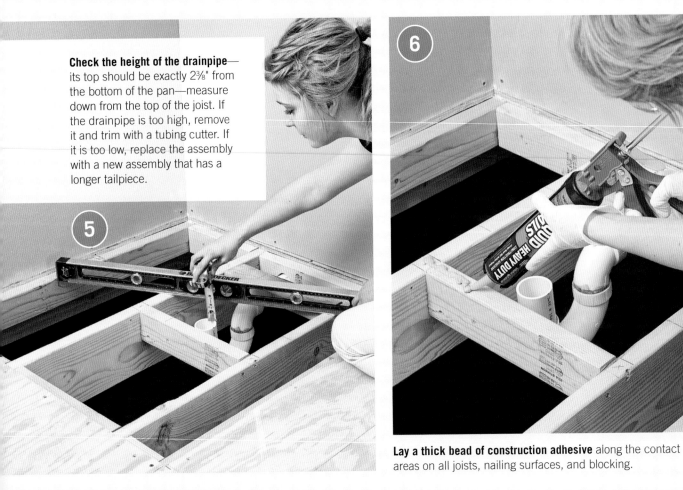

Lay a thick bead of construction adhesive along the contact areas on all joists, nailing surfaces, and blocking.

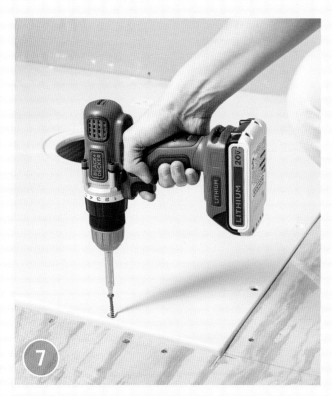

(7)

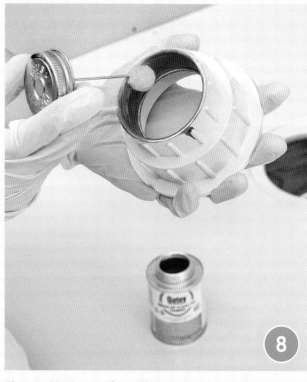

(8)

Set the pan in place and screw it down, using at least 2 screws along each side. Do not overtighten the screws. If you've cut off the screwing flange on one or more sides to accommodate an unusual shape, drill ⅛" pilot holes in the cut edges at joist or blocking locations, and drive the screws through the holes.

Disassemble the supplied drain assembly. Be careful not to lose any of the screws. Place the drain tailpiece on the waste pipe under where the pan's drainhole will be located, and measure to check that it sits at the correct level. Solvent-glue the tailpiece to the end of the waste pipe.

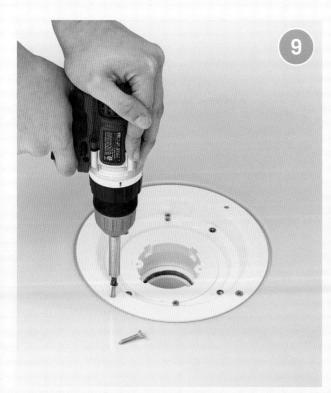

(9)

Thread the tail top piece into the tail through the drain flange. Use a speed square or other lever, such as spread channel lock pliers, to snugly tighten the tail top piece in place.

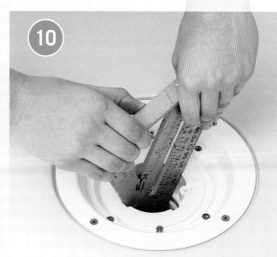

(10)

Position the supplied gaskets on top of the tailpiece (check the manufacturer's instructions; the gaskets usually need to be layered in the correct order). Set the drain flange piece on top of the tail, and into the drain hole in the pan. Drill ⅛" pilot holes through the flange and into the pan. Screw the flange to the pan.

(continued)

Install tile underlayment for the rest of the project area. If the underlayment is higher than the top of the pan once it is installed, you'll have to sand it to level, gradually tapering away from the pan.

Scrape any stickers or other blemishes off the pan with a putty knife. Lightly sand the entire surface of the pan using 120-grit sandpaper to help the sealant adhere. After you're done sanding, wipe down the sanded pan with a damp sponge. Make sure the entire area is clean.

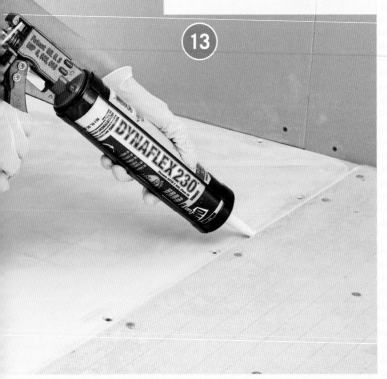

Seal the edge seams at the wall and between the pan and subfloor with waterproof latex sealant. Caulk any pan screw holes that were not used.

Cut strips of waterproofing tape to cover all seams in the tile underlayment (both walls and floor). Also cut strips for the joints where walls and floor meet. Open the pail of liquid waterproofing membrane and mix the liquid thoroughly. Beginning at the top and working down, brush a bed of waterproofing liquid over the seams. Before it dries, set the tape firmly into the waterproofing. Press and smooth the tape. Then brush a layer of waterproofing compound over the tape.

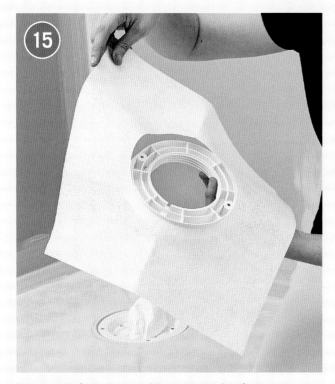

Trace a hole in the center of the waterproof drain gasket, using the bottom of the drain clamping donut. Cut the hole out using scissors. Be careful cutting the gasket because it is a crucial part of the drain waterproofing. Check the fit with the gasket against the underside of the clamping donut top flange.

Apply a thin coat of the waterproofing compound around the drain hole and to the back of the drain gasket. Don't apply too much; if the waterproofing is too thick under the gasket, it may not dry correctly.

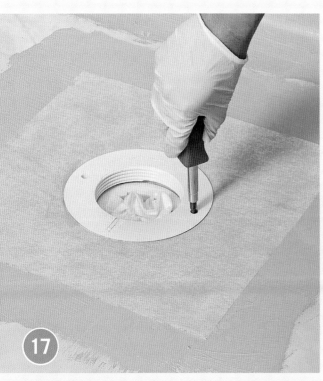

Put the gasket in place and brush a coat of the waterproofing over the gasket. Screw the clamping donut in place on the top of the drain and over the membrane. Hand-tighten the bolts and then cover the clamping donut with the waterproofing compound (avoid covering the slide lock for the drain grate).

Use a roller to roll waterproofing compound across the walls and over the entire pan surface. The ideal is 4mm thick (about the thickness of a credit card). Allow this first coat to dry for 2 hours, then cover with a second coat. This should conclude the waterproofing phase of the project and you're ready to begin laying tile once the waterproofing compound has dried thoroughly.

How to Install Tile for a Curbless Shower

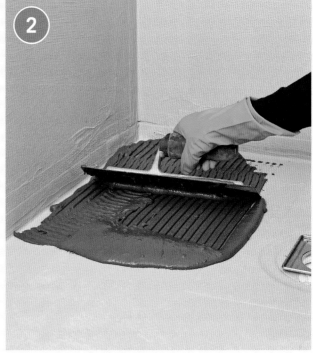

Set the floor tile first. Begin by placing a sample of the floor tile directly next to the drain so you can set the drain grate height to match. The adjustable mounting plate for the grate should be flush with the tops of the tile.

Begin laying floor tile in the corner of the shower. Lay a bed of thinset tile adhesive, using a notched trowel. The thinset container should specify the notch size (⅜" square notch is common).

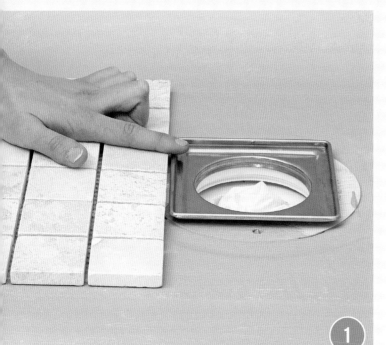

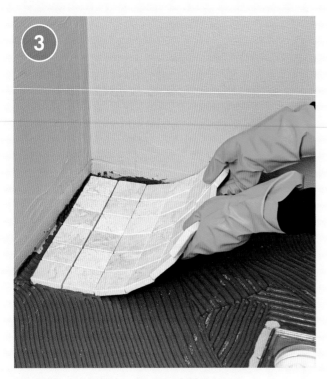

Install tile so a small square of untiled area is left around the drain opening (which, in the system seen here, is square, making for an easier cutting job).

Place the corner tile into the bed of thinset and press it to set it. Don't press down too hard or you will displace too much of the material. Continue laying tile, fanning out from the corner toward the drain opening. Leave space around the drain opening as it is likely you'll need to cut tiles to fit.

Mark the tiles that surround the drain opening for cutting. Leave a small gap between the tiles next to the drain grate mounting plate.

Cut the tiles along the trim lines using a tile saw. If you are not comfortable using a tile saw, score the tiles and cut them with tile nippers.

Apply thinset onto the shower pan, taking care not to get any on the drain grate mounting plate. You may need to use a small trowel or a putty knife to get into small gaps.

Set the cut tiles around the drain opening, doing your best to maintain even gaps that match the gaps in the rest of the floor. Once you've finished tiling around the drain, complete setting floor tile in the rest of the project area.

(continued)

Let the floor tile set overnight and then apply grout. Using a grout sponge, wipe the grout over the gaps so all gaps are filled evenly. After the grout dries, buff the floor with a towel to wipe up excess residue.

Snap the grate cover into the cover mounting plate (if you've stuffed a rag into the drain opening to keep debris out, be sure to remove it first). The grate cover seen here locks in with a small key that should be saved in case you need to remove the grate cover.

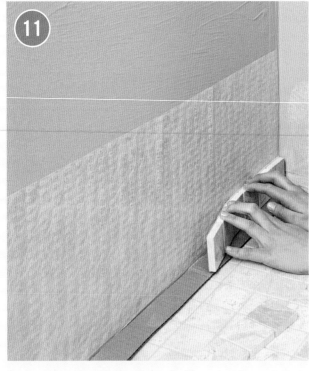

Begin setting the wall tile. Generally, it's easiest if you start at the bottom and work upward. Instead of thinset adhesive, an adhesive mat is being used here. This relatively new product is designed for walls and is rated for waterproof applications. It is a good idea to use a spacer (¼" thick or so) to get an even border at the bottoms of the first tiles.

In the design used here, a border of the same mosaic tile used in the floor is installed all around the shower area to make the first course. Dark brown accent tiles are installed in a single vertical column running upward, centered on the line formed by the shower faucet and showerhead. This vertical column is installed after the bottom border.

Next, another vertical column of accent tiles is installed on each side of the large, dark tiles. These columns are also laid using the floor tile, which connects the walls and floor visually in an effective way.

Finally, larger field tiles that match the floor tile used outside the shower area are installed up to the corner and outward from the shower area. Starting at the bottom, set a thin spacer on top of the border tiles to ensure even gaps.

Grout the gaps in the wall tiles. It's usually a good idea to protect any fittings, such as the shower faucet handle escutcheon, with painters tape prior to grouting. If you wish, a clear surround may be installed to visually define the shower area, as in the photo to the right, but because the shower pan is pitched toward the drain it really is not necessary.

Alcove Bathtubs

TOOLS & MATERIALS

Channel-type pliers	Shims
Hacksaw	Galvanized deck screws
Carpenter's level	Drain-waste-overflow kit
Pencil	1×3, 1×4, 2×4 lumber
Tape measure	Galvanized roofing nails
Saw	Galvanized roof flashing
Screwdriver	Thinset mortar
Drill	Tub & tile caulk
Adjustable wrench	Propane torch
Trowel	

Most of our homes are equipped with an alcove tub (usually 60 inches long) that includes a tub surround and shower function. By combining the tub and the shower in one fixture, you conserve precious bathroom floorspace and simplify the initial installation. Plus, you only have one bathing fixture that needs cleaning.

But because tub/showers are so efficient, they do get a lot of use and tend to have fairly limited lifespans. Pressed steel tubs have enamel finishes that crack and craze; plastic and fiberglass tubs get grimy and stained; even acrylic and composite tubs show wear eventually (and as with other fixtures, styles, and colors change too). Fortunately, today's acrylic and fiberglass tubs have more durable finishes than those made a decade or two ago.

If you are not completely remodeling the bathroom, plan to make the new tub fit with its surroundings. For instance, if you have wall tiles, you'll need to remove some of them in order to remove and replace the tub. Make sure you can buy new tiles that exactly match the size and color of the existing tiles. Also check the width of the new tub; if it is narrower than the old tub, it may leave an untiled space on the floor that you will need to fill.

Plumbing an alcove tub is a relatively difficult job because getting access to the drain lines attached to the tub and into the floor is often very awkward. Although an access panel is required by some codes, the truth is that many tubs were installed without them or with panels that are too small or hard to reach to be of much use. If you are contemplating replacing your tub, the first step in the decision process should be to find the access panel and determine if it is sufficient. If it is not (or there is no panel at all), consider how you might enlarge it. Often, this means cutting a hole in the wall on the adjoining room and also in the ceiling below. This creates more work, of course, but compared to the damage caused by a leaky drain from a subpar installation, making an access opening is little inconvenience.

By replacing a dingy old alcove tub with a fresh new one, you can make the tub and shower area as pleasant to use as it is efficient.

Left hand tub

Right hand tub

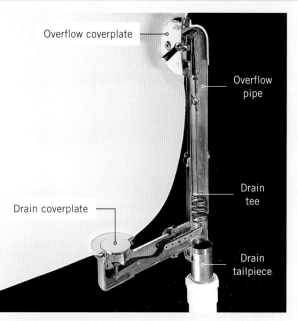

Overflow coverplate

Overflow pipe

Drain coverplate

Drain tee

Drain tailpiece

Choose the correct tub for your plumbing setup.
Alcove-installed tubs with only one-sided aprons are sold as either "left-hand" or "right-hand" models, depending on the location of the predrilled drain and overflow holes in the tub. To determine which type you need, face into the alcove and check whether the tub drain is on your right or your left.

A drain-waste-overflow kit with stopper mechanism must be purchased separately and attached after the tub is set. Available in both brass and plastic types, most kits include an overflow coverplate, an overflow pipe that can be adjusted to different heights, a drain tee fitting, an adjustable drain tailpiece, and a drain coverplate that screws into the tailpiece.

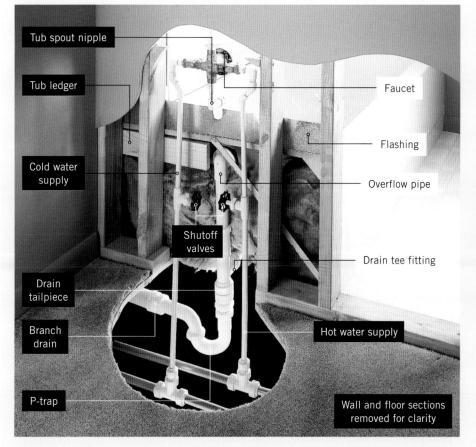

Tub spout nipple

Tub ledger

Cold water supply

Faucet

Flashing

Overflow pipe

Shutoff valves

Drain tailpiece

Branch drain

Drain tee fitting

Hot water supply

P-trap

Wall and floor sections removed for clarity

The supply system for a bathtub includes hot and cold supply pipes, shutoff valves, a faucet and handle(s), and a spout. Supply connections can be made before or after the tub is installed.

The drain-waste-overflow system for a bathtub includes the overflow pipe, drain tee, P-trap, and branch drain. The overflow pipe assembly is attached to the tub before installation.

How to Remove an Alcove Bathtub

Cut the old supply tubes, if you have access to them, with a reciprocating saw and metal cutting blade or with a hacksaw. Be sure to shut off the water supply at the stop valves first. Cut the shower pipe just above the faucet body and cut the supply tubes just above the stop valves.

Remove the faucet handles, tub spout, shower head and escutcheon, and arm. For the spout, check the underside for a set screw and loosen it if you find one. Then, insert a long screwdriver into the spout and turn the spout counterclockwise.

Remove the drain plug, working from the tub side. If the tub has a pop-up drain with linkage, twist the plug to disengage the linkage, and pull the plug and linkage out (inset). You may be able to use the handles of channel-type pliers to unscrew the flange, but a strainer wrench, also called a "dumbbell" tool, works better.

Remove the overflow coverplate (photo above) and then withdraw the pop-up drain linkage through the overflow opening (photo below).

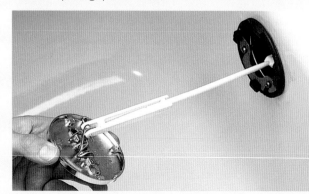

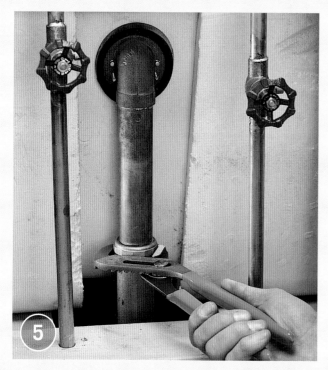

Disconnect the overflow pipe from the drain assembly and remove both parts (your access may not be as unrestricted as seen here). If you need to cut the pipes, go ahead and do it. In most cases, it is difficult to maneuver the tub out with the DWO assembly still attached.

Cut the wall to a line about 6" above the tub rim. Alcove tubs are fastened to the wall studs with nails driven through or above a flange that protrudes up from the rim. You'll need to remove a bit of the wall covering so you can remove the fasteners.

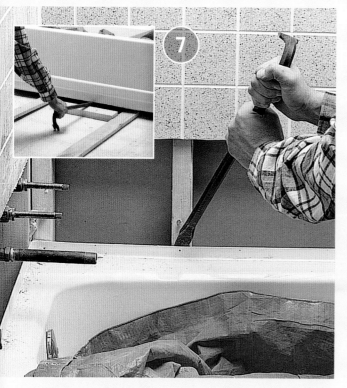

If you can, pry out fasteners and then pull the tub away from the walls by levering between the back rim of the tub and the back wall of the alcove. If it resists, check for adhesive caulk or even flooring blocking the bottom of the apron. If needed, raise the tub and slide a pair of 1 × 4 runners under the skirt edge (inset photo) to make it easier to slide out.

OPTION: Cut stubborn tubs in half to wrangle them out of the alcove. This has the added benefit of making the tubs easier to get out the door, down the stairs, and into the dumpster. If the tub is cast iron, you won't be able to cut it, and because it's so heavy, removing it intact will be difficult. You can break it apart much easier, however, using a sledgehammer. Wear protective clothing and eyewear, and cover everything in the room with a dropcloth before you start swinging.

How to Install a New Alcove Tub

Prepare for the new tub. Inspect and remove old or deteriorated wall surfaces or framing members in the tub area. In just about every case, it makes sense to go ahead and strip off the old alcove wallcoverings and ceiling down to the studs so you can replace them. This also allows you to inspect for hidden damage in the wall and ceiling cavities. Plus, many codes no longer allow the use of moisture-resistant drywall (greenboard) in tub and shower areas. Cementboard should be used instead.

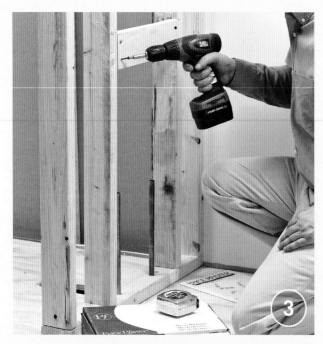

Check the height of the crossbraces for the faucet body and the showerhead. If your family members needed to stoop to use the old shower, consider raising the brace for the showerhead. Read the instructions for your new faucet/diverter and check to see that the brace for the faucet body will conform to the requirements (this includes distance from the surround wall as well as height). Adjust the brace locations as needed.

Check the subfloor for level—if it is not level, use pour-on floor leveler compound to correct it (ask at your local flooring store). Make sure the supply and drain pipes and the shutoff valves are in good repair and correct any problems you encounter. If you have no bath fan in the alcove, now is the perfect time to add one.

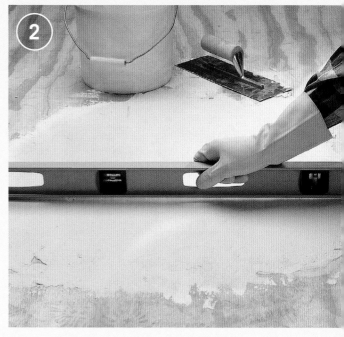

Begin by installing the new water supply plumbing. Measure to determine the required height of your shower riser tube and cut it to length. Attach the bottom of the riser to the faucet body and the top to the shower elbow.

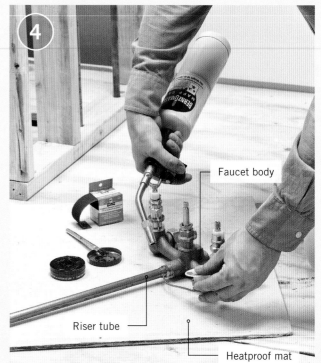

Faucet body

Riser tube

Heatproof mat

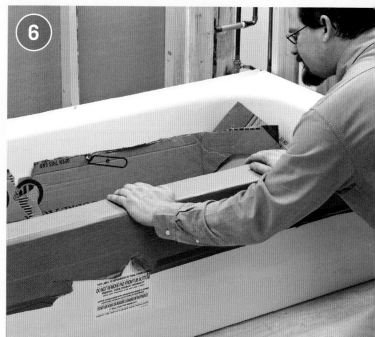

Attach the faucet body to the cross brace with pipe hanger straps. Then, attach supply tubing from the stop valves to the faucet body, making sure to attach the hot water to the left port and cold to the right port. Also secure the shower elbow to its cross brace with a pipe strap. Do not attach the shower arm yet.

Slide the bathtub into the alcove. Make sure tub is flat on the floor and pressed flush against the back wall. If your tub did not come with a tub protector, cut a piece of cardboard to line the tub bottom, and tape pieces of cardboard around the rim to protect the finish from shoes and dropped tools.

Mark locations for ledger boards. To do this, trace the height of the top of the tub's nailing flange onto the wall studs in the alcove. Then remove the tub and measure the height of the nailing flange. Measure down this same amount from your flange lines and mark the new ledger board location.

Install 1 × 4 ledger boards. Drive two or three 3"-galvanized deck screws through the ledger board at each stud. All three walls should receive a ledger. Leave an open space in the wet wall to allow clearance for the DWO kit. Measure to see whether the drain will line up with the tub's DWO. If not, you may need to cut and reassemble the drain.

(continued)

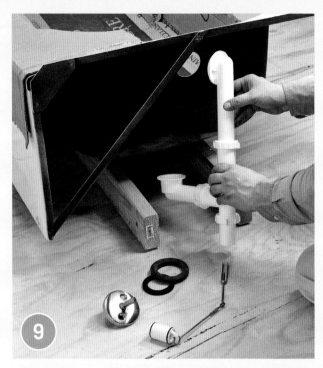

Drain strainer

Install the drain-waste-overflow (DWO) pipes before you install the tub. Make sure to get a good seal on the slip nuts at the pipe joints. Follow the manufacturer's instructions to make sure the pop-up drain linkage is connected properly. Make sure rubber gaskets are positioned correctly at the openings on the outside of the tub.

Thread the male-threaded drain strainer into the female-threaded drain waste elbow. Wrap a coil of plumber's putty around the drain outlet underneath the plug rim first. Hand tighten only.

Attach the overflow coverplate, making sure the pop-up drain controls are in the correct position. Tighten the mounting screws that connect to the mounting plate to sandwich the rubber gasket snugly between the overflow pipe flange and the tub wall. Then, finish tightening the drain strainer against the waste elbow by inserting the handle of a pair of pliers into the strainer body and turning.

Working with a helper, place the tub in position, taking care not to bump the DWO assembly. If the DWO assembly does not line up with the drainpipe, remove the tub and adjust the drain location. Many acrylic, fiberglass, and steel tubs will have a much firmer feeling if they are set in a bed of sand-mix concrete. Check manufacturer's instructions, and pour concrete or mortar as needed. Set the tub carefully back in the alcove.

Attach the drain outlet from the DWO assembly to the drain P-trap. This is the part of the job where you will appreciate that you spent the time to create a roomy access panel for the tub plumbing. Test the drain and overflow to make sure they don't leak. Also test the water supply plumbing, temporarily attaching the handles, spout, and shower arm so you can operate the faucet and the diverter.

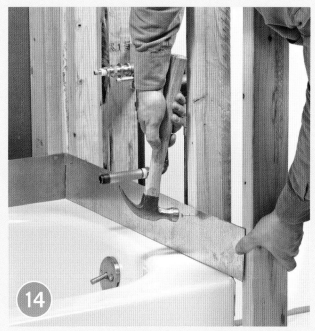

Drive a 1½" galvanized roofing nail at each stud location, just over the top of the tub's nailing flange. The nail head should pin the flange to the stud. Be careful here—an errant blow or overdriving can cause the enameled finish to crack or craze.

OPTION: You may choose to drill guide holes and nail through the flange instead.

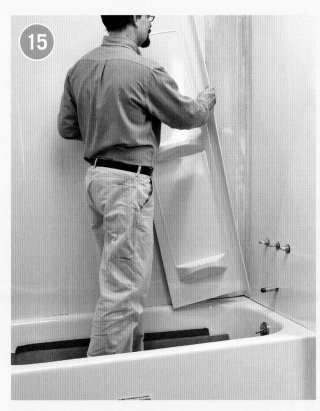

Install the wallcoverings and tub surround. You can also make a custom surround from tileboard or cementboard and tile. Many codes no longer allow the use of moisture-resistant drywall in tub and shower enclosures: choose cementboard instead.

Install fittings. First, thread the shower arm into the shower elbow and attach the spout nipple to the valve assembly. Also attach the shower head and escutcheon, the faucet handle/diverter with escutcheon, and the tub spout. Use thread lubricant on all parts.

Sliding Tub Doors

TOOLS & MATERIALS

Measuring tape
Pencil
Hacksaw
Miter box
Level
Drill
Center punch
Razor blade
Marker
Masonry bit for tile wall
Phillips screwdriver
Caulk gun
Masking tape
Silicone sealant & remover
Tub door kit
Masking tape

Curtains on your bathtub shower are a hassle. If you forget to slide them closed, mildew sets up shop in the folds. And every time you brush against them, they stick to your skin. Shower curtains certainly don't add much elegance or charm to a dream bath. Neither does a deteriorated door. Clean up the look of your bathroom, and even give it an extra touch of elegance, with a new sliding tub door.

When shopping for a sliding tub door, you have a choice of framed or frameless. A framed door is edged in metal. The metal framing is typically aluminum but is available in many finishes, including those that resemble gold, brass, or chrome. Glass options are also plentiful. You can choose between frosted or pebbled glass, clear, mirrored, tinted, or patterned glass. Doors can be installed on ceramic tile walls or onto a fiberglass tub surround.

A sliding tub door framed in aluminum gives the room a sleek, clean look and is just one of the available options. A model like this fits into a 60-inch alcove, so it can replace a standard tub, as long as you can provide access to the plumbing and an electrical connection.

How to Install Sliding Tub Doors

Remove the old door if there is one, then inspect the walls and tub ledge for plumb and level. Also remove any remaining old caulk or residue.

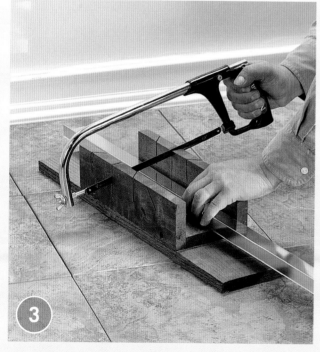

Measure the distance between the finished walls along the top of the tub ledge. Refer to the manufacturer's instructions for figuring the track dimensions. For the product seen here, 3/16" is subtracted from the measurement to calculate the track dimensions.

Using a hacksaw and a miter box, carefully cut the track to the proper dimension. Center the track on the bathtub ledge with the taller side out and so the gaps are even at each end. Tape into position with masking tape.

Place a wall channel against the wall with the longer side out and slide into place over the track so they overlap. Use a level to check the channel for plumb, and then mark the locations of the mounting holes on the wall with a marker. Repeat for the other wall channel. Remove the track.

(continued)

Drill mounting holes for the wall channel at the marked locations. In ceramic tile, nick the surface of the tile with a center punch, use a ¼" masonry bit to drill the hole, and then insert the included wall anchors. For fiberglass surrounds, use a ⅛" drill bit; wall anchors are not necessary.

Apply a bead of silicone sealant along the joint between the tub and the wall at the ends of the track. Apply a minimum ¼" bead of sealant along the outside leg of the track underside.

Position the track on the tub ledge and against the wall. Attach the wall channels using the provided screws. Do not use caulk on the wall channels at this time.

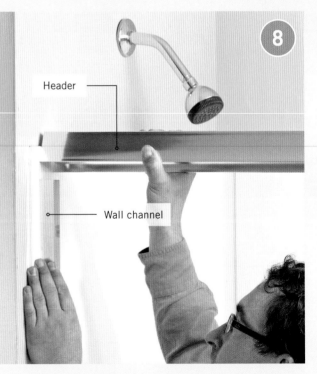

Header

Wall channel

Cut and install the header. At a location above the tops of the wall channels, measure the distance between the walls. Refer to the manufacturer's instructions for calculating the header length. For the door seen here, the length is the distance between the walls minus ¹⁄₁₆". Measure the header and carefully cut it to length using a hacksaw and a miter box. Slide the header down on top of the wall channels until seated.

9

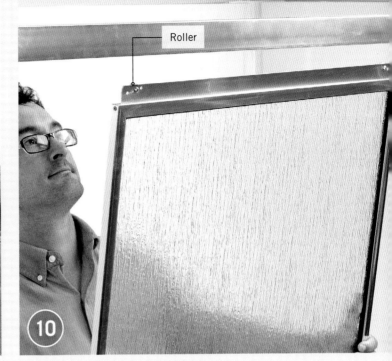

Roller

Mount the rollers in the roller mounting holes. To begin, use the second-from-the-top roller mounting holes. Follow the manufacturer's instructions for spacer or washer placement and orientation.

10

Carefully lift the inner panel by the sides and place the rollers on the inner roller track. Roll the door toward the shower end of the tub. The edge of the panel should touch both rubber bumpers. If it doesn't, remove the door and move the rollers to different holes. Drive the screws by hand to prevent overtightening.

12

11

Lift the outer panel by the sides with the towel bar facing out from the tub. Place the outer rollers over the outer roller track. Slide the door to the end opposite the shower end of the tub. If the door does not contact both bumpers, remove the door and move the rollers to different mounting holes.

Apply a bead of clear silicone sealant to the inside seam of the wall and wall channel at both ends and to the U-shaped joint of the track and wall channels. Smooth the sealant with a fingertip dipped in water.

Jetted Tub

TOOLS & MATERIALS

Plumbing tools	Shims
Utility knife	TFE paste or other thread lubricant
4-foot level	
Square-edge trowel	1 × 4 lumber
Drill or power driver	Plumber's putty
Channel-type pliers	1½" galvanized deck screws
Hacksaw	
Level	1" galvanized roofing nails
Circular saw	Dry-set mortar
Drill	Trowel
Screwdriver	Silicone caulk
Adjustable wrench	Jetted tub
Drain-waste-overflow assembly	Faucet
	Plumbing supplies
Rubber gaskets	Joint compound

A jetted spa, often called a whirlpool tub or a hot tub, is basically a bathtub that's plumbed to recirculate water, air, or both, creating an effect known as hydromassage. Hydromassage increases blood flow, relieves pressure on joints and muscles, and relieves tension. Interior hydromassage tubs usually have a water pump that blows a mixture of air and water through jets located in the tub body. Many fixtures include an in-line water heater to maintain water temperature. Jetted spas that circulate only warm air, not water (sometimes called "air-jet tubs") make it safe to use bath oils, bubble bath, and bath salts in the spa. The use of these products is discouraged in tubs that recirculate water as they can be harmful to the tub's integral plumbing.

A jetted spa model with no heater requires only a single 120-volt dedicated circuit with GFCI protection. Models with heaters normally require either multiple dedicated 120-volt circuits or a 240-volt circuit. Like normal bathtubs, jetted tubs can be installed in a variety of ways. Here, we install a drop-in tub (no nailing flange) in a three-wall alcove. This may require the construction of one or two new stub walls to house the supply and drain plumbing and for mounting a deck-mounted faucet.

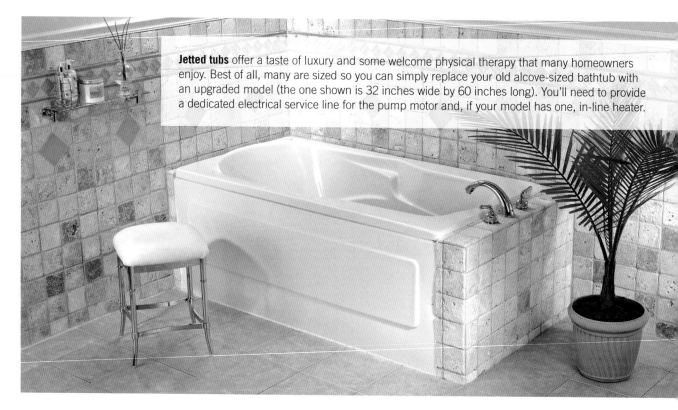

Jetted tubs offer a taste of luxury and some welcome physical therapy that many homeowners enjoy. Best of all, many are sized so you can simply replace your old alcove-sized bathtub with an upgraded model (the one shown is 32 inches wide by 60 inches long). You'll need to provide a dedicated electrical service line for the pump motor and, if your model has one, in-line heater.

WHIRLPOOLS

Installing a whirlpool is very similar to installing a bathtub, once the rough-in is completed. Completing a rough-in for a whirlpool requires that you install a separate GFCI-protected electrical circuit for the pump motor. Some building codes specify that a licensed electrician be hired to wire whirlpools; check with your local building inspector.

Select your whirlpool before you do rough-in work, because exact requirements will differ from model to model. Select your faucet to match the trim kit that comes with your whirlpool. When selecting a faucet, make sure the spout is large enough to reach over the tub rim. Most whirlpools use "widespread" faucets because the handles and spout are separate, and can be positioned however you like, even on opposite sides of the tub. Most building centers carry flex tube in a variety of lengths for connecting the faucet handles and spout.

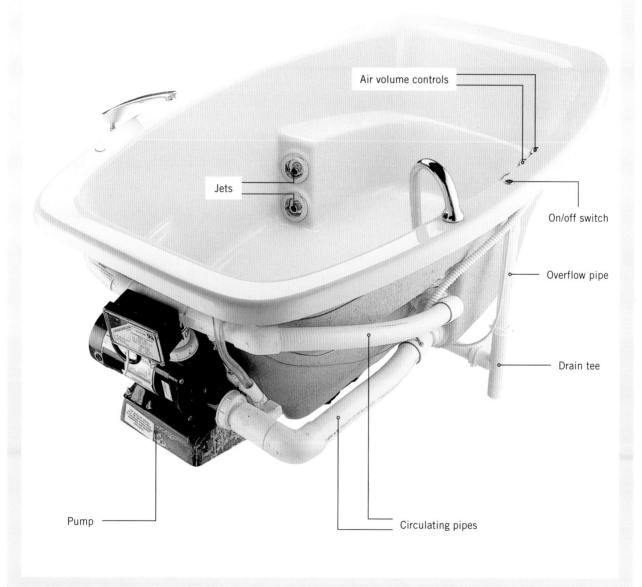

Air volume controls

Jets

On/off switch

Overflow pipe

Drain tee

Pump

Circulating pipes

A whirlpool circulates aerated water through jets mounted in the body of the tub. Whirlpool pumps move as much as 50 gallons of water per minute to create a relaxing hydromassage effect. The pump, pipes, jets, and most of the controls are installed at the factory, making the actual hookup in your home quite simple.

Tub Installation Options

Outdoor hot tubs can be inset into a deck or installed in a framed platform that can be built on just about any surface. Before installing an outdoor hot tub on a deck consult a structural engineer to inspect the deck and evaluate its ability to support such a heavy item. In most cases you will need to enhance the deck undercarriage to support a hot tub.

Ledger boards may be tacked to the stud walls in the tub installation area. These are for leveling purposes only and are not intended to support the weight of the tub and its contents. Support should be left to the subfloor and joists. If you are installing a tub where there previously was none, check with a building inspector to confirm that the structural members in the installation area are adequate.

A stub wall may be required at one or both ends of the tub so you can create an access panel to the pump. Stub walls also may be used to install supply and drain plumbing and to mount an electrical box to supply power to the pump motor or heater. The stub wall should not be used to support the tub rim.

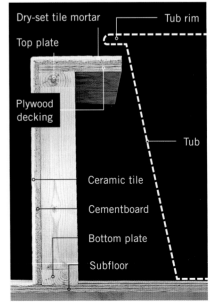

Dry-set tile mortar — Tub rim

Top plate

Plywood decking

Tub

Ceramic tile

Cementboard

Bottom plate

Subfloor

A drop-in tub has no apron and is designed to be installed in a framed deck. These decks, typically finished with cementboard and tile, are largely cosmetic and should contain access panels as required by the tub manufacturer. Often, they house a deck-mounted faucet. The deck is not intended to support the tub rim, so leave a small gap between the finished deck and the tub.

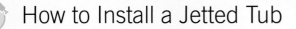

How to Install a Jetted Tub

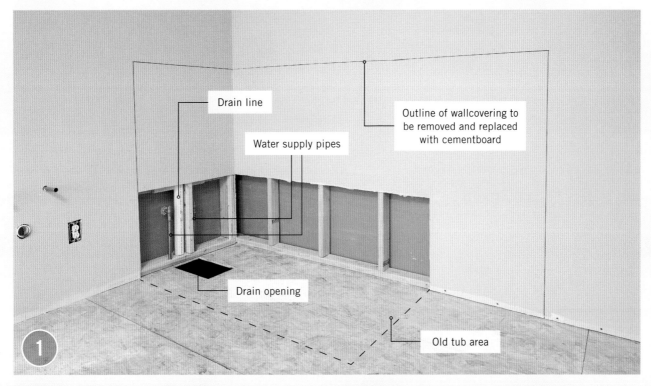

- Drain line
- Water supply pipes
- Outline of wallcovering to be removed and replaced with cementboard
- Drain opening
- Old tub area

1

Remove the old tub (see pages 92 to 93). It is always easiest to replace a tub with one of the same size and orientation. However, if you are upgrading to a jetted tub consider choosing one that is larger than the standard tub you are replacing. In many cases, a wider tub may be installed with very minimal adjustment to the plumbing. The 32"-wide by 60"-long whirlpool tub that is being installed in this project is the same size as the old tub, but in order to accommodate a small deck at the head of the tub (for mounting the faucet set) the drain pipe needed to be extended outward 12 inches. Also, a dedicated 20-amp electrical circuit needed to be installed for the pump.

NOTE: The model of tub you select, as well as the overall installation method (See page 103), will determine the exact sequence of steps necessary to install, plumb, and wire your tub. Always read the manufacturer's instructions closely and make certain to follow them.

2

Remove the tub apron (if it has a removable apron) and set the tub so it fits against the stud walls in the installation area. Shim underneath the tub so it is perfectly level (some models have adjustable feet).

Mark the height of the tub rim or flange onto the wall studs and then remove the tub. If you are using leveling ledgers (See page 103) you can attach them to the studs directly below the lines. In the installation seen here, a small stub wall will be made for the head and the foot of the tub. If this is your plan, measure from the floor to your reference lines to determine how tall you should build your stub wall or walls.

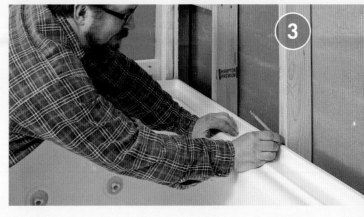

3

(continued)

Build a small wall frame for the head and the foot using ¾" plywood and 2 × 4s or 2 × 6s. Size the walls so they will be a small fraction of an inch shorter than the reference lines near the head and foot locations; include the thickness of the tile backer you are using in the height. The tub seen here has a vertical flange all the way around the rim, so the tile on the tops of the finished walls should just overlap the flange. Secure the wall frames by toe-nailing at floor joist locations.

Tub flange reference line

Extend the old drain hole in the subfloor if necessary. Because of the 12"-wide stub wall at the tub head, the new tub is a foot further away from the wall than the old tub.

Make plumbing connections for the new drain line and P-trap, making sure that the new drain pipe has the correct minimum slope and that the trap is positioned so it will align precisely with the tailpiece on the tub drain kit.

Install electrical boxes and run new circuits if needed to supply power to the tub. If you are not comfortable doing your own wiring, hire a professional electrician. The tub seen here does not have an in-line water heater so it requires electrical service for the pump motor only—a dedicated 20-amp circuit with GFCI protection. Orient the electrical boxes so the receptacle they contain will be easily accessible from the access panel opening in the walls or tub skirt.

OPTION: Install wall-mounted controls for turning the pump on and off and for setting the temperature controls if your tub has a heater. You will need to have all new wiring inspected and approved by your local electrical inspector.

Attach the drain/overflow pipe assembly to the tub prior to installation, using rubber gaskets and pipe joint compound. Measure the distance the drain tailpiece will need to drop to connect with the drain trap and trim the tailpiece to fit (inset photo).

Drain strainer

Overflow coverplate

Secure the drain/overflow assembly by tightening the overflow coverplate and the drain strainer onto the assembly from inside the tub.

Mix a batch of thinset mortar and shovel it in a 1"-thick layer in the tub installation area, limiting the material to just those areas that will contact the tub bottom. In many cases, the tub has several pads adhered to the underside that function as feet.

TIP: Moisten the subfloor so it does not draw water out of the ghinset too quickly.

(continued)

Slide or lower the tub into the installation area, taking care not to disturb the drain/overflow assembly. Make sure the drain tailpiece aligns exactly over the P-trap opening. Seat the tub or tub feet into the mortar bed—apply pressure as needed until the tub aligns with your leveling reference marks or ledgers.

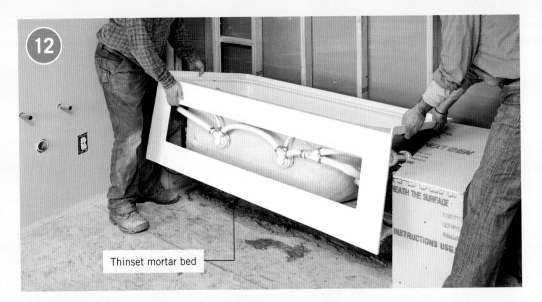

Thinset mortar bed

Doublecheck to make sure the tub is level. If it is too low in any spot, add thinset mortar underneath the tub or foot at that spot. Let the mortar dry overnight.

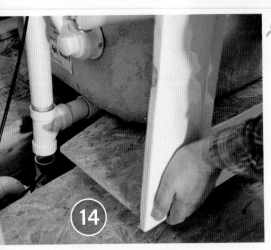

Connect the drain tailpiece from the drain-waste-overflow kit mounted on the tub to the trap in the drain opening. You should be able to access this connection if you reach through the apron area in the front of the tub skirt.

TIP

Test the drain system to make sure it does not leak. Using a hose, first add a small amount of water and visually inspect the slip fittings and the area around the drain body. If it looks good, fill the tub up past the overflow line to make sure the overflow pipe seal does not leak. Drain the tub.

Plug the pump motor into the dedicated, GFCI circuit. Reattach the tub apron.

How to Finish a Jetted Tub Area

Install a vapor barrier around the tub area by stapling 6-mil plastic sheeting to the wall studs. This is not intended as a waterproofing measure and is not a substitute for a waterproof membrane if you are creating a shower surround.

Install wall surface coverings in the tub area. Most codes now require that you use cementboard for this purpose, regardless of whether or not you are installing tile. Once all of the surfaces, both horizontal and vertical, in the tub area are covered with tile substrate, begin making your layout lines for the tile.

Install the spout supply valves and hook them up to the supply risers. Tubs are not predrilled for faucets as sinks are, so you'll need to decide whether to drill holes for the valves in the tub rim using a step bit, or to mount the faucet in the platform or the rim of the support wall.

Install your finished wall coverings (tile in most cases).

Attach the spout and the valve handles and test the supply system. To clear any debris from the lines, remove the spout aerator and run both hot and cold water for a minute or so.

Bidets

Bidets are becoming ever more popular in the United States. Maybe that's because they can give an ordinary bathroom a European flare that so many of us find alluring. Go to Europe, Asia, or South America and you'll see how much people—both men and women—can come to rely on bidets. Some fans of this bathroom fixture think those who don't use bidets are unhygienic.

With the trend moving toward larger and more luxurious bathrooms, many Americans are becoming intrigued by this personal hygiene appliance. The standard model features hot and cold faucets, and either a movable nozzle located by the faucet handles or a vertical sprayer located near the front of the bowl. Most bidets are outfitted with a pop-up drain. You can also buy a combination toilet and bidet if space is an issue.

Installing a bidet is very much like installing a sink. The only difference is that the bidet can have the waste line plumbed below the floor, like a shower. But like sinks, bidets may have single or multiple deck holes for faucets, so be certain to purchase compatible components.

TOOLS & MATERIALS

Tape measure
Drill
Adjustable wrench
Level
Silicone sealant
(2) ⅜" shutoff valves
(2) ⅜" supply lines
P–trap
Tubing cutter
Plumber's putty
Thread tape
Bidet
Bidet faucet

A bidet is a useful companion to a toilet, and it is a luxury item you and your family will appreciate. It's also a bit of a novelty you will enjoy sharing. For people with limited mobility, a bidet is an aide to independent personal sanitation.

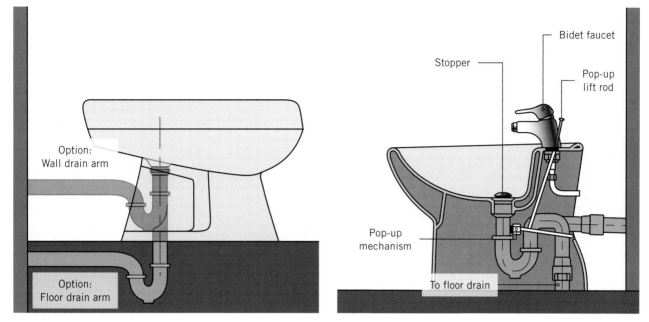

Bidet drains have more in common with sink drains than with toilet drains. Some even attach to a drain arm in the wall, with a P-trap that fits between the fixture drain tailpiece and the arm. Other bidets drain into a floor drain outlet with a trap that's situated between the tailpiece and the branch drain line.

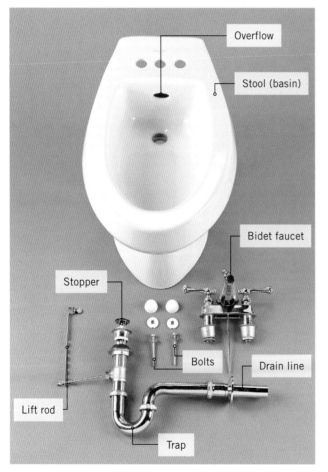

A bidet requires a special faucet that allows you to mix hot and cold water to a temperature you find comfortable. It has a third knob to control the water pressure. The aerator and spout pivot to allow you to adjust the spray to a comfortable height.

OPTION: You can get all the features of a bidet on your existing toilet with a number of aftermarket bidet seats. These seats feature heaters, sprayers, and dryers in basic or deluxe versions. Installation is easy and no additional space is needed.

How to Install a Bidet

Rough-in supply and drain lines according to the manufacturer's specifications. If you do not have experience installing home plumbing, hire a plumber for this part of the job. Apply a coil of plumber's putty to the base of the bidet faucet, and then insert the faucet body into the mounting holes. Thread the washers and locknut onto the faucet body shank and hand tighten. Remove any plumber's putty squeeze-out.

Apply a roll of plumber's putty around the underside of the drain flange. Wrap the bottom ⅔ of the flange threads with three layers of Teflon tape. Make sure to wrap the tape clockwise so that tightening the nut will not bunch up the tape. Insert the flange in the drain hole, place the gasket and washer, and then thread the nut onto the flange. Do not fully tighten.

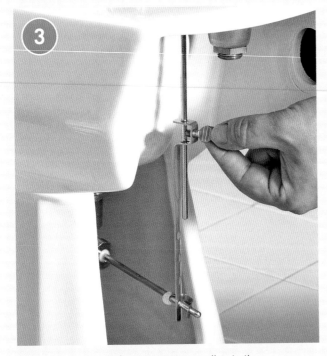

Install the pop-up drain apparatus according to the manufacturer's instructions.

Place the bidet in its final location, checking that supply and drain lines will be in alignment. Mark the locations of the two side-mounting holes through the predrilled holes on the stool and onto the floor.

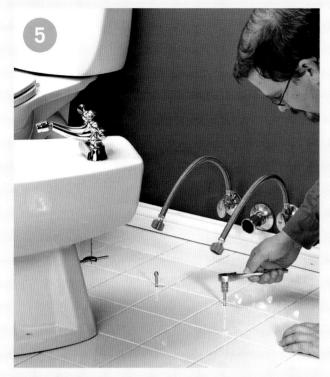

Remove the bidet and drill ³⁄₁₆" pilot holes at the marks on the floor. Drive the floor bolts (included with the bidet basin) into the holes. Position the bidet so the floor bolts fit into the bolt holes in the base.

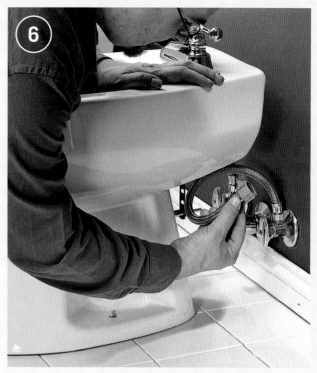

Connect the water supply risers to the bidet faucet using compression unions. Make sure to hook the hot and cold risers up to the correct ports on the faucet.

Hook up the drain line by attaching the P-trap to the drain tailpiece. The trap is then attached to a branch drain line coming out of the wall or floor in the same manner as a sink drain.

Remove the aerator so any debris in the supply line will clear and then turn on the water and open both faucets. Check for leaks in lines and fix, if found. Assemble the bolt caps and thread them onto the floor bolts.

NOTE: Do not dispose of paper in the bidet—return to the toilet to dry off after using the bidet for cleaning.

Urinals

Most people consider a urinal to be a commercial or industrial bathroom accessory, so why would you want one in your home—and in your dream bathroom no less? The answer is in the many advantages a urinal has to offer and the fact that most major bathroom fixture manufacturers are now producing urinals designed for residential installation.

A urinal doesn't take up much space and it uses much less water per flush than a standard toilet: .5 to 1.0 gallon of water per flush for the urinal, as opposed to the low-flow toilet's 1.6 gallons of water per flush. You also have the option of a waterless urinal, a real boon in water-scarce areas. A urinal also has the emotional benefit of ending the "up versus down" toilet seat debate. Finally, a urinal is generally easier to keep clean than a toilet because splashing is minimized.

In today's homes with large multiple bathrooms and his and hers master baths, there are plenty of places you can choose to install a urinal. Of course, the perfect place is where it will get used the most: in the bathroom closest to the TV if the guys congregate at your house to watch sporting events; or in the bathroom closest to boys' bedrooms if you've got a passel of them.

Urinals are great water savers and are becoming increasingly popular in today's dream bathroom.

TOOLS & MATERIALS

Tape measure	Miter box	Drywall tape
Adjustable wrench	Hex wrenches	Drywall compound
Pencil	Smooth-jawed spud wrench	2 × 6 lumber
Level	Slotted screwdriver	PVC 2" drainpipe
Sealant tape	Urinal flushometer	PVC 2" male threaded drain outlet
Utility knife	Emery cloth	½" copper pipe
Drywall saw	Wire brush	Urinal
Tubing cutter	Allen wrench	Sealant tape
Hacksaw	Drywall	

For the ultimate in water-conservation, you can now purchase a home urinal that uses zero water. A waterless urinal is never flushed, so you'll save about a gallon of water per usage. Naturally, waterless urinals are plumbed into your drain line system. But where typical plumbing fixtures rely on fresh water to carry the waste into the system, the waterless system relies simply on gravity for the liquid waste to find its way out of the fixture and into the drain. The secret is a layer of sealing liquid that is lighter than the water and forms a skim coat over the urine. When the urine enters the trap it displaces the sealing liquid, which immediately reforms on the surface to create a layer that seals in odors. The Kohler fixture seen here (see Resources, page 298) is an example of the sealing liquid system. Other waterless urinals use replaceable cartridges.

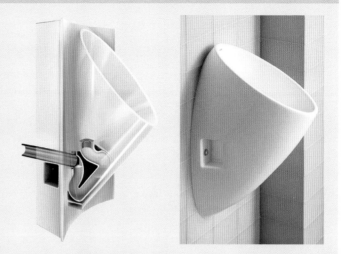

A layer of sealing liquid forms a skim coat that floats on top of the liquid to trap odors.

Flushing Options for Urinals

A manual flush handle is still the most common and least expensive flushing mechanism for urinals. It is reliable but not as sanitary as touchless types such as the flushometer on page 119.

Motion sensors automatically flush touchless urinals, which is a great improvement in sanitation. These tend to be more expensive, however, and are more likely to develop problems. Also, because they flush automatically when users step away from the fixture, they don't allow you to conserve water by limiting flushing.

How to Install a Urinal

Remove the drywall or other surface coverings between the urinal location and the closest water supply and waste lines. Remove enough wall surface to reveal half of the stud face on each side of the opening to make patch work simpler.

2 × 6 mounting board

Following the manufacturer's directions for the urinal and flushometer, determine the mounting height of the urinal, and mark the location of the supply and waste lines. For this installation, the 2" waste line is centered 17½" above the finished floor. Cut 5½ × 1½" notches in the wall studs centered at 32" above the finished floor surface, then attach a 2 × 6 mounting board.

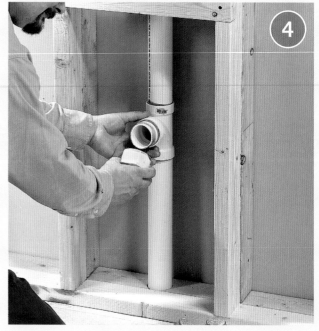

Install the copper cold water supply line according to the manufacturer's specifications. Here, it is 4¾" to the side of the fixture centerline and 45" from the finished floor (11½" from the top of the fixture). Cap the stub-out 3" from the finished wall surface.

Install the 2" drainpipe and vent pipe, making sure that the centerline of the drain outlet is positioned correctly (here, 17½" above the finished floor and 4¾" to the side of the supply line). Attach the male threaded waste outlet to the drain pipe. It should extend beyond the finished wall surface. Replace the wall covering and finish as desired.

Apply Teflon tape to the waste outlet. Thread the female collar onto the waste outlet until it is firmly seated and the flanges are horizontally level. Place the gasket onto the female collar. The beveled surface of the gasket faces toward the urinal.

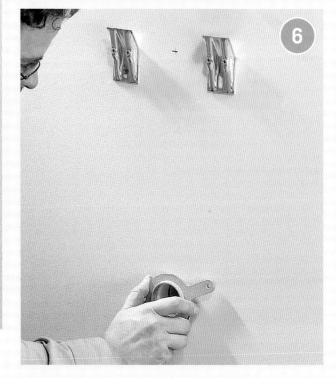

Attach the mounting brackets 32" above the floor, 3¼" to the sides of the centerline of the waste outlet.

Determine the distance from the centerline of the water inlet on the top of the urinal, called the spud, to the finished wall. Subtract 1¼" from this distance and cut the water supply pipe to that length using a tubing cutter. Turn off the water before cutting. After cutting, deburr the inside and outside diameter of the supply pipe. Attach the threaded adapter to the cut pipe.

Hang the urinal on the brackets, being careful not to bump the porcelain as it chips easily. Thread the screws through the washers, the holes in the urinal, and into the collar. Tighten the screws by hand, then one full turn with an adjustable wrench. Do not overtighten.

(continued)

INSTALLING FIXTURES & FAUCETS ● 117

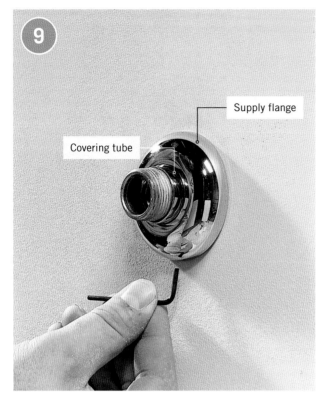

9

Covering tube

Supply flange

Measure from the wall surface to the first thread of the adapter. Using a hacksaw and a miter box or a tubing cutter, cut the covering tube to this length. Slide the covering tube over the water supply pipe. Slide the supply flange over the covering tube until it rests against the wall. Tighten the setscrew on the flange with an Allen wrench.

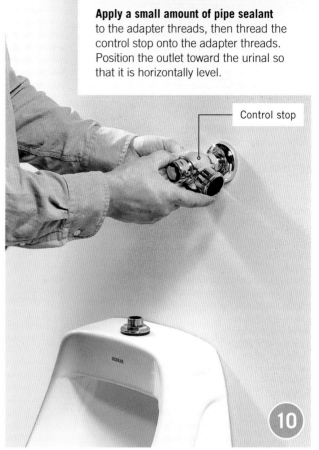

Apply a small amount of pipe sealant to the adapter threads, then thread the control stop onto the adapter threads. Position the outlet toward the urinal so that it is horizontally level.

Control stop

10

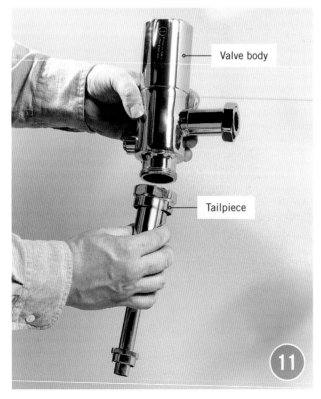

Valve body

Tailpiece

11

Hand tighten the tailpiece into the flushometer valve body.

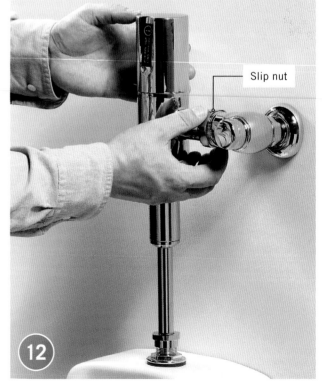

Slip nut

12

Hand tighten the slip nut that connects the valve body to the control stop.

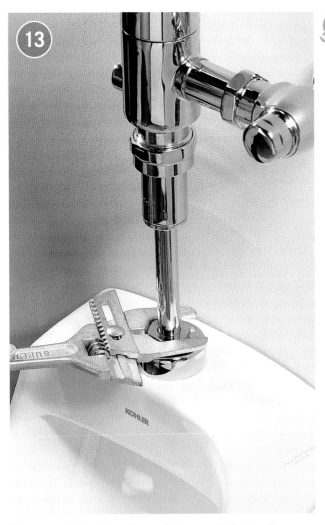

(13)

Use a smooth-jawed spud wrench to securely tighten the tailpiece, vacuum breaker, and spud couplings.

For maximum sanitation, choose a urinal flush mechanism with an electronic sensor, like the Kohler flushometer being installed here. The electronic eye on this type of flush mechanism senses when a user approaches the fixture and then commands the fixture to flush when the user steps away. This eliminates the need to touch the handle before the user has the opportunity to wash his hands.

(14) **While testing the flush,** adjust the supply stop screw counter-clockwise until adequate flow is achieved.

Water Softeners

If your house has hard water coursing through its pipes, then you've got a couple of problems. Not only does your water do a poor job of dissolving soap, but you also have plenty of scale deposits on dishes, plumbing fixtures, and the inside of your water heater.

Softeners fix these problems by chemically removing the calcium and magnesium that are responsible for the hard water (usually described as over 17 grains of minerals per gallon). These units are installed after the water meter but before the water line branches off to appliances or fixtures, with one exception: Piping to outside faucets should branch off the main line before the softener because treating outside water is a waste of money.

Softeners come with an overflow tube and a purge tube to rinse out the minerals that are extracted from the water. These tubes should drain to a floor drain or to a laundry sink basin, which is the better approach if the sink is close by. Remember to leave an air gap between the tube and the sink or floor drain. Do not connect the tube directly to a drain or vent pipe.

KNOW YOUR TYPES OF SALT

Salt for water softeners comes in three basic types: rock salt, solar salt (crystals), and evaporated salt (pellets). Rock salt is a mineral that's mined from salt deposits. Solar salt is a crystalline residue left behind when seawater is evaporated naturally. It sometimes is sold as pellets or blocks. Evaporated salt is similar to solar salt, but the liquid in the brine is evaporated using mechanical methods. Rock salt is cheapest but leaves behind the most residue and therefore requires more frequent brine tank cleaning. Evaporated salt pellets are the cleanest and require the least maintenance.

A modern water softener is a single appliance, with the softener resting on top of the salt storage tank.

TOOLS & MATERIALS

Tape measure	Propane torch	Steel wool	Solder
Tubing cutter	Slip-joint pliers	Soldering flux	4"-thick concrete blocks

3-VALVE BYPASS

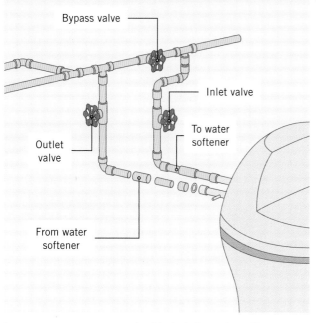

Bypass valve

Inlet valve

To water softener

Outlet valve

From water softener

In some areas you are required to install a water softener with three valves, as shown. This arrangement allows you to bypass the water softener, so water can run to the house when the softener is disconnected.

SOFTENED WATER

From your plumbing's point of view, the best water softening strategy is to position the softener close to the main, cold-only supply line (as seen here). Doing this results in both hot and cold water being softened. But because some homeowners object to the altered taste and increased salinity of softened water, the softener may be installed after the hot and cold lines have split from the main supply line. This way, the water may be softened immediately before it enters the heater, and the cold water remains unsoftened.

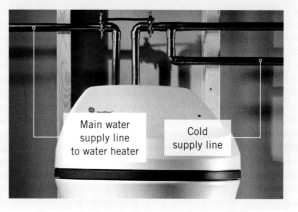

Main water supply line to water heater

Cold supply line

How to Install a Water Softener

Install the bypass valve in the softener's head. One side of the valve goes in the inlet port and the other fits into the outlet port. This valve is held in place with simple plastic clips or threaded couplings.

NOTE: Check local codes for bypass requirements.

The overflow tube is usually connected to the side of the softener's tank. Run this tube, along with the discharge tube, to a floor drain or a laundry sink.

(continued)

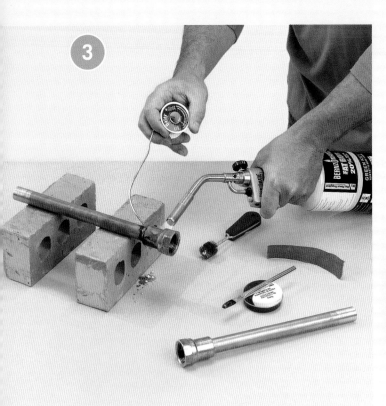

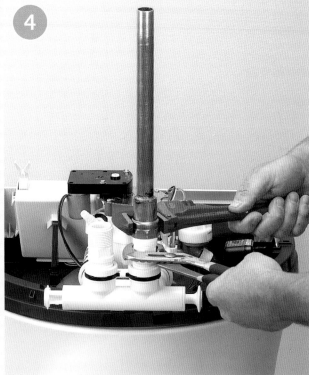

Measure the distance between the bypass ports on the tank to the cold water supply line. Cut copper tubing to fit this space and solder appropriate fittings onto both ends.

Use two wrenches to tighten the tube nuts, one holding the valve stable. Don't overtighten, or you may break plastic parts in the valve.

Connect the copper tubing from the softener to the water supply lines. Clean all fittings and pipes with steel wool. Then, apply soldering flux to the parts and solder them together with a propane torch.

To maintain electrical bonding in a metal supply tube system, connect the copper lines with a bonding clamp.

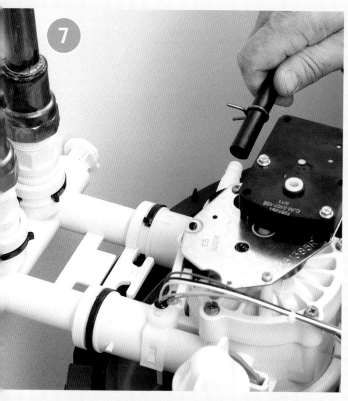

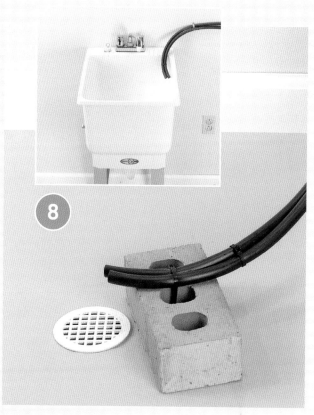

Install the plastic tubing discharge tube on the head of the water softener following the manufacturer's directions.

Run the tank overflow hose and the drain tube to a nearby floor drain or utility sink (not into a drain or vent pipe). The hoses should be secured so they don't flop around, and their ends must be at least 1½" above a drain.

Follow manufacturer's instructions to purge the air from the water softener. First run water with the valve in the bypass position, then pull the valve out so it is in the service position.

Turn on the water supply and make sure the installation works properly. If you see any leaks, fix them. Then add the water softening pellets to the top of the unit in the ratios explained on the package.

Hot Water Dispenser

There are boxes and boxes of beverages and food that need only a trickle of hot water to achieve their destiny: coffee, tea, hot chocolate, instant soup, hot cereals, and just plain old hot water and lemon to name a few. And there's no faster way to get this hot water than with a hot water dispenser. These units are designed to fit in the spare hole on many kitchen sink decks. But, if you don't have one, you can replace your spray hose with the dispenser. Or, if you want to keep the hose, just drill an extra hole in your sink or countertop to accommodate the dispenser faucet.

NOTE: Installing this appliance requires both plumbing and wiring work. If you are unsure of your skills in these areas, hire a professional. (Be sure to check your local codes before starting.)

A dispenser requires an always-hot (unswitched) electrical receptacle under the sink. You could install a new receptacle with both plugs always hot, as shown in the steps, or the receptacle for the food disposer could be wired so that one plug (for the disposer) is controlled by a switch and the other (for the dispenser) is always hot.

On-demand hot water is not only a convenience, it can help to conserve both energy and water.

TOOLS & MATERIALS

Power drill with ¾"-dia. bit	Wire connectors
Utility knife	Saddle valve
Wire stripper	Brass plug to fill spray hose port on kitchen faucet
Screwdrivers	
Adjustable wrench	Teflon tape
14/2 NM electrical cable	Hot water dispenser kit
Flexible cable conduit	Cable connectors
Duplex electrical box	15-amp circuit breaker (to match service panel breakers)
Conduit box connector	
Switched receptacle	
Measuring tape	Tubing cutter

SPLIT & SWITCHED RECEPTACLE FOR BOTH FOOD DISPOSER & HOT-WATER DISPENSER

There are several ways to split a receptacle so that one plug is hot and one is switched. Here, power enters the switch box first, and three-wire cable is run from the switch box to the receptacle box. Connect all the ground wires. At the receptacle box, remove the connecting tab between the two brass terminals; connect the red and black wires to the brass terminals; and connect the white (neutral) wire to the silver terminal. At the switch box, splice the white wires together; connect the red wire to one terminal; and connect the black wires to the other terminal via a pigtail.

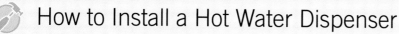
How to Install a Hot Water Dispenser

Drill an access hole for a new power cable (in flexible conduit) in the bottom of the sink compartment cabinet. Use a drill and a ¾"-dia. bit. Go into the basement and drill a hole up through the flooring that will align with the first hole (or make other arrangements to run circuit wire as you see fit).

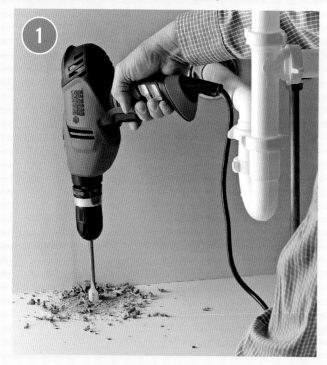

①

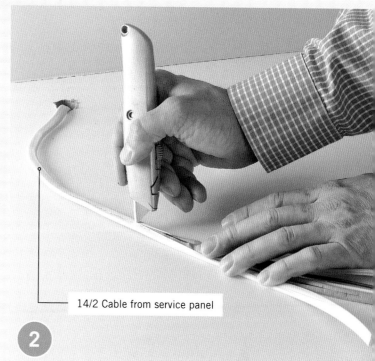

②

14/2 Cable from service panel

Fish a 14/2 or 12/2 cable from the electric service panel up through the hole in the floor. Strip the sheathing from the cable with a utility knife. Also strip the insulation from the wires with a wire stripper. Do not nick the wire insulation.

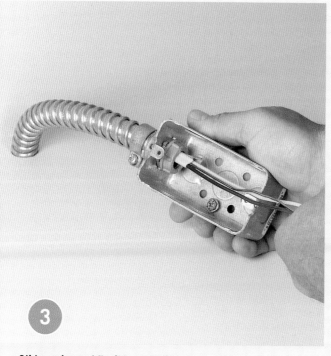

③

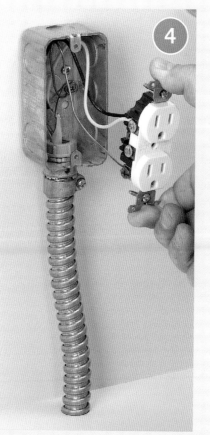

④

Install a receptacle. Mount a duplex metal box on the cabinet wall. Connect the ground wire to the receptacle's grounding terminal. Connect the black (hot) wire to the brass terminal, and the white (neutral) wire to the silver terminal. Mount the receptacle onto the box and add a coverplate. If the circuit does not have GFCI protection, install a GFCI receptacle.

Slide a piece of flexible conduit over the wires, so the wires are protected from the point they leave the cabinet floor to when they enter the electrical box. Attach the conduit to the box with a box connector so at least 8" of wire reaches into the box.

(continued)

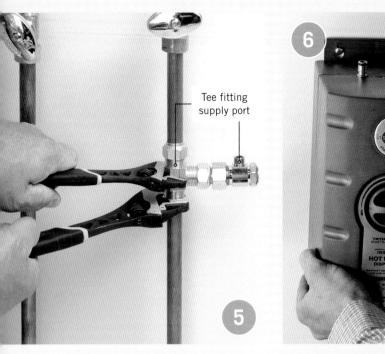

Tee fitting
supply port

Tie into water supply. Water for the dispenser comes from the cold water supply line under the kitchen sink. Mount a tee on this pipe, below its shutoff valve, by alternately tightening the tee bolts on both sides with a wrench.

Determine the best place for the dispenser heater, usually on the back cabinet wall, so its pigtail plug will reach the switched receptacle. Screw its mounting bracket to the wall and hang the heater on this bracket.

To replace a spray hose with the dispenser faucet, remove the nut that holds the sprayer to the sink. Then remove the end of the hose from its port on the bottom of the faucet, using an adjustable wrench. This will free the hose so it can be pulled out from above the sink. Plug the spray hose part on the faucet.

The dispenser faucet is designed to fit into a standard sink hole. To install it, just squeeze its supply tubes together so they can fit into the hole, and drop it in place. The unit is held securely by a washer and locking screw that is tightened from below the sink.

Tie into water supply. Shut off the water and open nearby faucets to drain the pipe. Under the sink, cut into the cold-water pipe and install a compression or soldered tee fitting. Install a compression stop valve onto the fitting. Tighten the nuts, shut off the valve, and turn the water back on to test for leaks.

Attach the two copper water tubes to the heater with compression fittings. Tighten them with a wrench. On the model seen here, the heater unit has three tubes. One supplies cold water to the heater, one supplies hot water to the faucet, and a third clear plastic hose acts as a vent and is attached to an expansion tank within the heater.

Slide the end of the plastic vent tube onto the nipple on top of the tank and attach it according to the manufacturer's instructions. On some models a spring clip is used for this job; other models require a hose clamp.

Install the heater power supply cable in the service panel. Begin by turning off the main power breaker. Then, remove the outside door panel and remove one of the knockout plates from the top or side of the box. Install a cable clamp inside this hole, push the cable through the clamp, and tighten the clamp to secure the cable.

NOTE: Hire an electrician if you are not experienced with wiring.

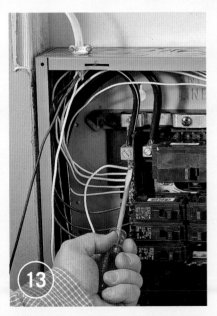

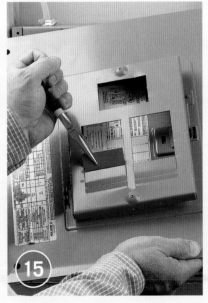

Strip the sheathing from the cable inside the panel and remove the insulation from the ends on the black and white cable wires. Loosen a lug screw on the neutral bus bar and push the white wire under the lug. Attach the ground wire to the grounding bus bar. Tighten both these screws securely.

Loosen the lug screw on a standard 15-amp breaker and put the end of the black (hot) cable wire under this lug. Tighten the lug with a screwdriver. Then install the breaker in the hot bus bar by pushing it into place.

Once a new breaker is installed, the service panel cover has to be modified to fit over it. Break out the protective plate that covers the breaker position with pliers. Screw the cover to the panel, and turn on the main breaker. Turn on the water supply to the dispenser and plug it into the receptacle. Turn on the receptacle switch, wait fifteen minutes, and check that the system is working properly.

Icemakers

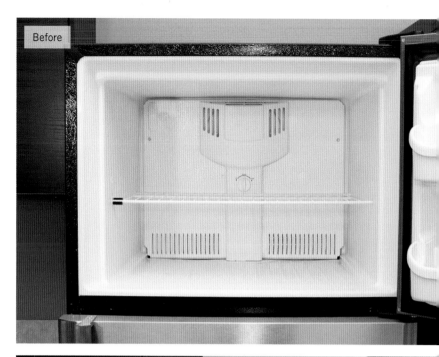

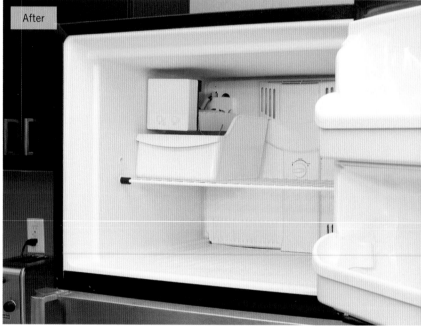

A built-in icemaker is easy to install as a retrofit appliance in most modern refrigerators. If you want to have an endless supply of ice for home use, you'll wonder how you ever got along without one.

Most expensive refrigerators come with icemakers as standard equipment, and practically every model features them as an option (a refrigerator with an icemaker usually costs about $100 more). It is also possible to purchase an icemaker as a retrofit feature for your old fridge.

Hooking up an existing icemaker to a cold-water supply involves drilling holes and connecting to a cold-water pipe. Most often, a pipe can be found in the basement below the kitchen, perhaps under the kitchen sink. To make the connection, some local codes allow the installation of a saddle tee valve, but many do not, and a compression tee valve is not difficult to install, as we show. In many kitchens the flexible line running from the valve to the fridge is copper, but reinforced icemaker tubing is easier to install and less likely to kink or crack. To be sure everything fits, you can buy a connection kit from the refrigerator manufacturer.

If you have an older refrigerator with no icemaker and you'd like it to have one, all is not lost. Inspect the back of the unit, behind the freezer compartment. If your refrigerator has the required plumbing to support an icemaker, you will see a port or a port that is covered with backing. In that case, all you need to do is take the make and model information to an appliance parts dealer and they can sell you an aftermarket icemaker. Plan to spend $100 to $200.

TOOLS & MATERIALS

Screwdrivers	Electric drill and assorted bits	Open-end or adjustable wrench
Nut drivers		
Needle-nose pliers	Icemaker kit (or icemaker tubing with ferrules and nuts)	Tee fitting or saddle valve
Duct or masking tape		Long ½"-inch drill bit
Channel-type pliers		Electrician's tape
Putty knife		

An icemaker receives its supply of water for making cubes through a ¼" copper supply line that runs from the icemaker to a water pipe. The supply line runs through a valve in the refrigerator and is controlled by a solenoid that monitors the water supply and sends the water into the icemaker itself, where it is turned into ice cubes. The cubes drop down into a bin, and as the ice level rises, they also raise a bail wire that's connected to a shutoff. When the bin is full, the bail wire will be high enough to trigger a mechanism that shuts off the water supply.

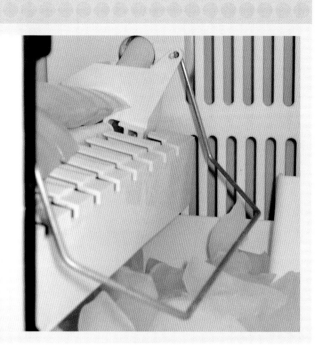

Aftermarket automatic icemakers are simple to install as long as your refrigerator is icemaker ready. Make sure to buy the correct model for your appliance and do careful installation work—icemaker water supply lines are very common sources for leaks.

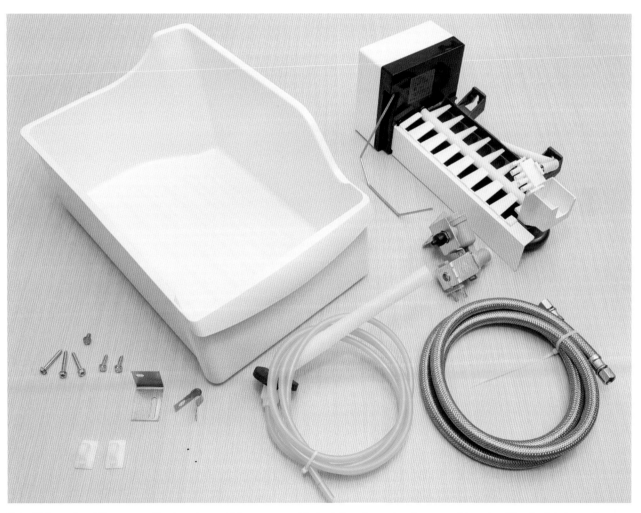

Retrofit icemaker kits come with almost everything you need to install an icemaker in your refrigerator. The flexible icemaker supply line needs to be purchased separately. Larger home centers keep retrofit icemakers for the more popular model in stock. You can find units for most pre-plumbed refrigerators through appliance parts stores or online.

①

Locate a nearby cold-water pipe, usually in the basement or crawl space below the kitchen. Behind the refrigerator and near the wall, use a long ½" bit to drill a hole through the floor. Do not pull the bit out.

②

From below, fasten icemaker tubing to the end of the drill bit by wrapping firmly with electrician's tape. From above, carefully pull the bit up to thread the tubing up into the kitchen.

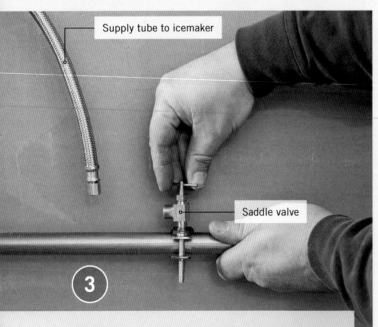

Supply tube to icemaker

Saddle valve

③

Shut off the water and open nearby faucets to drain the line. Cut into a cold-water pipe and install a compression tee valve or a saddle valve. Tighten all the nuts, close the valve and nearby faucets, and restore water to test for leaks.

④

Connect the tubing. Arrange the tubing behind the fridge so you have about 6 ft. of slack, making it easy to pull the fridge out for cleaning. Insert the tubing into the valve and tighten the nut. To finish the installation, connect the tubing to the refrigerator. Keep the tubing neatly coiled and kink-free for future maintenance.

How to Install a Retrofit Icemaker

Remove all the contents from the refrigerator and freezer.
Unplug the unit and pull it away from the wall so you can
access the back easily. On the back of the refrigerator, remove
or pierce the protective sheet that covers the port for the
water inlet tube, following any directions printed on the sheet.

NOTE: If you cannot locate these openings your refrigerator
is not preplumbed for an icemaker.

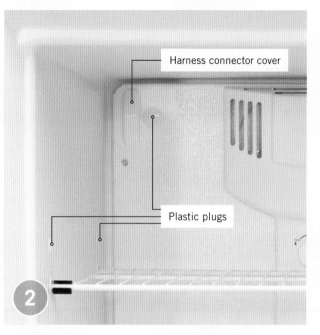

Harness connector cover

Plastic plugs

Inside the freezer compartment, remove the plastic plugs and
covers in the upper left. Use a plastic putty knife to pry plugs
from the access holes (the model seen here has three: one
on the back wall and two on the side wall). This model also
has a plastic cover over the harness connector opening that is
removed by unscrewing a small hex screw.

Join the water inlet tube to the water supply tubing that came
with the kit, slipping the foam sealing gasket onto the threads
of the water inlet tube. Hand-tighten the compression fitting
and then tighten one-half-turn with a wrench or pliers. Do not
overtighten. Insert the water inlet into the opening on the back
of the appliance until the flange on the inlet tube is seated
squarely at the mouth of the opening.

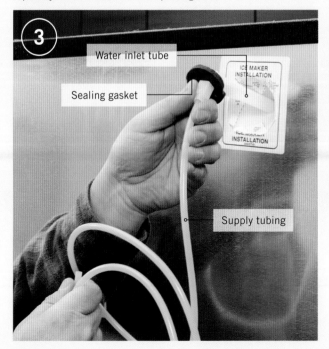

Water inlet tube

Sealing gasket

Supply tubing

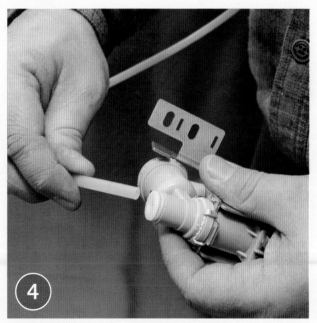

Remove the access panel at the bottom of the backside of the
refrigerator. The icemaker kit will include a water valve that
is connected to both the water supply and the system wiring
(the wiring harness). You'll find it easier if you make these
connections prior to mounting the valve onto the appliance.
First, insert the free end of the icemaker supply tubing you
connected at the top into the port on the water valve.

(continued)

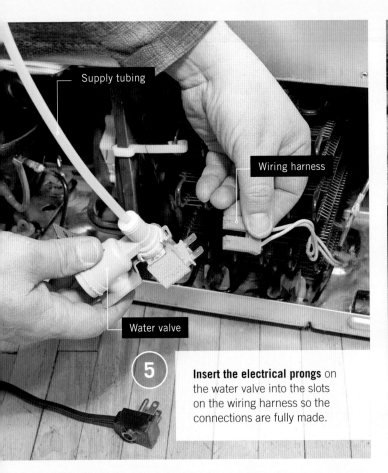

Supply tubing

Wiring harness

Water valve

5 **Insert the electrical prongs** on the water valve into the slots on the wiring harness so the connections are fully made.

6 **Secure the water valve** to the back of the refrigerator at the spot indicated in the instruction manual. There should be pre-punched holes that align with the screw holes in the mounting flange of the water valve. Use self-tapping screws to attach the valve.

7 **Attach a cold water supply tube** to the inlet port on the water valve. Use flexible, reinforced tubing such as the stainless steel reinforced tubing seen here. Tighten the nut on the supply tube with channel-type pliers.

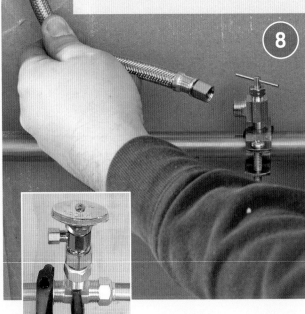

8 **Attach the other** end of the supply tubing to a cold water supply line from the home water supply system (see page 130). You may use either a saddle valve (piercing or nonpiercing) or a tee valve with a shutoff (inset photo). Most professionals would recommend the tee valve as these are regarded as less prone to leakage.

Inside the freezer compartment, locate the tip of the water inlet tube that was inserted into the back of the refrigerator.

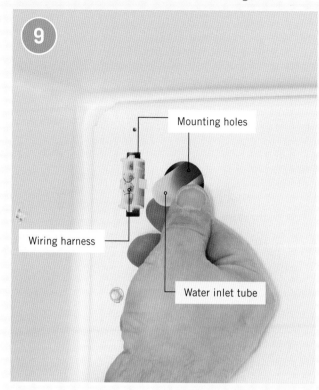

Mounting holes

Wiring harness

Water inlet tube

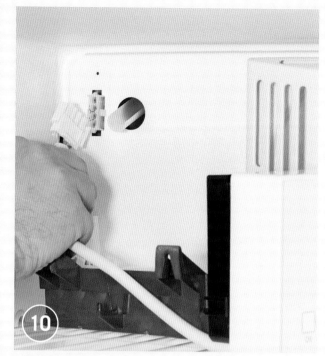

Set the icemaker unit inside the freezer. Some models (such as this one) have a small, adjustable leveling bracket that should be attached to the bottom of the unit first. Connect the plug from the icemaker unit securely into the wiring harness.

The icemaker unit is supported by two hanger screws driven into the predrilled holes in the side wall of the freezer compartment. Drive the hanger screws partway into the holes, leaving enough screw shank exposed that you can fit the hanger mounts on the icemaker over the screw heads.

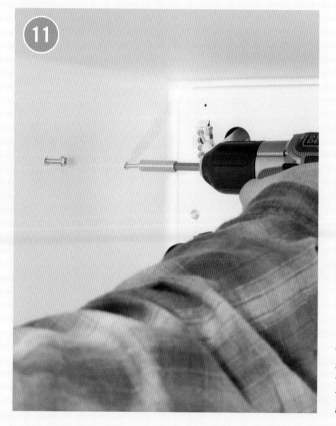

Hang the icemaker on the mounting screws. Adjust the leveling bracket until you can see that the unit is level. Tighten the mounting screws only until the unit is snug against the side wall. Make sure the water inlet tube is aligned over the fill cup at the back of the unit. Position the ice container underneath the icemaker and follow the manufacturer's directions for testing. Reattach the back acess panel and return the appliance to position.

Pot Filler

Kitchen design trends are moving ever closer to replicating commercial kitchens in the home. One example of this trend is the pot filler. A long-neck faucet that mounts to the wall behind or onto the counter beside the cooktop, a pot filler allows you to dispense water directly into large pots on the cooktop. This saves lugging pots of water from the sink to the stove.

Although horizontally mounted models are available, most pot fillers are attached to the wall. Almost all are designed for cold water only. Some have two valves, one at the wall and another at the end of the spout. Other models can be turned on with a foot pedal for safe, hands-free use.

A pot filler will require code-approved supply pipe (½" in most cases) connected with a permanent union at another supply line or the main. The best time to run a new supply is during a remodel. But retrofitting a new supply line and mounting a pot filler is not too difficult as a standalone project. Using PEX supply pipe will make running the new supply line in finished walls easier.

A pot filler is a cold-water tap that you install above your cooktop so you can add water to large stock pots without having to carry a full pot of water around the kitchen.

TOOLS & MATERIALS

Hack saw	PEX fittings
PEX tools	Reciprocating saw
PEX pipe	Drywall tools
Pot filler	Pipe joint compound
Protector plates	Drywall patching materials

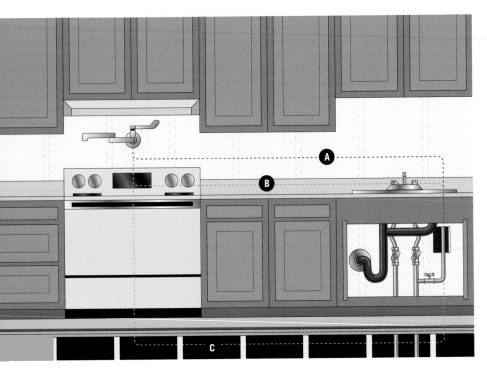

Plan the route for the new supply line. In most cases, you will enter the stud cavity of the wall and run a new line directly upward, past the backsplash height of the countertop (A). If the countertop backsplash is removable, avoid wallboard patching by installing the tubing behind the backsplash (B). You may also be able to run the supply line underneath the kitchen if there is an unfinished basement (C).

How to Install a Pot Filler

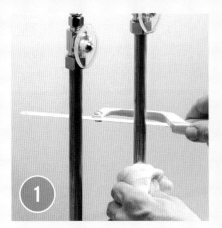

Shut off the water supply and locate the cold water supply riser at the kitchen sink. Cut into the riser and install a tee fitting, or replace the existing shutoff valve on the riser with a multiple-outlet shutoff valve, with an outlet for ½" supply pipe for the pot filler.

Plan the route for the new supply line beginning at the tee fitting and working toward the cooktop area. Determine the height of the new line and then snap chalklines from the sink to the cooktop. With the electrical power shut off, remove wall coverings 2" above and below the chalkline and at the location for the pot filler outlet. Make sure the location is high enough that the pot filler spout will clear your tallest stockpot.

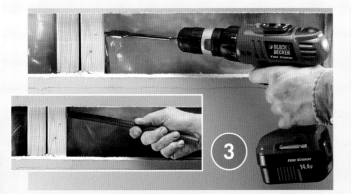

Drill ¾" holes in the framing for the supply tubes. Install protector plates if the holes are within 1¼" of the stud edge. Run ½" PEX from the supply riser through the holes to the pot filler location (inset). Attach nailing plates to protect the pipes.

Attach the new PEX supply line to the tee fitting at the supply riser, installing an accessible shutoff valve on the new line.

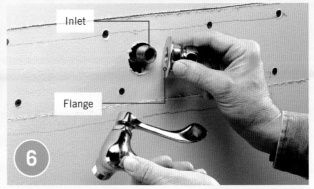

At the cooktop, install the faucet union as specified by the manufacturer. Add blocking as needed. The pot filler installed here attaches to a drop-ear L-fitting, mounted to blocking. Apply pipe joint compound to the faucet inlet and thread it on to the L-fitting.

Cut and install the drywall patch. Fit the flange over the inlet. Apply pipe joint compound to the threads of the faucet body. Assemble and adjust the faucet according to the manufacturer's instructions. Test the faucet before refinishing the drywall.

Reverse-Osmosis Water Filters

Not all water is created equal. Some water tastes better than other water. Some water looks better than other water. And some has more impurities. Because no one wants to drink bad water, the bottled water business has exploded over the past twenty years. Home filtration systems have also grown by leaps and bounds, in part because there are so many different types of filters available.

For example, sediment filters will remove rust, sand, and suspended minerals, like iron. A carbon filter can remove residual chlorine odors, some pesticides, and even radon gas. Distillation filters can remove bacteria and organic compounds, while a traditional water softener can neutralize hard water. But many of the most toxic impurities, heavy metals like mercury, lead, cadmium, and arsenic are best

Reverse-osmosis filters can be highly effective for removing specific contaminants from drinking water. Because the filtration process wastes a lot of fresh water, it's a good idea to have your water professionally tested before investing in an RO system.

removed with a reverse-osmosis (RO) system like the one shown here.

These filters are designed to treat cooking and drinking water. The system holds the treated water in a storage tank and delivers it to a sink-mounted faucet on demand. RO units feature multiple filter cartridges, in this case a pre-filter unit, followed by the RO membrane, and then a carbon post-filter.

TOOLS & MATERIALS

Plastic gloves	Teflon tape
Screwdrivers	Saddle valve
Electric drill	Rubber drain saddle
Adjustable wrench	

POINT-OF-USE FILTERS

Point-of-use water filtration systems are typically installed in the sink base cabinet, with a separate faucet from the main kitchen faucet. The setup shown here has an extra filter to supply a nearby refrigerator icemaker.

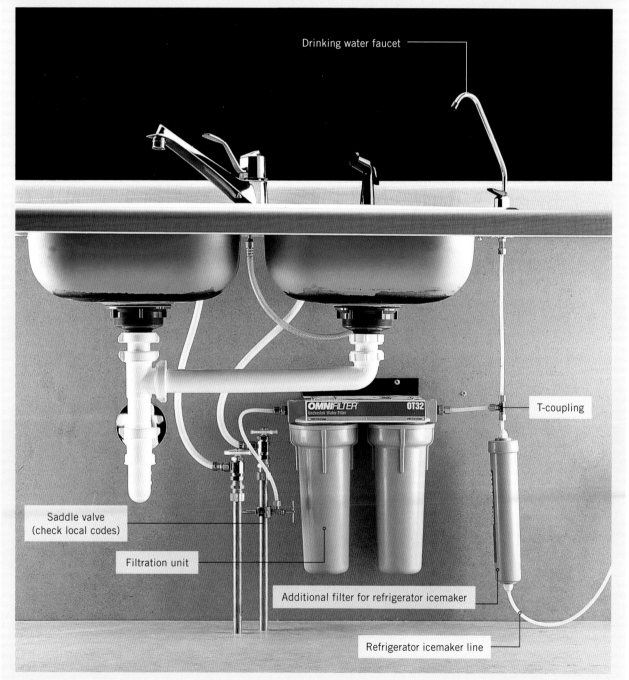

Drinking water faucet

T-coupling

Saddle valve (check local codes)

Filtration unit

Additional filter for refrigerator icemaker

Refrigerator icemaker line

How to Install a Reverse-Osmosis Water Filter

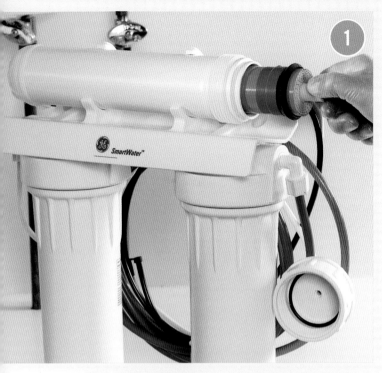

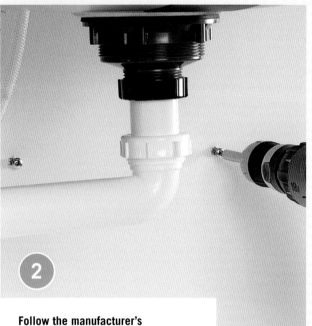

Install the RO membrane filter. It is shipped in a separate bag that is filled with anti-bacterial fluid. Wearing plastic gloves, remove the cartridge from the bag and install it in the filter unit. Make sure to touch only the ends of the cartridge when you handle it or you can damage the membrane.

Follow the manufacturer's instructions to establish the best location for the filter inside your kitchen sink cabinet. Drive mounting screws into the cabinet wall to support the unit.

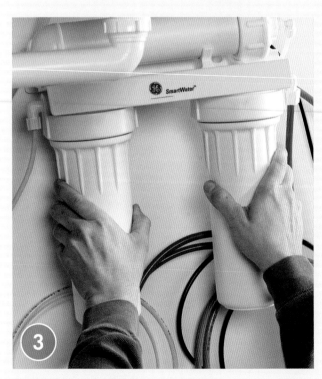

Assemble the entire filtration system and then hang it on the cabinet wall. The best system layout may be to locate the filter on one wall and the storage tank on the opposite wall.

Attach valve to the side of the storage tank. Just wrap its threads a couple of times with Teflon tape and screw the valve into the tank. Finger tighten it, then turn it one more turn with an adjustable wrench.

Connect the filter to the tank with plastic tubing. Some units use a compression fitting; this one uses a push-type collar. Simply insert the hose into the collar until it stops. Pull back gently to make sure it is firmly attached.

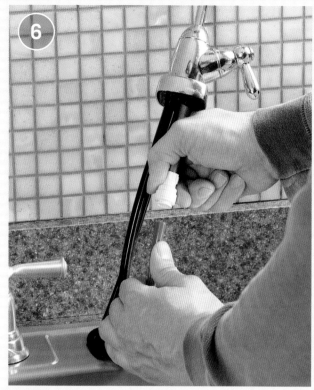

Connect the water storage tank and faucet with plastic tubing. Here, a push-type compression fitting on the end of the tubing was used. To install it, push the end of the fitting over the bottom of the faucet shank until the fitting bottoms out.

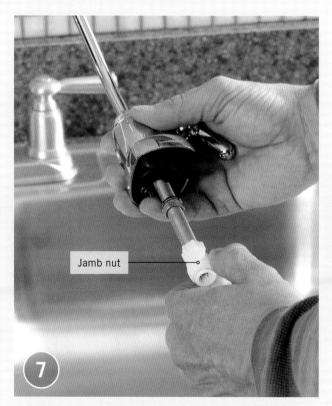

Jamb nut

The filter faucet comes with a jamb nut and sometimes a plastic spacer (as with this unit) that goes on the shank of the faucet before the jamb nut. After the nut is finger tight, snug it securely with an adjustable wrench.

Mount the faucet in the sink deck, following the manufacturer's instructions.

(continued)

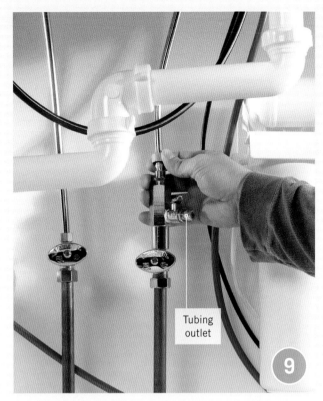

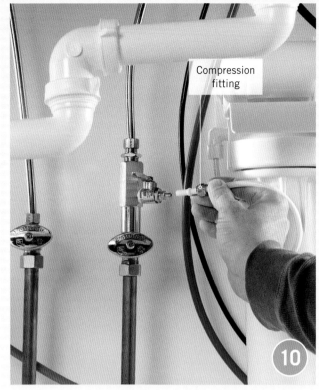

The water supply to the filter comes from the cold-water supply line that services the kitchen sink faucet. The easiest way to tap into the supply line is to replace the shutoff valve at the supply riser with a new valve containing an additional outlet for tubing.

Attach the filter supply tube to the port on the shutoff valve with a compression fitting. Push the end of the tubing onto the valve, then push the ferrule against the valve and thread the compression nut into place. Finger tighten it, then turn it one more full turn with a wrench.

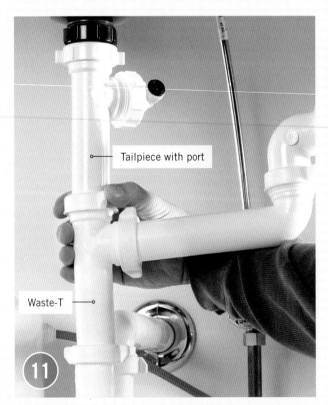

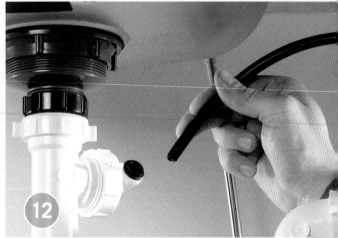

Attach the tubing from the drain to the auxiliary port on the tailpiece. Finish up by turning on the water and checking the system for leaks. Be sure to filter and drain at least two tanks of water, to clean any contaminants from the system, before drinking the water.

NOTE: The inlet device mounted on the auxiliary tailpiece port here is designed for reverse-osmosis filters and contains an internal check valve. Install an inline check valve in the drain tube if you don't already have one.

The filter must also be tied into the drain system. The best way to do this is to replace the drain tailpiece with a new drain tailpiece that contains an auxiliary port.

INSTALLING A WHOLE-HOUSE WATER FILTRATION SYSTEM

A whole-house water filtration system is installed along the supply pipe carrying water to the house, located after the water meter, but before any other appliances in the pipe line. A whole-house system reduces the same elements as an undersink system and can also help reduce the iron flowing into the water softener, prolonging its life.

Always follow the manufacturer's directions for your particular unit. If your electrical system is grounded through the water pipes, make sure to install ground clamps on both sides of the filtration unit with a connecting jumper wire. Globe valves should be installed within 6" of the intake and the outtake sides of the filter.

Filters must be replaced every few months, depending on type of manufacturer. The filtration unit cover unscrews for filter access.

A whole-house water filtration system: (A) intake side, (B) supply pipe from the water meter pipe, (C) outlet side to the house supply pipe, (D) filter, and (E) filtration unit cover.

Shut off main water supply and turn on faucets to drain pipes. Position unit after water meter, but before any other appliances in supply pipe. Measure and mark pipe to accomodate the filtration unit. Cut pipe at marks with a pipe cutter. Join water meter side of pipe with intake side of unit, and house supply side of pipe with outtake side of unit. Tighten with a wrench.

Install a filter and screw filtration unit cover to bottom of the filtration unit. Attach a jumper wire to pipes on other side of unit, using pipe clamps. Open main water supply lines to restore the water supply. Allow faucets to run for a few minutes, as you check to make sure that the system is working properly.

Frost-proof Sillcocks

If you live in a part of the world where sub-freezing temperatures occur for extended periods of time, consider replacing your old sillcock (outdoor faucet) with a frost-proof model. In this project we show you how to attach the new sillcock using compression fittings, so no torch or molten solder is required. Before freezing weather arrives, be sure to disconnect the hose from a frost-proof sillcock. If you don't, water that may remain in the hold and in the sillcock's shaft (or that may be created by condensation) may freeze and crack the shaft.

Compression fittings are ok to use in accessible locations, like between open floor joists in a basement. Your building code may prohibit their use in enclosed walls and floors. To see if your sillcock can be replaced according to the steps outlined here, see the facing page.

Did that outside faucet freeze again? Replace it with one that you never have to turn off in the winter.

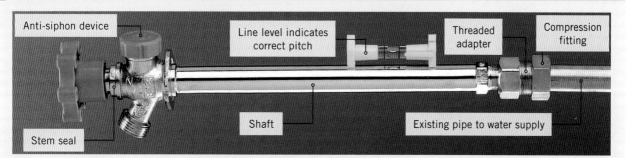

The frost-proof sillcock shown here can stay active all winter because the stem washer turns off the water in the warm interior of the house. The shaft needs to be pitched slightly down toward the outside to allow water to drain from the shaft. This supply pipe is connected to the threaded adapter with a compression fitting, which is secured to the pipe with two wrenches. Do not use the steps that follow if any of the following apply:

- Your pipes are made from steel instead of copper.

- The length of the pipe from the sillcock to where you can comfortably work on it is greater than 12".

- The pipe has a valve or change of direction fitting within 10" of the existing sillcock.

- The existing supply pipe is ⅝" outside diameter as measured with an adjustable wrench, and you are unable to make the hole in the wall bigger to accommodate the thicker shaft of the frost-proof sillcock. (For example, the hole is in a concrete foundation.)

How to Replace a Hose Bib with a Frost-proof Sillcock

Turn off the water to your outside faucet at a shutoff found inside the house or basement behind the faucet. Open the faucet and a bleeder valve on the shutoff to drain any remaining water from the pipe.

When you are sure the water flow has been stopped, use a tubing cutter to sever the supply pipe between the shutoff valve and the faucet. Make this first cut close to the wall. Tighten the tubing cutter onto the pipe. Both wheels of the cutter should rest evenly on the pipe. Turn the cutter around the pipe. The line it cuts should make a perfect ring, not a spiral. If it doesn't track right, take it off and try in a slightly different spot. When the cutter is riding in a ring, tighten the cutter a little with each rotation until the pipe snaps.

(continued)

Remove the screws holding the flange of the old sillcock to the house and pull it and the pipe stub out of the hole. Measure the outside diameter of the pipe stub. It should be either ⅝", which means you have ½" nominal pipe, or ⅞", which means you have ¾" nominal pipe. Measure the diameter of the hole in the joist. (If it's less than an inch, you'll probably need to make it bigger.) Measure the length of the pipe stub from the cut end to where it enters the sillcock. This is the minimum length the new sillcock must be to reach the old pipe. Record all this information.

Spot where supply tubing was cut

3/4" I.D. / 7/8" O.D.

Find a spot on the supply pipe where you have good access to work with a fitting and wrenches. The point of this is to help you select a new sillcock that is the best size for your project. In most cases, you'll have only two or three 6" to 12" shaft sizes to pick from. In the example above, we can see that the cut section of pipe is 6" long and the distance from the cut end to a spot with good access on the intact pipe is 3", so a new sillcock that's 9" long will fit perfectly.

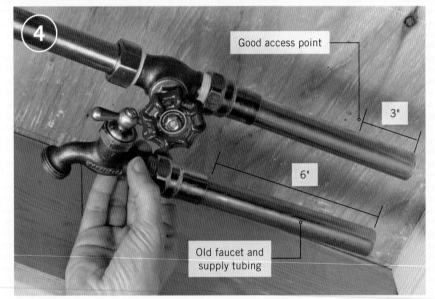

Good access point

3"

6"

Old faucet and supply tubing

If you need to replace old pipe with a larger diameter size, simplify the job of enlarging the sillcock entry hole into your home with a simple drill guide. First, drill a perpendicular 1⅛" diameter hole in a short board. From outside, hold the board over the old hole so the tops are aligned (you can nail or screw it to the siding if you wish). Run the drill through your hole guide to make the new, wider and lower hole in the wall.

Drill guide

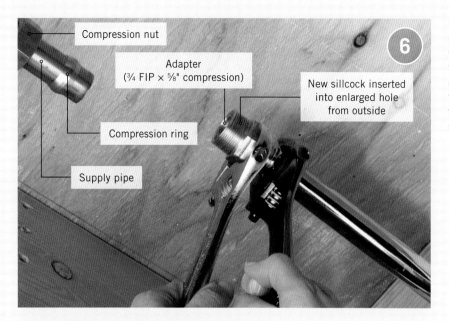

Compression nut

Adapter
(¾ FIP × ⅝" compression)

New sillcock inserted
into enlarged hole
from outside

Compression ring

Supply pipe

6

Insert the sillcock into the hole from the outside. Cut the supply pipe where it will meet the end of the sillcock. From the inside, wrap Teflon tape clockwise onto the threads of the sillcock. Stabilize the sillcock with one wrench and fully tighten the adapter onto the threaded sillcock with the other wrench.

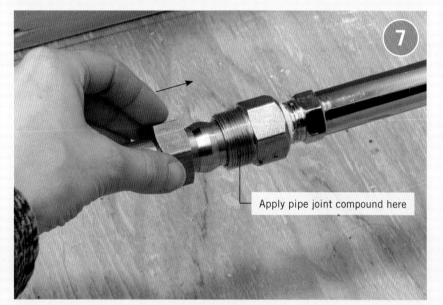

Apply pipe joint compound here

7

Insert the end of the supply pipe into the adapter and pull them together. Spin the sillcock shaft so the faucet outside is oriented correctly (there should be a reference line on the bottom or top of the shaft). Apply pipe joint compound to the male threads on the adapter body. Hand thread the nut onto the adapter body. Stabilize the adapter body with one wrench, then tighten the compression nut with the other about two full turns past hand tight.

8

Turn the water back on. With the sillcock off and then on, check for leaks. Tighten the compression nut a little more if this union drips with the sillcock off. From outside the house, push the sillcock down against the bottom of the entry hole in the wall. Drill small pilot holes into the siding through the slots on the sillcock flange. Now, pull out on the sillcock handle in order to squeeze a thick bead of silicone caulk between the sillcock flange and the house. Attach the sillcock flange to the house with No. 8 or No. 10 corrosion-resistant screws.

Pedestal Sinks

Pedestal sinks move in and out of popularity more frequently than other sink types, but even during times they aren't particularly trendy they retain fairly stable demand. You'll find them most frequently in small half baths, where their little footprint makes them an efficient choice. Designers are also discovering the appeal of tandem pedestal sinks of late, where the smaller profiles allow for his-and-hers sinks that don't dominate visually.

The primary drawback to pedestal sinks is that they don't offer any storage. Their chief practical benefit is that they conceal plumbing some homeowners would prefer not to see.

The sink is mounted onto the wall via a screw-attached metal bracket, and the pedestal is actually installed after the sink is hung and its purpose is only decorative. But other pedestal sinks (typically on the higher end of the design scale) have structurally important pedestals that do most or all of the bearing for the sink.

If you squeeze the plumbing tightly together, you may be able to hide the trap, stop valves, and supply tubes. Most of the time, however, at least some of these things will show. In that case, spend a bit more for classy-looking plumbing components.

Pedestal sinks are available in a variety of styles and are a perfect fit for small half baths. They keep plumbing hidden, lending a neat, contained look to the bathroom.

How to Install a Pedestal Sink

Wall surface shown cut away for clarity

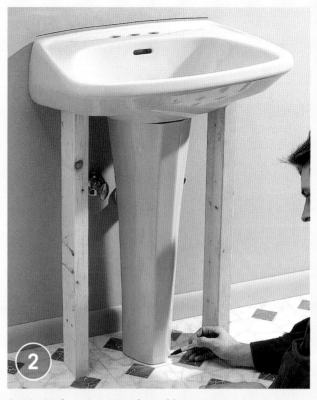

Install 2 × 6 blocking between the wall studs, behind the planned sink location where you will drive screws to mount the sink. Cover the wall with water-resistant drywall. Waste and supply lines may need to be moved, depending on the sink.

Set the basin and pedestal in position and brace it with 2 × 4s. Outline the top of the basin on the wall, and mark the base of the pedestal on the floor. Mark reference points on the wall and floor through the mounting holes found on the back of the sink and the bottom of the pedestal.

Set aside the basin and pedestal. Drill pilot holes in the wall and floor at the reference points, then reposition the pedestal. Anchor the pedestal to the floor with lag screws.

Attach the faucet, then set the sink on the pedestal. Align the holes in the back of the sink with the pilot holes drilled in the wall, then drive lag screws and washers into the wall brace using a ratchet wrench. Do not overtighten the screws.

Hook up the drain and supply fittings. Caulk between the back of the sink and the wall when installation is finished. You may choose to apply caulk between the sink and the wall, or between the bottom of the pedestal and the floor.

Wall-Hung Vanities

TOOLS & MATERIALS

Studfinder   Level
Drill   Vanity

Think of a wall-mounted sink or vanity cabinet and you're likely to conjure up images of public restrooms where these conveniences are installed to improve access for floor cleaning. However, wall-hung sinks and vanities made for home use are very different from the commercial installations.

Often boasting high design, beautiful modern vanities and sinks come in a variety of styles and materials, including wood, metal, and glass. Some attach with decorative wall brackets that are part of the presentation; others look like standard vanities, just without legs. Install wall-hung sinks and vanities by attaching them securely to studs or wood blocking.

Today's wall-hung sinks are stylish and attractive, but they require mounting into studs or added blocking to keep them secure.

How to Install a Wall-Hung Vanity Base

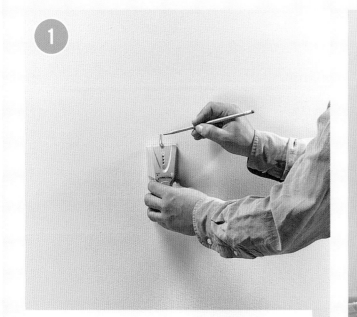

Remove the existing sink or fixture and inspect the wall framing. Also determine if plumbing supply and waste lines will need to be moved to accommodate the dimensions of the new fixture. Locate the studs in the sink location with a stud finder.

Hold the sink or cabinet in the installation area and check to see if the studs align with the sink or sink bracket mounting holes. If they do, skip to step 3. If the studs do not align, remove the wallboard behind the mounting area. Install 2 × 6 blocking between studs at the locations of the mounting screws. Replace and repair wallboard.

Blocking

Mark the locations of the mounting holes on the wall using a template or by supporting the sink or vanity against the wall with a temporary brace (made here from scrap 2 × 4s) and marking through the mounting holes.

Drill pilot holes at the marks. Have a helper hold the vanity in place while you drive the mounting screws. Hook up the plumbing (see pages 150 to 157).

Vessel Sinks

The vessel sink harkens back to the days of washstands and washbowls. Whether it's round, square, or oval, shallow or deep, the vessel sink offers great opportunity for creativity and proudly displays its style. Vessel sinks are a perfect choice for a powder room, where they will have high visibility.

Most vessel sinks can be installed on any flat surface—from a granite countertop to a wall-mounted vanity to an antique dresser. Some sinks are designed to contact the mounting surface only at the drain flange. Others are made to be partially embedded in the surface. Take care to follow the manufacturer's instructions for cutting holes for sinks and faucets.

A beautiful vessel sink demands an equally attractive faucet. Select a tall spout mounted on the countertop or vanity top or a wall-mounted spout to accommodate the height of the vessel. To minimize splashing, spouts should directly flow to the center of the vessel, not down the side. Make sure your faucet is compatible with your vessel choice. Look for a centerset or single-handle model if you'll be custom drilling the countertop—you only need to drill one faucet hole.

TOOLS & MATERIALS

Jigsaw
Trowel
Pliers
Wrench
Caulk gun and caulk
Sponge
Drill
Vanity or countertop
Vessel sink
Pop-up drain
P-trap or bottle trap and drain kit
Faucet
Phillips screwdriver

Vessel sinks are available in countless styles and materials, shapes, and sizes. Their one commonality is that they all need to be installed on a flat surface.

Vessel Sink Options

This glass vessel sink embedded in a "floating" glass countertop is a stunning contrast to the strong and attractive wood frame anchoring it to the wall.

The natural stone vessel sink blends elegantly into the stone countertop and is enhanced by the sleek faucet and round mirror.

The stone vessel sink is complemented by the wall-hung faucet. The rich wood vanity on which it's perched adds warmth to the room.

Vitreous china with a glazed enamel finish is an economical and durable choice for a vessel sink (although it is less durable than stone). Because of the flexibility of both the material and the glaze, the design options are virtually unlimited with vitreous china.

How to Install a Vessel Sink

Secure the vanity cabinet or other countertop that you'll be using to mount the vessel sink.

1

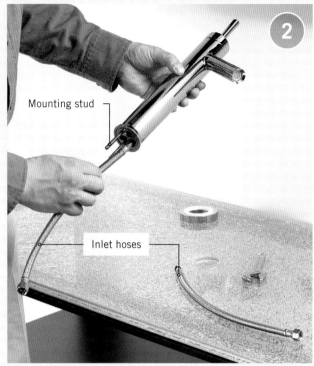

2

Mounting stud

Inlet hoses

Begin hooking up the faucet. Insert the brass mounting stud into the threaded hole in the faucet base with the slotted end facing out. Hand tighten, and then use a screwdriver to tighten another half turn. Insert the inlet hoses into the faucet body and hand tighten. Use an adjustable wrench to tighten another half turn. Do not overtighten.

Place the riser ring on top of the O-ring over the faucet cutout in the countertop. From underneath, slide the rubber gasket and the metal plate over the mounting stud. Thread the mounting stud nut onto the mounting stud and hand tighten. Use an adjustable wrench to tighten another half turn.

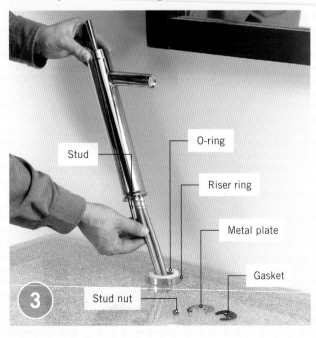

Stud

O-ring

Riser ring

Metal plate

Gasket

3

Stud nut

4

To install the sink and pop-up drain, first place the small metal ring between two O-rings and place over the drain cutout.

Place the vessel bowl on top of the O-rings. In this installation, the vessel is not bonded to the countertop.

Put the small rubber gasket over the drain hole in the vessel. From the top, push the pop-up assembly through the drain hole.

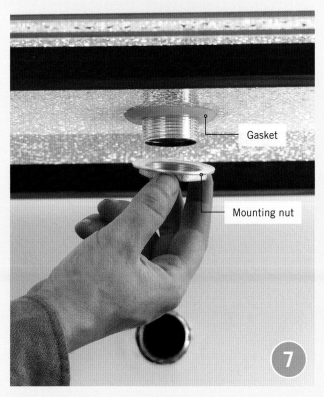

Gasket

Mounting nut

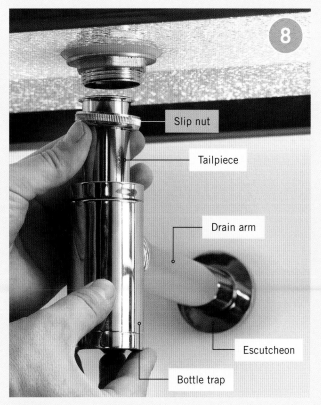

Slip nut

Tailpiece

Drain arm

Escutcheon

Bottle trap

From underneath, push the large rubber gasket onto the threaded portion of the pop-up assembly. Thread the nut onto the pop-up assembly and tighten. Use an adjustable wrench or basin wrench to tighten an additional half turn. Thread the tailpiece onto the pop-up assembly.

Install the bottle trap. Loosen the rings on the top and outlet of the bottle trap. Slide the drum trap top hole over the tailpiece. Slide the drain arm into the side outlet, with the flat side of the rubber gasket facing away from the trap. Insert the drain arm into the wall outlet. Hand tighten the rings.

Wall-Mounted Sinks

There are many benefits to a wall-mounted sink that, depending on your situation and needs, will offset the inherent lack of storage space. In contrast to the footprint of a traditional vanity-mounted sink, wall-mounted units can save space on the sides and in front of the fixture. More importantly, they are an essential addition to a Universal Design bathroom where wheelchair accessibility is a key consideration. It's why these particular fixtures are sometimes called "roll-under" sinks.

All that practicality aside, early models at the lower end of the price spectrum were somewhat unattractive because their designs simply left the drain tailpiece, trap, and supply shut-off valves in plain sight. But there's no need for you to settle for a less-than-handsome wall-mounted sink. Manufacturers have developed two solutions to the problem of exposed plumbing. Some are designed with a bowl that conceals supply line shut-offs, replacing the trap with sleekly designed tailpieces and squared off trap bends. The other solution, and one more widely available, is a wall-mounted pedestal that covers the plumbing. Sinks with this feature are sometimes called "semi-pedestal."

We've opted to illustrate the installation of just such a sink in the instructions that follow. Keep in mind that different manufacturers sometimes use very different mounting procedures. In any case, the idea remains the same: strongly secure the sink to studs or blocking, so that it is completely stable and will not fall.

The most involved part of the installation process is usually rerouting water supply and drain lines as necessary. You should hire a licensed plumber for this if you're not comfortable with the work. Once the plumbing is in place, the installation is quick and easy.

TOOLS & MATERIALS

Carpenter's level	Phillips screwdriver
Adjustable wrenches	Standard screwdriver
Pipe wrench	Jigsaw
Channel-type pliers	Basin wrench
Cordless power drill and bits	Tape measure
Tubing cutting	Hacksaw
	2 × 8 lumber

Although a wall-mounted sink offers many benefits—accessibility to wheelchair users among them—there's no need to sacrifice chic style for that functionality. Photo courtesy of American Standard. (See Resources, page 298)

How to Install a Wall-Mounted Sink

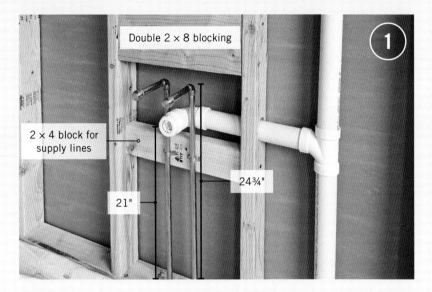

Double 2 × 8 blocking

2 × 4 block for supply lines

21"

24¾"

1

Remove the existing sink if any. Remove wall coverings as necessary to install blocking for mounting the sink. Reroute water supply and drain lines as necessary, according to the sink manufacturer's directions. The sink in this project required the centerpoints of the waste pipe be 21", and the supply lines 24¾" up from the finished floor. If unsure of your plumbing skills or code requirements, hire a professional plumber for this part of the project. Install blocking between the studs for attaching the mounting bracket for the sink. A doubled 2 × 8 is installed here. Have your plumbing inspected, if required by your municipality, before you install the drywall and finished wall surface.

2

Drill guide holes for the mounting bolts if your sink is a direct-mount model, as this one is. Some wall-hung sinks are hung from a mounting bracket. The bolts used to hang this sink are threaded like lag screws on one end, with a bolt end that projects from the wall. The guide holes should be spaced exactly as the manufacturer specifies so they align with the mounting holes in the back mounting flange on the sink.

TIP: Protect tile surfaces with masking tape in the drilling areas to avoid chip-out.

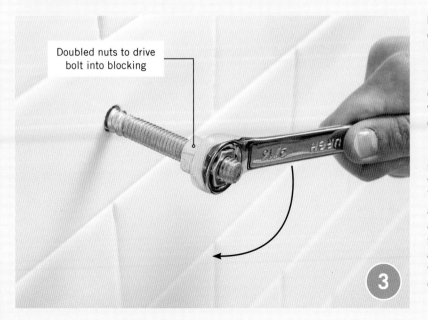

Doubled nuts to drive bolt into blocking

3

Drive the threaded mounting bolts (screw end first) into the guide holes. There should be pilot holes (smaller than the guide holes) driven into the blocking. To drive this hardware, spin a pair of nuts onto the bolt end and turn the bolt closest to you with a wrench. Drive the mounting bolt until the end is projecting out from the wall by a little more than 1½". Remove the nuts. Install the pop-up drain in the sink, and then slide the sink over the ends of the mounting bolts so the mounting flange is flush against the wall. You'll want help for this. Thread the washers and nuts onto the ends of the mounting bolts and hand-tighten. Check to make sure the sink is level and then tighten the nuts with a socket or wrench, reaching up into the void between the basin and the flange. Don't overtighten—you could crack the sink flange.

(continued)

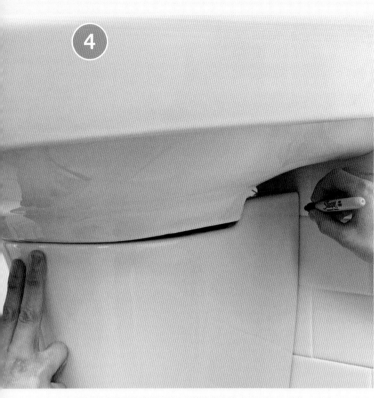

Have a helper hold the sink pedestal (in this model, a half-pedestal) in position against the underside of the sink. Mark the edges of the pedestal on the wall covering as reference for installing the pedestal-mounting hardware. Remove the pedestal.

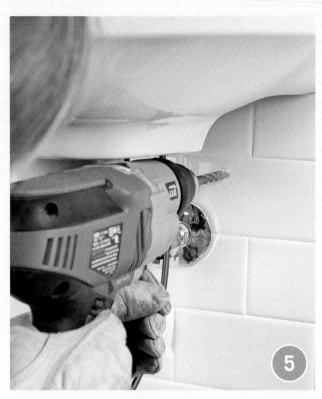

Remove the pedestal and drill the pilot holes for the pedestal-mounting bolts, which work much in the same way as the sink-mounting bolts. Drill guide and pilot holes then drive the mounting bolts, leaving about 1¼" of the bolt end exposed.

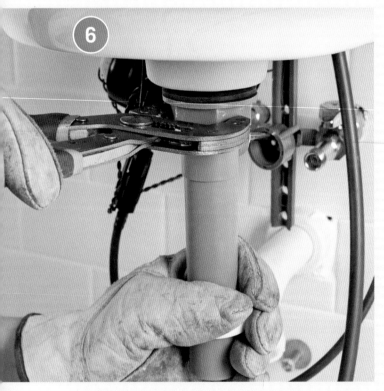

Install the drain and drain tailpiece on the sink. Also mount the faucet body to the sink deck if you have not done so already. Also attach the drain trap arm to the drain stub out in the wall and attach shutoff valves to the drain supply lines. You'll find instructions for doing all of these jobs elsewhere in this book.

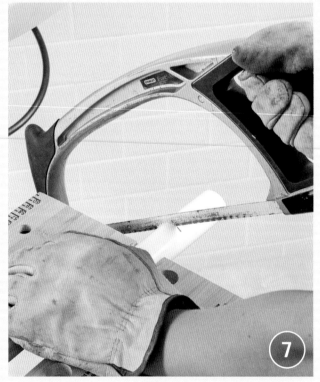

Complete the drain connection by installing a P-trap assembly that connects the tailpiece and the trap arm. Also connect the drain pop-up rod that projects out of the tailpiece to the pop-up plunger mechanism you've already installed.

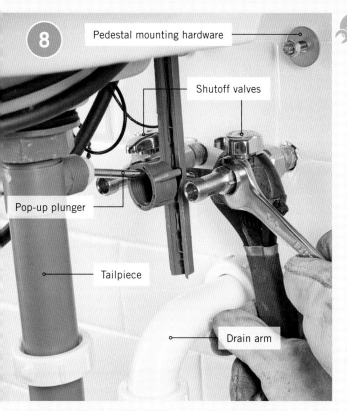

8

Pedestal mounting hardware

Shutoff valves

Pop-up plunger

Tailpiece

Drain arm

Make sure the shutoff valve fittings are tight and oriented correctly, and then hook up the faucet supply risers to the shutoff valves. Turn on the water supply and test.

To quickly and easily find an undersink leak, lay bright white paper or paper towels under the pipes and drain connections. Open the water supply valves and run water in the sinks. It should be clear exactly where the water dripped from by the location of the drip on the paper.

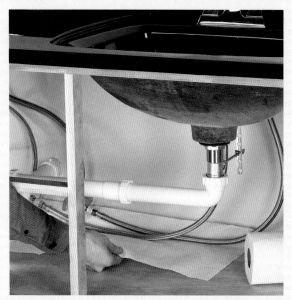

9

Slide the pedestal into place on the mounting studs. Working through the access space under the sink, use a wrench to tighten the mounting nut over the washer on the stud. Carefully tighten the nut until the pedestal is held securely in place. Be careful not to overtighten the nut.

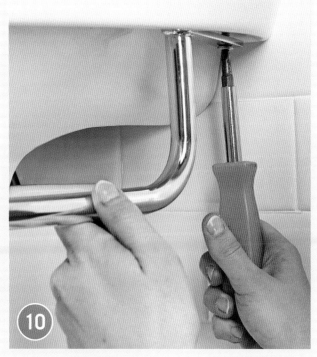

10

Attach the towel bar to the sink by first pushing the well nuts into the holes on the underside of the sink rim. Set the bar in place, and screw in the attachment screws on both sides, just until snug.

Plumbing a Double-Bowl Vanity

Side-by-side sinks are a bathroom luxury, especially for busy couples (which accounts for why they are called "his-and-her" sinks) or busy bathrooms. Although the basics of installing a vanity for a double sink are structurally the same as a single-bowl vanity, the plumbing requires modification to accommodate the extra fixture.

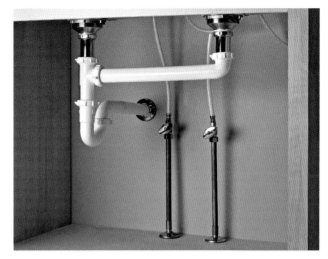

Double-bowl vanities have drain plumbing that's very similar to double-bowl kitchen sinks. In most cases, the drain tailpieces are connected beneath one of the tailpieces at a continuous waste tee. The drainline from the second bowl must slope downward toward the tee. From the tee, the drain should have a trap (usually a P-Trap) that connects to the trap arm coming out of the wall.

How to Plumb a Double Sink

Shut off the supply valves located under the sink. Disconnect and remove the supply lines connecting the faucet to the valves. Loosen the P-trap nuts at both ends and remove the P-trap.

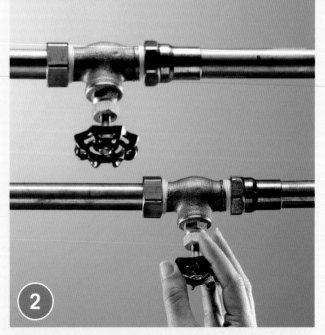

Remove the existing countertop and vanity. Turn off the house water supply at the main shut-off valve. Drain the remaining water by opening the faucet at the lowest point in the house. Use a hacksaw to remove existing undersink shutoff valves.

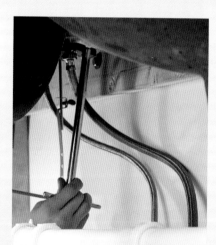

Secure the new vanity in place by screwing it to the wall.
Lay a bead of caulk along the underside and back edge of the countertop, where it will contact the vanity and wall. Set the countertop in place and check it for level. If your sinks are not integral, install them according to the type of sink you're using.

Slide the new dual-outlet valve onto the hot water supply line, pass the nut and compression washer over the pipe, and tighten with a wrench. Install the dual-outlet valve on the cold supply line in the same way.

Seat the faucets for the double sinks as you would for a single sink, by applying a bead of putty on the underside of the bases (unless they are to be used with gaskets instead of putty). Secure them in place by tightening the locking nuts on the underside of the faucets.

Connect a new PVC P-trap to the undersink drain pipe, and attach a tee connector to the trap. Extend PVC connections to the drain assemblies of both sinks.

Connect the pop-up stopper linkage.
Connect the cold water supply lines to the appropriate faucet tailpieces and repeat with the hot water supply lines. Turn on the main water supply, remove the faucet aerator, and run the water in the sinks. Check for leaks and replace the aerator.

Hands-Free Bathroom Faucets

If you've ever washed your hands in an airport bathroom, chances are you've already come across a hands-free faucet. Developed to conserve water and stop the spread of disease, these faucets have quickly become ubiquitous in commercial facilities across the country and around the world.

But now homeowners can enjoy the benefits of hands-free faucets in their own bathrooms. Although not as widely available as standard faucets, different hands-free units are beginning to appear in the aisles of large home centers and hardware stores nationwide. These feature varying technologies depending on the manufacturer.

The most common type of commercial hands-free bathroom faucet relies on an infrared motion sensor, much like those in home security systems. When something solid passes within the sensor's range, the faucet turns on for a predetermined period of time. Home units operate a little differently. They include motion sensing and "touch-on, touch-off" units. The model we selected for this installation project uses an electrical field sensor that reacts to the stored charge in every human body, called *capacitance*. Whether motion- or touch-activated, these home faucets rely on an electrical field created by a solenoid connected to the faucet body. When a human hand disrupts the electrical field, the faucet turns on or off. Touch faucets operate the same, but the faucet body itself is the electrical field.

For most of these types of faucets, water temperature and flow rate are set manually before the faucet is "programmed." Then it's a case of tapping the faucet body or waving a hand near it to start or stop the flow.

Although these faucets are pricier than standard manual models, they represent a leap forward for people with motor-skill difficulties, or for preventing disease spread between family members using a busy bathroom in a crowded house. The good news is that they are not much more challenging to install than a standard faucet—with the exception of units that are hardwired into the home's electrical system. Hardwired units should be installed by a licensed professional.

TOOLS & MATERIALS

Faucet and hardware	Teflon tape
Adjustable wrenches	Flashlight
Channel-type pliers	

A touch-on, touch-off faucet such as this can save water, make life easier for children and physically challenged users, and they come in a nice selection of style and finish options.

How to Install a Hands-Free Faucet

Check the parts in the box against the instruction sheet part list. Remove the center from the base gasket as necessary and thread the base's LED wire through the hole in the gasket. Seat the gasket into the groove in the insulator base and ensure that is snug and level.

NOTE: If your vanity deck has multiple holes, you'll need to use the supplied escutcheon plate. Run the LED wire through the escutcheon hole and seat the insulator base on top of the escutcheon (make sure the LED light is facing forward).

Slide the mounting bracket into place under the sink, on the mounting post. Be sure that the LED wire and supply lines are not crimped by the bracket. The mounting bracket needs to be oriented correctly; check the manufacturer's instructions to ensure it's situated in the right way, and secured with the metal side down.

Ensure the LED wire is not crimped and thread the mounting post nut on the mounting post. Hand tighten. Check again that the faucet body is positioned correctly on the top of the sink and the LED light is facing forward. Tighten the mounting nut with a wrench, or with the tool supplied by the manufacturer, as shown here.

(continued)

Insert the outlet tube into the top of the solenoid until it is snugly attached. Secure the tube in place with the metal clip provided. These clips can often be attached more than one way, so check the instructions to make sure you've installed the clip correctly. Then lightly pull on the solenoid to ensure the tube is firmly attached and won't come free under pressure.

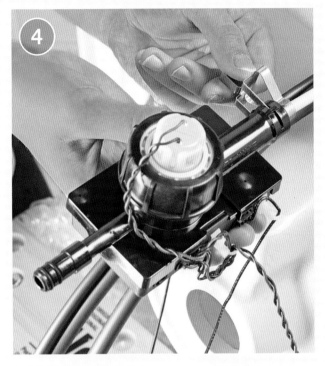

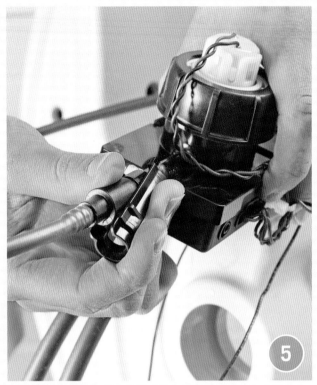

Slide the feeder hose into the bottom of the solenoid until it is snug. Snap the attachment clip in place to secure the hose, and again pull gently on the hose to make sure the clip is secure.

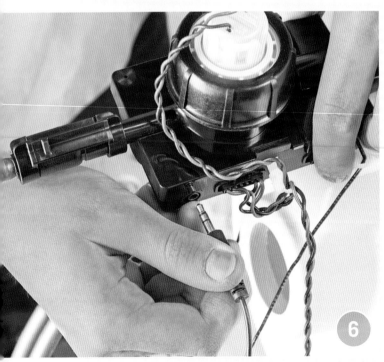

Touch the cold supply knob or another ground with your hand to dissipate any residual static charge. Remove the protective cap or endpiece from the end of the LED wire hanging from the faucet. Plug the prong of the wire into the hole in the solenoid. Make sure it is all the way in (on this model, you push until you hear a click).

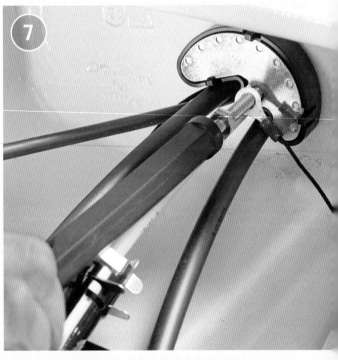

Slide the solenoid ground wire onto the mounting post and secure it in place with a nut. Tighten the nut with a wrench, ensuring that the wires don't twist together. Put the batteries in the battery box and then connect the wire from the solenoid to the connection on the battery box. Secure the battery box to the cabinet floor, wall, or underside of the sink according to the manufacturer's directions, and the type of vanity you have.

Connect the water lines for your hands-free faucet as you would with any faucet, using the supplied ferrules and check valves in place of the existing hardware on the stops. Insert the new ferrule and screw the check valve in place, hand tight. Then tighten the nut just one turn with a wrench. Attach the cold and hot lines to the proper check valves on the cold and hot stops—they must be connected to the appropriate stop (the ends of the faucet body supply lines will usually be marked as they are in this case—either with a color or other designation to signify which stop the supply line goes to). Attach the cold supply line to the check valve first, then repeat with the hot supply line. Snug to hand tight and then use a wrench to tighten one full turn more. Loop supply lines rather than cutting them.

Turn the faucet handle to the closed position and remove the aerator (use the manufacturers' supplied tool for this). Turn on both water supplies. Turn on the water for about 1 min. Turn off the water and reinstall the aerator. Check the solenoid, stops, and faucet for leaks.

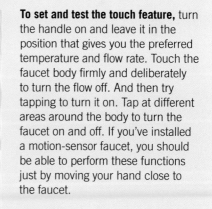

To set and test the touch feature, turn the handle on and leave it in the position that gives you the preferred temperature and flow rate. Touch the faucet body firmly and deliberately to turn the flow off. And then try tapping to turn it on. Tap at different areas around the body to turn the faucet on and off. If you've installed a motion-sensor faucet, you should be able to perform these functions just by moving your hand close to the faucet.

Kitchen Sinks

Most drop-in, self-rimming kitchen sinks are easily installed. Drop-in sinks for do-it-yourself installation are made from cast iron coated with enamel, stainless steel, enameled steel, acrylic, fiberglass, or resin composites. Because cast-iron sinks are heavy, their weight holds them in place and they require no mounting hardware. Except for the heavy lifting, they are easy to install. Stainless steel and enameled-steel sinks weigh less than cast-iron and most require mounting brackets on the underside of the countertop. Some acrylic and resin sinks rely on silicone caulk to hold them in place.

If you are replacing a sink, but not the countertop, make sure the new sink is the same size or larger. All old silicone caulk residue must be removed with acetone or denatured alcohol, or else the new caulk will not stick.

TOOLS & MATERIALS

Caulk gun
Spud wrench
Screwdriver
Sink
Sink frame
Plumber's putty or silicone caulk
Mounting clips
Jigsaw
Pen or pencil

SHOPPING TIPS

- When purchasing a sink, you also need to buy strainer bodies and baskets, sink clips, and a drain trap kit.
- Look for basin dividers that are lower than the sink rim—this reduces splashing.
- Drain holes in the back or to the side make for more usable space under the sink.
- When choosing a sink, make sure the predrilled openings will fit your faucet.

Drop-in sinks, also known as self-rimming sinks, have a wide sink flange that extends beyond the edges of the sink cutout. They also have a wide back flange to which the faucet is mounted directly.

How to Install a Self-Rimming Sink

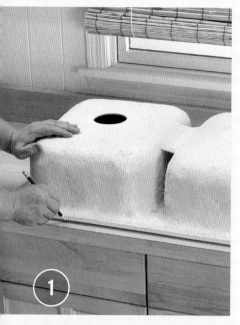

1

Invert the sink and trace around the edges as a reference for making the sink cutout cutting lines, which should be parallel to the outlines, but about 1" inside of them to create a 1" ledge. If your sink comes with a template for the cutout, use it.

2

Drill a starter hole and cut out the sink opening with a jigsaw. Cut right up to the line. Because the sink flange fits over the edges of the cutout, the opening doesn't need to be perfect, but as always you should try to do a nice, neat job.

3

Attach as much of the plumbing as makes sense to install prior to setting the sink into the opening. Having access to the underside of the flange is a great help when it comes to attaching the faucet body, sprayer, and strainer, in particular.

4

Apply a bead of silicone caulk around the edges of the sink opening. The sink flange most likely is not flat, so try and apply the caulk in the area that will make contact with the flange.

5

Place the sink in the opening. Try to get the sink centered right away so you don't need to move it around and disturb the caulk, which can break the seal. If you are installing a heavy cast-iron sink, it's best to leave the strainers off so you can grab onto the sink at the drain openings.

6

For sinks with mounting clips, tighten the clips from below using a screwdriver or wrench (depending on the type of clip your sink has). There should be at least three clips on every side. Don't overtighten the clips—this can cause the sink flange to flatten or become warped.

Standpipe Drains

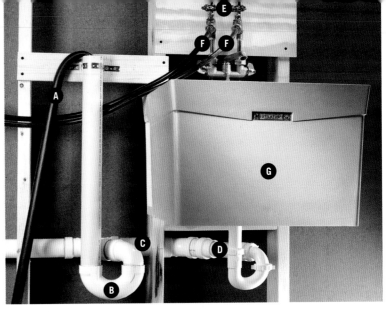

A standpipe drain allows you to drain a water-consuming appliance (usually a washing machine) directly into the waste system, instead of into a utility tub (also called a laundry tray). This eliminates the possibility of the sink drain plugging and causing the sink basin to overflow (most utility sinks do not have an overflow hole).

Some standpipes come with attached P-traps and can be purchased at many home centers.

A 2-inch pipe is required by most building codes. The top of the standpipe should be at least 18 inches high but no more than 42 inches above the floor. Hose bibs are installed in the hot and cold supply lines at the utility sink to provide the water supply to the washing machine.

A washing machine with standpipe drain: washing machine drain hose (A), 2" standpipe drain with trap (B), waste line (C), utility sink drain pipe (D), hot and cold supply lines with hose bibs (E), rubber supply hoses to washing machine (F), and utility sink (G).

TOOLS & MATERIALS

Reciprocating saw	2 × 4 backer	Threaded tee fittings
Utility knife	2½" deck screws	Torch
Waste wye fitting	½" screws	Sheet metal
Primer & solvent glue	Pipe strap	Teflon tape
90° elbow	Hose bibs	Rubber supply hose
2" standpipe with trap	Solder	

How to Install a Washing Machine Standpipe Drain

Provide venting for the standpipe and/or the utility sink. Some locales allow you to install an unvented standpipe, but most building departments now require some sort of venting. In an extreme case, you may need to run a new vent up through the roof.

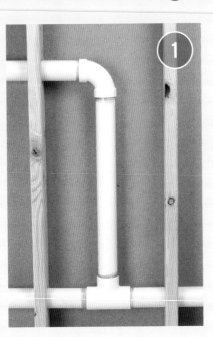

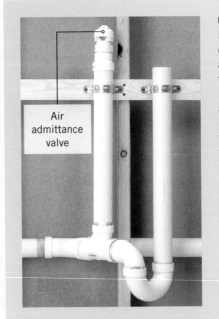

Air admittance valve

OPTION: Your building department may allow you to vent the standpipe by installing an air admittance valve (AAV). Consult with your inspector to be sure you locate the AAV in a code-approved manner. If you are installing a utility sink instead of a standpipe, you may be able to install an AAV onto the drain trap under the sink.

2

Measure and mark the size and location of a waste wye fitting in the drain line. Remove the marked section, using a reciprocating saw. Make cuts as straight as possible.

Utility sink drain pipe

3

Use a utility knife to remove rough burrs on the cut ends of the pipe. Dry-fit the waste wye fitting into the drain line to make sure it fits properly, then attach the wye fitting using primer and solvent cement.

4

Dry-fit a 90° elbow and a 2" standpipe with trap to the waste wye fitting. Make sure the top of the standpipe is between 18 and 42" above the floor. Solvent-cement all the pipes in place.

5

Attach a 2 × 4 backer behind the top of the standpipe for support, using 2½" deck screws. Fasten standpipe to the wood support, using a length of pipe strap and ½" screws. Insert the washing machine's rubber drain hose into the standpipe.

How to Hook Up a Washing Machine Box

Install hose bibs in the utility sink supply lines. Turn off water main and drain pipes. Cut into each supply pipe 6" to 12" from faucet. Solder threaded tee fittings into each supply line. Protect wood from torch flame with two layers of sheet metal. Wrap Teflon tape around threads of hose bibs, and screw them into tee fittings. Connect a rubber supply hose from each bib to the appropriate intake port on the washing machine.

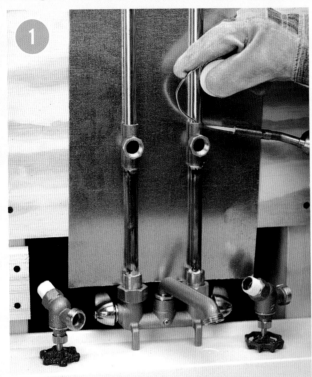

From washer

To washer

Recessed washing machine boxes are available for finished utility rooms. The supply pipes and standpipe drain run to one central location. The washing machine's hose bibs, supply hoses, and drain hose must remain easily accessible.

SAFE WASHING MACHINE WATER SUPPLY

Washing machine hoses usually last a long time, but "usually" isn't good enough. Because a damaged hose may drip or even gush for a long time before it's discovered, especially in a room that's infrequently used, it is recommended that hoses be replaced every year or two.

For more peace of mind, consider two valve options. A self-adjusting valve eliminates constant pressure on the hoses, and so lengthens their life. It turns on only when the machine is being used. An automatic laundry shutoff valve removes water pressure on the hoses when the machine is not in use.

The self-adjusting valve shown is installed with the plumbing inside a wall, for a neat look. Remove drywall, if there is any, to expose the framing. Install the valve at the recommended height by nailing its adjustable wings to studs on each side. Run the supply pipes and the drain line between studs, and attach to the valve and test. Then apply drywall and add the cover plate.

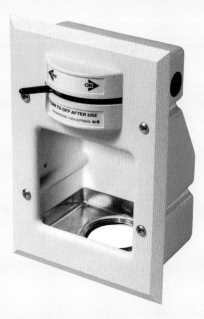

How to Install a Utility Sink

Assemble the sink. Work with the sink upside-down. For many models, the legs simply slip into slots at the corners.

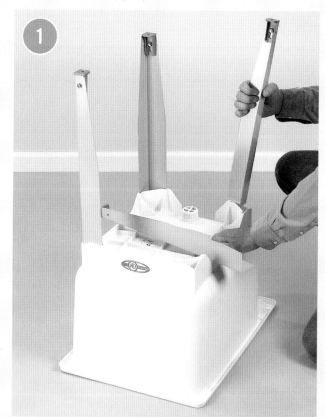

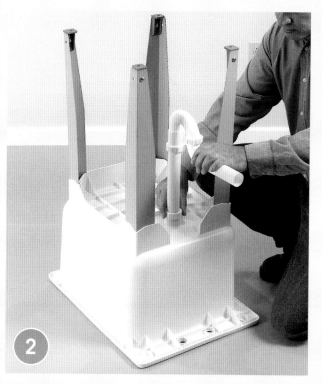

Attach the trap. Turn the sink sideways and install the strainer body: apply a rope of plumber's putty to the underside of the flange, then tighten the nut on the underside of the sink. Assemble the drain trap. These plastic fittings can be tightened by hand.

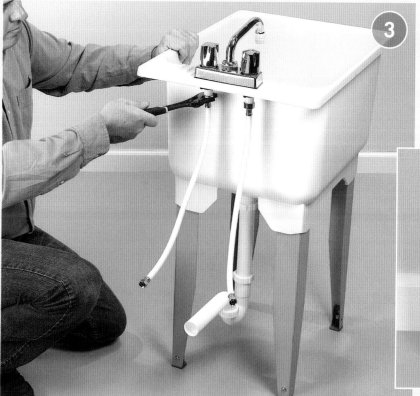

Install and hook up the faucet. Turn the sink right-side-up and install the faucet in the sink's holes, run flexible supply lines to the hot and cold inlets, and tighten with a wrench. Drive screws through the holes in the legs to anchor the sink to the floor (below). If you have a concrete floor, you'll need a masonry bit and masonry screws.

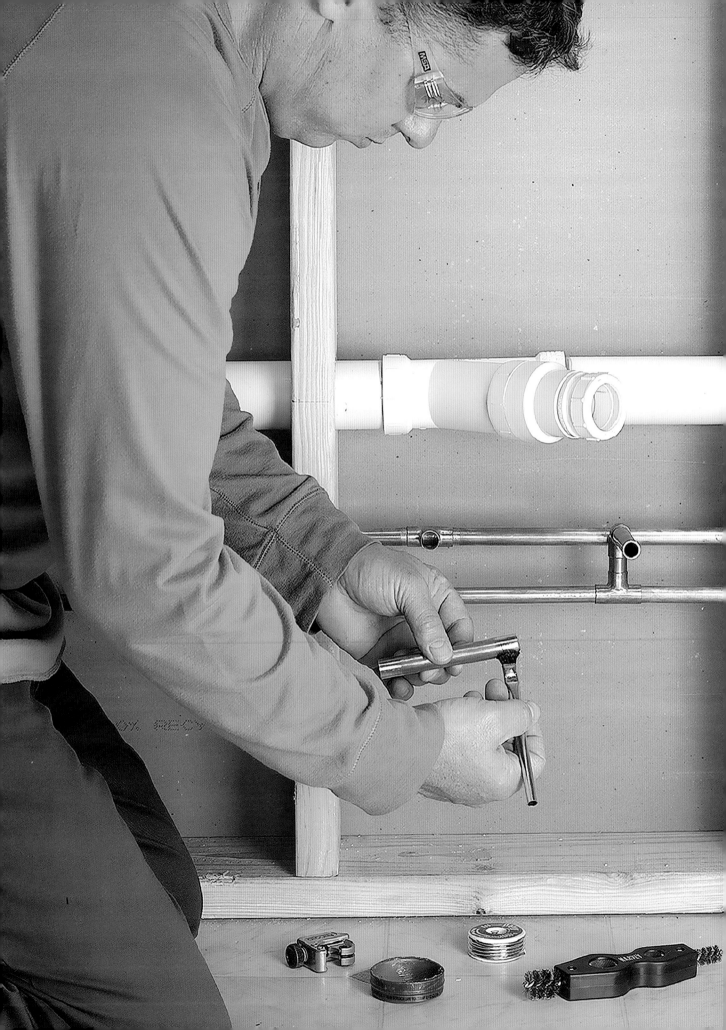

Installing Plumbing Lines

Installing new plumbing lines is not as difficult as most homeowners may believe. If you are building a new addition or will be working in brand-new stud walls, you can simplify the job immeasurably by planning ahead and designing your walls to hold the plumbing. The most important design consideration is that a wet wall wall (a wall containing drain and/or supply plumbing) should be built using 2 × 6 framing members, not 2 × 4. The extra width allows you to cut notches or access holes in the framing members without removing so much material that your walls fail to pass construction codes.

In addition to wall thickness, the other chief consideration when planning a new plumbing line is where (and how) it will tie into your existing plumbing system. As a general rule you want to locate the tie-in points so they are as close as possible to existing drain and supply pipes. But you also need to factor in access—if you have an exposed drain pipe in the floor below, you'll be glad you chose to tie into it rather than a pipe in a finished wall next door, even if it means the new lines are a bit longer.

Installing new plumbing lines takes planning, preparation, and a permit. Involve your local plumbing inspector from the outset. He or she will have good suggestions and help steer you in a wise direction. Plus, they will need to visit your home at least once during the process to inspect and approve your work, so it is always a good idea to treat the inspector as a partner.

In this chapter:
- Installation Basics
- Planning Plumbing Routes
- Sample Plumbing Layouts
- Tips for Installing New Plumbing Lines

Installation Basics

A major plumbing project is a complicated affair that often requires demolition and carpentry skills. Bathroom or kitchen plumbing may be unusable for several days while completing the work, so make sure you have a backup bathroom or kitchen space to use during this time.

To ensure that your project goes quickly, always buy plenty of pipe and fittings—at least 25% more than you think you need. Making several extra trips to the building center is a nuisance and can add many hours to your project. Always purchase from a reputable retailer that will allow you to return leftover fittings for credit.

The how-to projects on the following pages demonstrate standard plumbing techniques but should not be used as a literal blueprint for your own work. Pipe and fitting sizes, fixture layout, and pipe routing will always vary according to individual circumstances. When planning your project, carefully read all the information in the planning section. Before you begin work, create a detailed plumbing plan to guide your work and help you obtain the required permits. Don't depend on manufacturer specs to plan the installations of fixtures and the running of pipes; always check local codes. They may vary from the specs, and are generally more stringent.

Use 2 × 6 studs to frame "wet walls" when constructing a new bathroom or kitchen. Thicker walls provide more room to run drain pipes and main waste-vent stacks, making installation much easier.

Installing New Plumbing

Use masking tape to mark the locations of fixtures and pipes on the walls and floors. Read the layout specifications that come with each sink, tub, or toilet, then mark the drain and supply lines accordingly. Position the fixtures on the floor, and outline them with tape. Measure and adjust until the arrangement is comfortable to you and meets minimum clearance specifications. If you are working in a finished room, prevent damage to wallpaper or paint by using self-adhesive notes to mark the walls.

Consider the location of cabinets when roughing in the water supply and drain stub-outs. You may want to temporarily position the cabinets in their final locations before completing the drain and water supply runs.

Install control valves at the points where the new branch supply lines meet the main distribution pipes. By installing valves, you can continue to supply the rest of the house with water while you are working on the new branches.

(continued)

MAXIMUM HOLE & NOTCH CHART

FRAMING MEMBER	MAXIMUM HOLE SIZE	MAXIMUM NOTCH SIZE
2 × 4 loadbearing stud	1⁷⁄₁₆" diameter	⅞" deep
2 × 4 non-loadbearing stud	2⅛" diameter	1⁷⁄₁₆" deep
2 × 6 loadbearing stud	2¼" diameter	1⅜" deep
2 × 6 non-loadbearing stud	3⁵⁄₁₆" diameter	2³⁄₁₆" deep
2 × 6 joists	1⅞" diameter	⅞" deep
2 × 8 joists	2⅜" diameter	1¼" deep
2 × 10 joists	3¹⁄₁₆" diameter	1½" deep
2 × 12 joists	3¾" diameter	1⅞" deep

The framing member chart shows the maximum sizes for holes and notches that can be cut into studs and joists when running pipes. Where possible, use notches rather than bored holes, because pipe installation is usually easier. When boring holes, there must be at least ⅝" of wood between the edge of a stud and the hole, and at least 2" between the edge of a joist and the hole. Joists can be notched only in the end ⅓ of the overall span; never in the middle ⅓ of the joist. When two pipes are run through a stud, the pipes should be stacked one over the other, never side by side.

Create access panels so that in the future you will be able to service fixture fittings and shutoff valves located inside the walls. Frame an opening between studs, then trim the opening with wood moldings. Cover the opening with a removable plywood panel the same thickness as the wall surface, then finish it to match the surrounding walls.

Protect pipes from punctures if they are less than 1¼" from the front face of wall studs or joists by attaching metal protector plates to the framing members.

Test-fit materials before solvent-cementing or soldering joints. Test-fitting ensures that you have the correct fittings and enough pipe to do the job, and can help you avoid lengthy delays during installation.

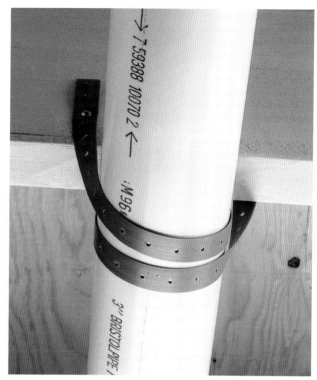

Support pipes adequately. Horizontal and vertical runs of DWV and water supply pipe must be supported at minimum intervals, which are specified by your local plumbing codes. A variety of metal and plastic materials are available for supporting plumbing pipes.

Use plastic bushings to help hold plumbing pipes securely in holes bored through wall plates, studs, and joists. Bushings can help to cushion the pipes, preventing wear and reducing rattling. Always use manufacturer-recommended bushings with metal wall studs (inset).

Install extra tee fittings on new drain and vent lines so that you can pressure-test the system when the building inspector reviews your installation. A new DWV line should have these extra tee fittings near the points where the new branch drains and vent pipes reach the main waste-vent stack.

Planning Plumbing Routes

The first, and perhaps most important, step when replacing old plumbing is to decide how and where to run the new pipes. Since the stud cavities and joist spaces are often covered with finished wall surfaces, finding routes for running new pipes can be challenging.

When planning pipe routes, choose straight, easy pathways whenever possible. Rather than running water supply pipes around wall corners and through studs, for example, it may be easiest to run them straight up wall cavities from the basement. Instead of running a bathtub drain across floor joists, run it straight down into the basement, where the branch drain can be easily extended underneath the joists to the main waste-vent stack.

In some situations, it is most practical to route the new pipes in wall and floor cavities that already hold plumbing pipes, since these spaces are often framed to provide long, unobstructed runs. A detailed map of your plumbing system can be very helpful when planning routes for new plumbing pipes (page 179).

The most complicated part of new plumbing service is often the venting for the DWV system. All fixtures must be vented in a code-approved manner, and these codes are at times daunting to learn. See page 184 for more information on planning vent runs. Where possible, run vent lines through walls or up to the attic, to tie into existing vents. If that is not allowed, you may need to run a vent pipe up through the roof. In some cases you can use air admittance valves instead of vent pipes.

To maximize their profits, plumbing contractors generally try to avoid opening walls or changing wall framing when installing new plumbing. But the do-it-yourselfer does not have these limitations. Faced with the difficulty of running pipes through enclosed spaces, you may find it easiest to remove wall surfaces or to create a newly framed space for running new pipes.

On these pages, you will see some common methods used to create pathways for replacing old pipes with new plumbing.

Build a framed chase. A chase is a false wall created to provide space for new plumbing pipes. It is especially effective for installing a new main drainage stack. On a two-story house, chases can be stacked one over the other on each floor in order to run plumbing from the basement to the attic. Once plumbing is completed and inspected, the chase is covered with wallboard and finished to match the room.

Planning Pipe Routes

Use existing access panels to disconnect fixtures and remove old pipes. Plan the location of new fixtures and pipe runs to make use of existing access panels, minimizing the amount of demolition and repair work you will need to do.

Convert a laundry chute into a channel for running new plumbing pipes. The door of the chute can be used to provide access to control valves, or it can be removed and covered with wall materials, then finished to match the surrounding wall.

Run pipes inside a closet. If they are unobtrusive, pipes can be left exposed at the back of the closet. Or, you can frame a chase to hide the pipes after the installation is completed.

Remove suspended ceiling panels to route new plumbing pipes in joist cavities. Or, you can route pipes across a standard plaster or wallboard ceiling, then construct a false ceiling to cover the installation, provided there is adequate height. Most building codes require a minimum of 7 ft. from floor to finished ceiling.

(continued)

Use a drill bit extension and spade bit or hole saw to drill through wall plates from unfinished attic or basement spaces above or below the wall.

Look for "wet walls." Walls that hold old plumbing pipes can be good choices for running long vertical runs of new pipe. These spaces are usually open, without obstacles such as fireblocks and insulation.

Probe wall and floor cavities with a long piece of plastic pipe to ensure that a clear pathway exists for running new pipe (left photo). Once you have established a route using the narrow pipe, you can use the pipe as a guide when running larger drain pipes up into the wall (right photo).

Remove flooring when necessary. Because replacing toilet and bathtub drains usually requires that you remove sections of floor, a full plumbing replacement job is often done in conjunction with a complete bathroom remodeling project.

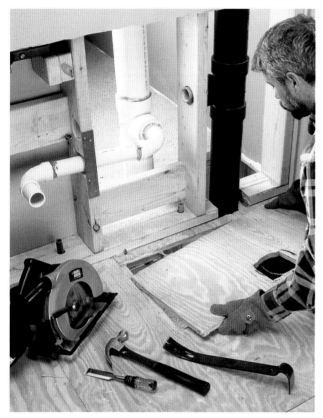

Remove wall surfaces when access from above or below the wall is not possible. This demolition work can range from cutting narrow channels in plaster or wallboard to removing the entire wall surface. Remove wall surfaces back to the centers of adjoining studs; the exposed studs provide a nailing surface for attaching repair materials once the plumbing project is completed.

Create a detailed map showing the planned route for your new plumbing pipes. Such a map can help you get your plans approved by the inspector, and it makes work much simpler. If you have already mapped your existing plumbing system, those drawings can be used to plan new pipe routes.

Sample Plumbing Layouts

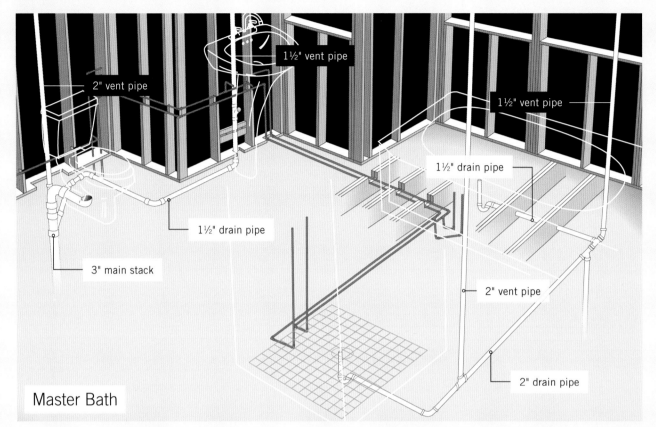

1½" vent pipe

2" vent pipe

1½" vent pipe

1½" drain pipe

1½" drain pipe

2" vent pipe

3" main stack

2" drain pipe

Master Bath

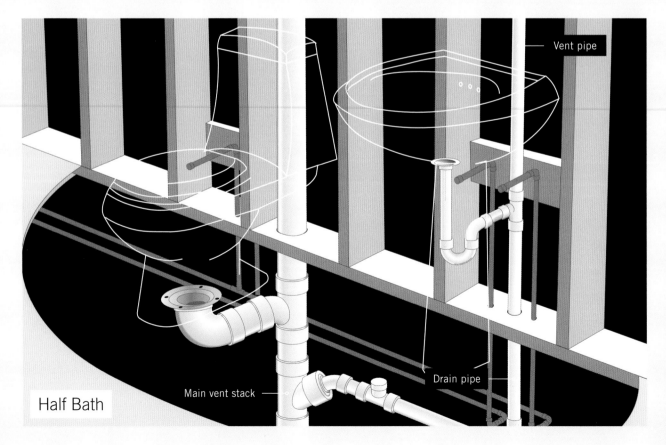

Vent pipe

Drain pipe

Main vent stack

Half Bath

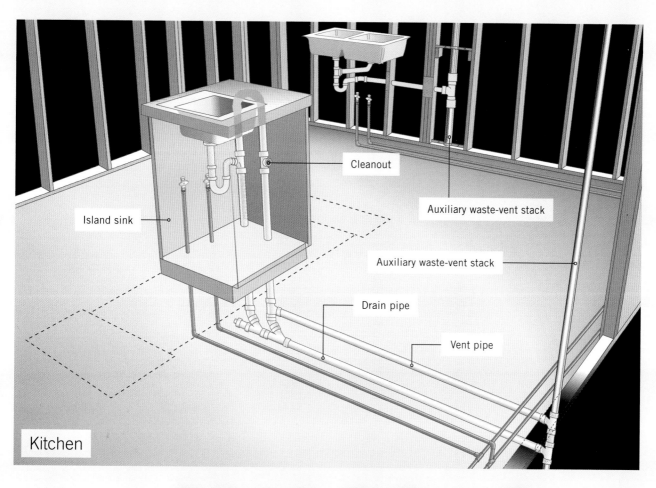

Island sink

Cleanout

Auxiliary waste-vent stack

Auxiliary waste-vent stack

Drain pipe

Vent pipe

Kitchen

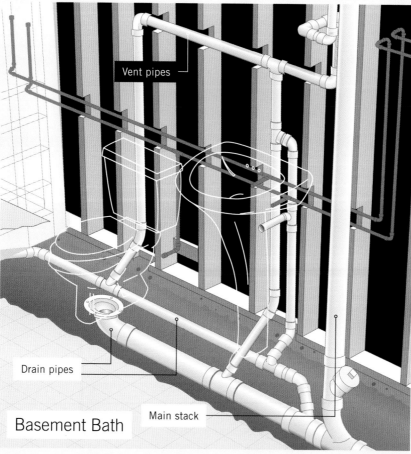

Vent pipes

Drain pipes

Main stack

Basement Bath

Tips for Installing New Plumbing Lines: Supply Lines

Remove the subfloor completely in the installation area if you are running new supply lines inside the floor cavity. Among other advantages, this allows you to dry-fit the complete layout before soldering or solvent-welding.

Support supply risers with a ¾"-thick backer board installed between floor joists. Secure the horizontal supply tubes to the backer with pipe straps. Risers should extend at least 6" above the finished floor.

When soldering copper, tack a piece of metal flashing between wall studs behind the work area to serve as a heat shield.

Use ¾-to-½" reducing tees to tap into ¾" branch supply lines. Most plumbing fixtures require only a ½"-dia. supply tube.

Use a tubing cutter to remove sections of branch supply lines.

Drill access holes directly into a cabinet base to allow supply risers to enter the cabinet. The holes should align with access holes for the risers in the subfloor.

Use a small level to make sure unattached riser pipes are plumb when marking cutting lines on mating horizontal branch lines.

Dry-fit as much of the new line as you can, whether the new pipes are copper or cpvc. Dry-fitting almost always yields more reliable results for DIYers than taking measurements as you go.

Tips for Installing New Plumbing Lines: Drain and Vent Lines

Drain and vent lines may be located in exterior walls, but if you live in a cold climate the walls must be well insulated, with ample insulation between the pipes and the exterior. Avoid running supply lines in an exterior wall in cold climates.

If installing a large whirlpool tub, cut away the subfloor to expose the full length of the joists under the tub, then screw or bolt a second joist, called a sister, against each existing joist. Make sure both ends of each joist are supported by load-bearing walls.

Lay large sections of plywood across the joists to create a stable work surface when installing plumbing lines in an open floor.

Use levels to check your work when installing new lines. This is especially important for meeting minimum slope requirements. It's also a good practice to ensure that visible lines stay parallel.

Install cleanouts at the ends of branch drain lines to create access points for augers in the event you need to remove a clog.

If a floor joist interferes with the toilet drain, cut away a short section of the joist and box-frame the area with double headers. The framed opening should be just large enough to install the toilet and sink drains.

CONNECTING NEW VENT PIPES TO A MAIN STACK

In the attic, cut into the main waste-vent stack and install a vent tee fitting, using banded couplings. The side outlet on the vent tee should face the new 2" vent pipe running down to the bathroom. Attach a test tee fitting to the vent tee.

NOTE: If your stack is cast iron, make sure to adequately support it before cutting into it.

Use elbows, vent tee fittings, reducers, and lengths of pipe as needed to link the new vent pipes to the test tee fitting on the main waste-vent stack. Vent pipes can be routed in many ways, but you should make sure the pipes have a slight downward angle to prevent moisture from collecting in the pipes. Support the pipes every 4 ft. or as required by local codes.

Tips for Installing New Plumbing Lines: Basement Bath

Score cutting lines into the concrete surfaces of the basement foundation floor before attempting to break out the concrete with a jackhammer (recommended) or cold chisel and mallet. This helps prevent the migration of cracks outside of the work area and makes for an overall neater job.

Use a jackhammer to break up and remove the basement foundation floor in the installation area so you can run new drain/sewer pipelines from the bathroom to the main drain. Wear a dust mask, hearing protection, and eye protection. It's also a good idea to cordon off the work areas from the rest of your home with sheet plastic to keep dust from traveling.

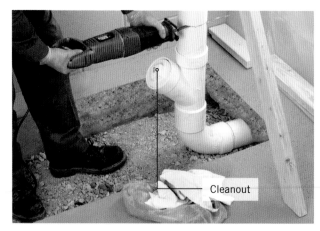

Cleanout

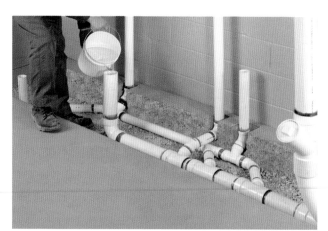

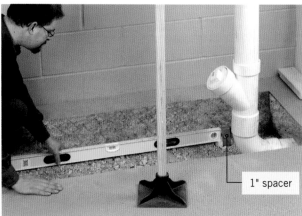

1" spacer

Replace the entire sweep elbow where the drain stack joins the sewer line. The union in the new sweep should have an opening to accommodate the new drain line.

After you've made all your new drain line connections, test the line by dumping water down the risers to make sure there are no leaks. Then, cover the new drain lines with a course of drainage rock followed by a layer of fresh concrete that's at least 4" thick.

Working with Gas Pipe

Running gas supply lines and making gas hookups are similar jobs to working with drain and supply plumbing. Given the extremely dangerous nature of handling natural gas and propane, however, you should approach these jobs with extreme caution. In fact, many jurisdictions do not allow homeowners to install gas pipe unless they happen to be certified in that area of expertise. Making the hookup from supply lines to gas fixtures is less regulated, but still dangerous. The availability of new flexible gas connectors has made the task simpler and eliminated some of the most troublesome aspects, including the use of flare fittings. If you choose to attempt any projects with gas connections, be sure to pay attention to the materials you'll use. Whether it is the copper supply tubes or the tape used to lubricate threaded connections, gas lines employ an entirely different set of gas-rated pipes, fittings, and materials.

Gas Consumption of Household Appliances

APPLIANCE	AVG. BTU'S PER HOUR	GAS CONSUMPTION PER HOUR*
50-gallon water heater	50,000	50 cu. ft.
Furnace	200,000	200 cu. ft.
Clothes dryer	35,000	35 cu. ft.
Range/oven	65,000	65 cu. ft.

*Based on output rate of 1,000 btu per cubic foot of fuel per hour. Your actual rate will likely differ. Check with your energy company.

Determine the flow rate for a branch line by adding the gas consumption per hour (use above data only if specific information is not printed on your appliance label) of each appliance. Although appliances may not run concurrently, it is advisable to select pipe size based on 100% flow rate. Note that distance traveled also plays an important role in selecting pipe size diameter (½", ¾", 1", 1¼", or 1½").

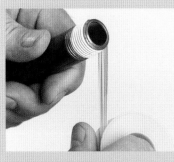

Wrap the male pipe threads with gas-rated Teflon tape before joining to fittings. Wind the tape clockwise (as you face the hole in the pipe), and wrap two or three windings. Alternatively, apply pipe joint compound to the threads.

Turn off the gas at the gas meter, using an adjustable wrench. The valve does not have a stop, so it can rotate indefinitely. The gas is off when the bar is perpendicular to the pipe.

Disconnect the existing appliance. If a flexible stainless-steel connector was used, discard it, as they can only be installed once. Remove the gas stub-out or flexible copper line back to the supply line.

Attach a male-threaded-to-flare adapter to the valve. Use two adjustable wrenches—one holding the valve in place and one tightening the fitting.

Attach the appliance connector tube to the valve. Make sure to buy a connector with ends that match the valve and the appliance port. In most cases, you may now use flexible stainless-steel connectors instead of soft copper tubing that requires flaring. But soft copper is allowed if you have the equipment to make a flare fitting joint and want to save a few dollars.

Hook up the appliance by attaching the other flare nut to the threaded gas inlet port on the appliance. Plug in the appliance's power cord. Turn on gas at the main meter and at the stop valve and test the flare fittings for leaks. Once you're certain all the joints are good, carefully slide the appliance into place.

Plumbing Repairs

Making plumbing repairs is a good deal easier today than it was a generation ago. Back then, a leaky faucet was repaired by disassembling the valve and repacking it with messy string. Today, you simply remove the old cartridge and pop in a new one. In older times, if your toilet was running you replaced a rubber gasket or washer. Today, you're more likely to simply remove and replace the entire flush mechanism, which is actually a good deal easier to do than fixing one discreet piece of the mechanism. But convenience always comes at a price. Locating the correct replacement parts can get tricky, and instead of a cheap washer or bit of graphite string, you usually have to pay for the whole replacement parts package.

Faucets and drains are the parts of your plumbing system that are most likely to need repairs. Faucets leak or drip and drains clog. If you add these repairs to fixing toilet problems, you've covered almost everything you're likely to face. This chapter includes thorough information on these common repairs, as well as several that you're less likely to encounter—but in the event that you do, you'll be prepared.

In this chapter:
- Common Toilet Problems
- Clogged Toilets
- Toilet Flanges
- Toilet Drain Lines
- Sink Faucets
- Kitchen Sprayers
- Fixing Leaky Tubs & Shower Faucets
- Single-Handle Tub & Shower Faucet with Scald Control
- Tubs & Showers
- Sink Drains
- Branch & Main Drains
- Supply Pipes
- Noisy Pipes

Common Toilet Problems

A clogged toilet is one of the most common plumbing problems. If a toilet overflows or flushes sluggishly, clear the clog with a plunger or closet auger. If the problem persists, the clog may be in a branch drain or a drainage stack (pages 244 to 245).

Most other toilet problems are fixed easily with minor adjustments that require no disassembly or replacement parts. You can make these adjustments in a few minutes, using simple tools (pages 192 to 198).

If minor adjustments do not fix the problem, further repairs will be needed. The parts of a standard toilet are not difficult to take apart, and most repair projects can be completed in less than an hour.

A recurring puddle of water on the floor around a toilet may be caused by a crack in the toilet base or in the tank. A damaged toilet should be replaced. Installing a new toilet is an easy project that can be finished in three or four hours.

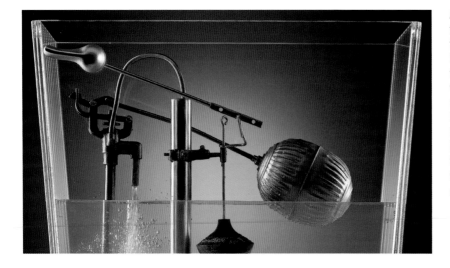

An older toilet may have a tank ball that settles onto the flush valve to stop the flow of water into the bowl. The ball is attached to a lift wire, which is in turn attached to the lift rod. A ballcock valve is usually made of brass, with rubber washers that can wear out. If the ballcock valve malfunctions, you might be able to find old washers to repair it, but replacing both the ballcock and the tank ball with a float-cup assembly and flapper is easier and makes for a more durable repair.

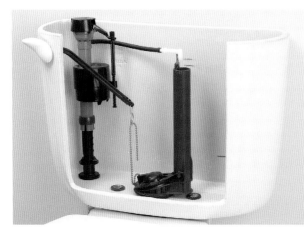

A modern float-cup valve with flapper is inexpensive and made of plastic, but is more reliable than an old ballcock valve and ball.

A pressure-assist toilet has a large vessel that nearly fills the tank. As water enters the vessel, pressure builds up. When the toilet is flushed, this pressure helps push water forcefully down into the bowl. As a result, a pressure-assist toilet provides strong flushing power with minimal water consumption.

PROBLEMS	REPAIRS
 Toilet handle sticks or is hard to push.	1. Adjust lift wires (page 192). 2. Clean and adjust handle (page 195).
Handle must be held down for entire flush.	1. Adjust handle (page 195). 2. Shorten lift chain or wires (page 192). 3. Replace waterlogged flapper.
 Handle is loose.	1. Adjust handle (page 195). 2. Reattach lift chain or lift wires to lever (page 192).
Toilet will not flush at all.	1. Make sure water is turned on. 2. Adjust lift chain or lift wires (page 192).
 Toilet does not flush completely.	1. Adjust lift chain (page 195). 2. Adjust water level in tank (page 194). 3. Increase pressure on pressure-assisted toilet.
Toilet overflows or flushes sluggishly.	1. Clear clogged toilet (page 206). 2. Clear clogged branch drain or drainage stack (page 244).
 Toilet runs continuously or there are phantom flushes.	1. Adjust lift wires or lift chain (page 192). 2. Replace leaky float ball (page 196). 3. Adjust water level in tank (page 194). 4. Adjust and clean flush valve (page 195). 5. Replace flush valve (page 198). 6. Replace flapper. 7. Service pressure-assist valve (page 204).
 Water on floor around toilet.	1. Tighten tank bolts and water connections (page 208). 2. Insulate tank to prevent condensation. 3. Replace wax ring (page 208). 4. Replace cracked tank or bowl.
Toilet noisy when filling.	1. Open shutoff valve completely. 2. Replace ballcock and float valve. 3. Refill tube is disconnected.
 Weak flush.	1. Clean clogged rim openings. 2. Replace old low-flow toilet.
Toilet rocks.	1. Replace wax ring and bolts (page 208). 2. Replace toilet flange (page 208).

Making Minor Adjustments

Many common toilet problems can be fixed by making minor adjustments to the handle and the attached lift chain (or lift wires).

If the handle sticks or is hard to push, remove the tank cover and clean the handle-mounting nut. Make sure the lift wires are straight.

If the toilet will not flush completely unless the handle is held down, you may have to remove excess slack in the lift chain.

If the toilet will not flush at all, the lift chain may be broken or may have to be reattached to the handle lever.

A continuously running toilet (page opposite) can be caused by bent lift wires, kinks in a lift chain, or lime buildup on the handle mounting nut. Clean and adjust the handle and the lift wires or chain to fix the problem.

How to Adjust a Toilet Handle & Lift Chain (or Lift Wires)

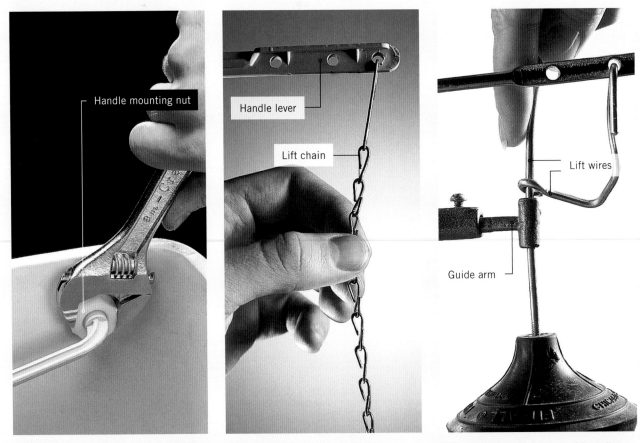

Clean and adjust handle-mounting nut so handle operates smoothly. Mounting nut has reversed threads. Loosen nut by turning clockwise; tighten by turning counterclockwise. Remove lime buildup with a brush dipped in vinegar.

Adjust lift chain so it hangs straight from handle lever, with about ½" of slack. Remove excess slack in chain by hooking the chain in a different hole in the handle lever or by removing links with needlenose pliers. A broken lift chain must be replaced.

Adjust lift wires (found on older toilets without lift chains) so that wires are straight and operate smoothly when handle is pushed. A sticky handle often can be fixed by straightening bent lift wires. You can also buy replacement wires, or replace the whole assembly with a float cup.

Phantom flushes? Phantom flushes are weak flushes that occur without turning the handle. The flapper may not be completely sealing against the flush valve's seat. Make sure the chain is not tangled, and that the flapper can go all the way down. If that does not solve the problem, shut off water and drain the tank. If the problem persists, the flapper may need to be replaced.

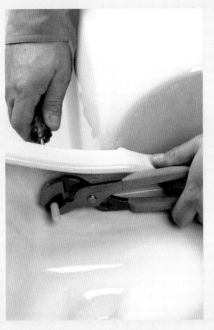

Seat loose? Loose seats are almost always the result of a loose nut on the seat bolts. Tighten the nuts with pliers. If the nut is corroded or stripped, replace the bolts and nuts or replace the whole seat.

Tank fills too slowly? The first place to check is the shutoff valve where the supply tube for the toilet is connected. Make sure it is fully open. If it is, you may need to replace the shutoff—these fittings are fairly cheap and frequently fail to open fully.

Seat uncomfortably low? Instead of going to the trouble of raising the toilet or replacing it with a taller model, you can simply replace the seat with a thicker, extended seat.

Bowl not refilling well? The rim holes may be clogged; many toilets have small holes on the underside of the bowl rim, through which water squirts during a flush. If you notice that some of these holes are clogged, use a stiff-bristled brush to clear out debris. You may need to first apply toilet bowl cleaner or mineral cleaner.

Toilet running? Running toilets are usually caused by faulty or misadjusted fill valves, but sometimes the toilet runs because the tank is leaking water into the bowl. To determine if this is happening with your toilet, add a few drops of food coloring to the tank water. If, after a while, the water in the bowl becomes colored, then you have a leak and probably need to replace the rubber gasket at the base of your flush valve.

Reset Tank Water Level

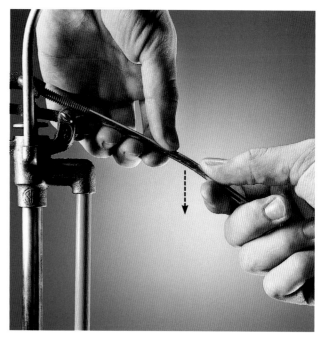

Tank water flowing into the overflow pipe is the sound we hear when a toilet is running. Usually, this is caused by a minor misadjustment that fails to tell the water to shut off when the toilet tank is full. The culprit is a float ball or cup that is adjusted to set a water level in the tank that's higher than the top of the overflow pipe, which serves as a drain for excess tank water. The other photos on this page show how to fix the problem.

A ball float is connected to a float arm that's attached to a plunger on the other end. As the tank fills, the float rises and lifts one end of the float arm. At a certain point, the float arm depresses the plunger and stops the flow of water. By simply bending the float arm downward a bit, you can cause it to depress the plunger at a lower tank water level, solving the problem.

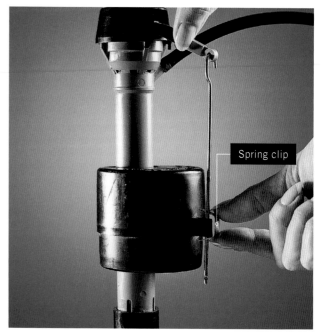

Spring clip

A diaphragm fill valve usually is made of plastic and has a wide bonnet that contains a rubber diaphragm. Turn the adjustment screw clockwise to lower the water level and counterclockwise to raise it.

A float cup fill valve is made of plastic and is easy to adjust. Lower the water level by pinching the spring clip with fingers or pliers and moving the clip and cup down the pull rod and shank. Raise the water level by moving the clip and cup upward.

WHAT IF THE FLUSH STOPS TOO SOON?

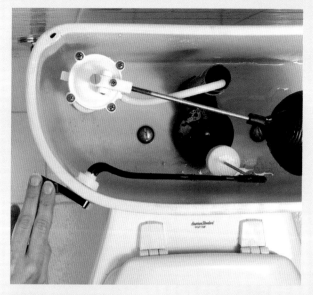

Sometimes there is plenty of water in the tank, but not enough of it makes it to the bowl before the flush valve shuts off the water from the tank. Modern toilets are designed to leave some water in the tank, since the first water that leaves the tank does so with the most force. (It's pressed out by the weight of the water on top.) To increase the duration of the flush, shorten the length of the chain between the flapper and the float (yellow in the model shown).

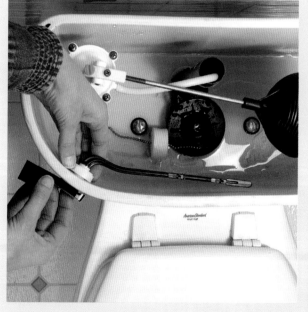

If the toilet is not completing flushes and the lever and chain for the flapper or tank ball are correctly adjusted, the problem could be that the handle mechanism needs cleaning or replacement. Remove the chain/linkage from the handle lever. Remove the nut on the backside of the handle with an adjustable wrench. It unthreads clockwise (the reverse of standard nuts). Remove the old handle from the tank.

The handle lever should pull straight up on the flapper. If it doesn't, reposition the chain hook on the handle lever. When the flapper is covering the opening, there should be just a little slack in the chain. If there is too much slack, shorten the chain and cut off excess with the cutters on your pliers.

Unless the handle parts are visibly broken, try cleaning them with an old toothbrush dipped in white vinegar. Replace the handle and test the action. If it sticks or is hard to operate, replace it. Most replacement handles come with detailed instructions that tell you how to install and adjust them.

How to Replace a Fill Valve

Toilet fill valves wear out eventually. They can be repaired, but it's easier and a better fix to just replace them. Before removing the old fill valve, shut off the water supply at the fixture stop valve located on the tube that supplies water to the tank. Flush the toilet and sponge out the remaining water. Loosen the nut and disconnect the supply tube, then loosen and remove the mounting nut.

If the fill valve spins while you turn the mounting nut, you may need to hold it still with locking pliers. Lift out the fill valve. In the case of an old ballcock valve, the float ball will likely come out as well. When replacing an old valve like this, you will likely also need to replace the flush valve (see pages 198–199).

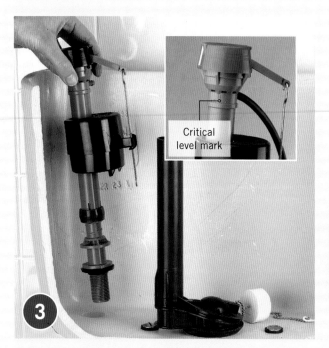

The new fill valve must be installed so the critical level ("CL") mark is at least 1" above the overflow pipe (see inset). Slip the shank washer on the threaded shank of the new fill valve and place the valve in the hole so the washer is flat on the tank bottom. Compare the locations of the "CL" mark and the overflow pipe.

Adjust the height of the fill valve shank so the "CL" line and overflow pipe will be correctly related. Different products are adjusted in different ways—the fill valve shown here telescopes when it's twisted.

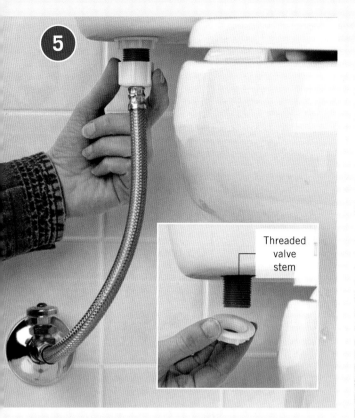

⑤

Threaded
valve
stem

Slip the valve's threaded end down through the tank. Push down on its shank (not the top) while tightening the locknut (inset). Hand tighten, then use a wrench to make an extra ¼ turn. Hook up the water supply tube, and tighten in the same way.

If the overflow pipe has a cap, remove it. Attach one end of the refill tube from the new valve to the plastic angle adapter and the other end to the refill nipple near the top of the valve. Attach the angle adapter to the overflow pipe. Cut off excess tubing with scissors to prevent kinking.

WARNING: Don't insert the refill tube into the overflow pipe. The outlet of the refill tube needs to be above the top of the pipe for it to work properly.

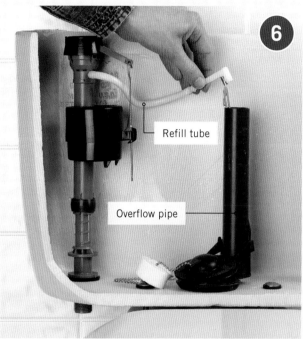

⑥

Refill tube

Overflow pipe

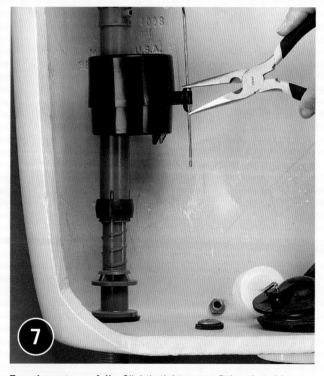

⑦

Turn the water on fully. Slightly tighten any fitting that drips water. Adjust the water level in the tank by squeezing the spring clip on the float cup with needlenose pliers and moving the cup up or down on the link bar. Test the flush.

OPTION: Newer diaphragm valves cost a bit more than float cups, but they boast quieter water flow. Install one the same way you would a float cup.

How to Replace a Flush Valve

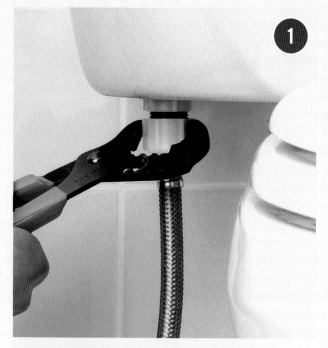

Before removing the old flush valve, shut off the water supply at the fixture stop valve located on the tube that supplies water to the tank. Flush the toilet and sponge out the remaining water. To make this repair you'll need to remove the tank from the bowl. Start by unscrewing the water supply coupling nut from the bottom of the tank.

Unscrew the bolts holding the toilet tank to the bowl by loosening the nuts from below. If you are having difficulty unscrewing the tank bolts and nuts because they are fused together by rust or corrosion, apply penetrating oil or spray lubricant to the threads, give it a few minutes to penetrate, and then try again. If that fails, slip an open-ended hacksaw (or plain hacksaw blade) between the tank and bowl and saw through the bolt (inset photo).

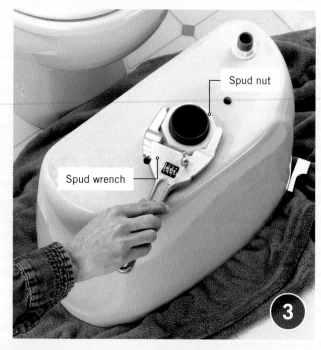

Spud nut

Spud wrench

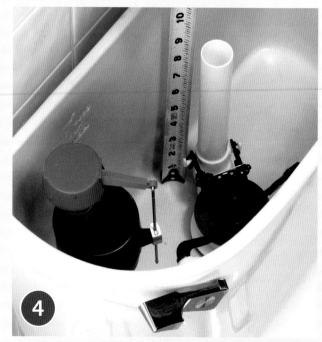

Unhook the chain from the handle lever arm. Remove the tank and carefully place it upside-down on an old towel. Remove the spud washer and spud nut from the base of the flush valve using a spud wrench or large channel-type pliers. Remove the old flush valve.

Place the new flush valve in the valve hole and check to see if the top of the overflow pipe is at least 1" below the critical level line (see page 194) and the tank opening where the handle is installed. If the pipe is too tall, cut it to length with a hacksaw.

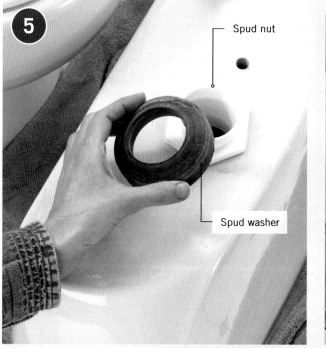

Position the flush valve flapper below the handle lever arm and secure it to the tank from beneath with the spud nut. Tighten the nut one-half turn past hand tight with a spud wrench or large channel-type pliers. Overtightening may cause the tank to break. Put the new spud washer over the spud nut, small side down.

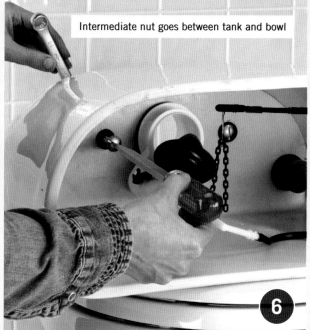

With the tank lying on its back, thread a rubber washer onto each tank bolt and insert it into the bolt holes from inside the tank. Then, thread a brass washer and hex nut onto the tank bolts from below and tighten them to a quarter turn past hand tight. Do not overtighten.

With the hex nuts tightened against the tank bottom, carefully lower the tank over the bowl and set it down so the spud washer seats neatly over the water inlet in the bowl and the tank bolts fit through the holes in the bowl flange. Secure the tank to the bowl with a rubber washer, brass washer, and nut or wing nut at each bolt end. Press the tank to level as you hand-tighten the nuts. Hook up the water supply at the fill valve inlet.

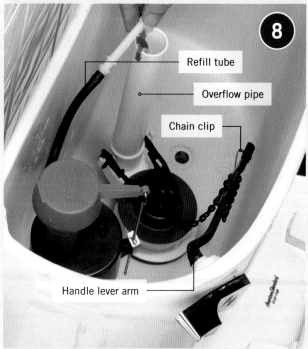

Connect the chain clip to the handle lever arm and adjust the number of links to allow for a little slack in the chain when the flapper is closed. Leave a little tail on the chain for adjusting, cutting off remaining excess. Attach the refill tube to the top of the overflow pipe the same way it had been attached to the previous refill pipe. Turn on the water supply at the stop valve and test the flush. (Some flush valve flappers are adjustable.)

Dual-flush Valves

Though dual-flush valves for modern toilets were invented in Australia in the 1980s, they didn't become prominent worldwide until the 1990s when water-saving technology became easier to install and implement. A dual-flush valve allows you to make a half flush when a small amount of water will suffice; when you need a stronger flush, you can turn the handle in the other direction for a full flush. This can save plenty of water—and money—over the course of a year (see chart below).

A typical retrofit unit comes with both a flush valve and a fill valve, can be installed in most toilet tanks, and is extremely affordable—often not more than $50. Like most standard toilet valves, dual-flush valves rely on the force of gravity to achieve a clean and powerful flush, and although models from different manufacturers may vary in their installation and design, they all work to achieve the same purpose—a more water-efficient flush for the environmentally minded and cost-savings savvy consumers. To use dual-flush technology, some units require you to pull up on the handle instead of down, while others are push-button activated. Stand-alone dual-flush valves can be purchased for home installation in a standard one-flush gravity-assisted toilet, or complete dual-flush-capable toilets can be purchased directly from manufacturers, and they come in a wide variety of styles and finishes to match most bathrooms.

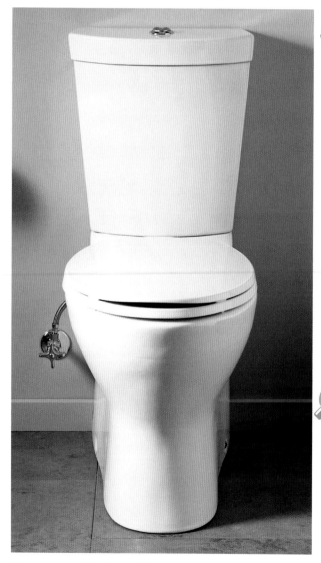

Conserve water (and money) with the push of a button (inset). Dual-flush valves can be installed in most standard toilets.

GET WITH THE (LOW) FLOW

GALLONS PER FLUSH (GPF)	SAVINGS IN GALLONS PER YEAR (GPY)
5.0	0
3.5	11,000 gpy from 5.0 gpf
1.6	25,300 gpy from 5.0 gpf to 1.6 gpf 14,100 gpy from 3.5 gpf to 1.6 gpf
1.28	27,700 gpy from 5.0 gpf to 1.28 gpf 16,500 gpy from 3.5 gpf to 1.28 gpf
1.0	29,000 gpy from 5.0 gpf to 1.0 gpf
	18,600 gpy from 3.5 gpf to 1.0 gpf

Water savings based on an average household of four, each flushing 5.1 times a day, 365 days a year.
Source: WaterSense, see Resources, p. 298

TOOLS & MATERIALS

Dual-flush valve assembly	Screwdriver
Replacement gasket	Teflon tape
Hex nut	Channel-lock pliers
Bolts	Wax pencil
Rubber washers	Bucket
Brass washers (if necessary)	Sponge
	Towel

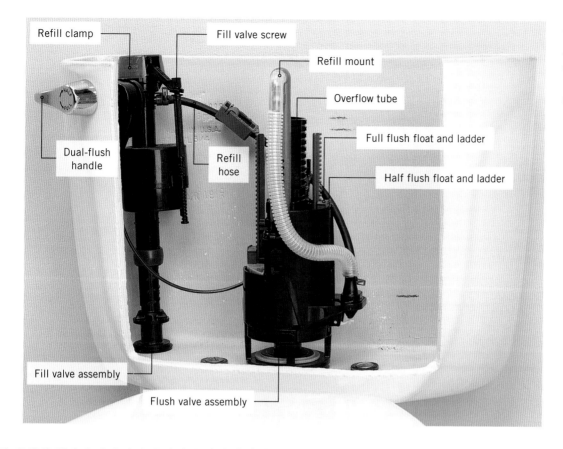

Refill clamp

Fill valve screw

Refill mount

Overflow tube

Dual-flush handle

Refill hose

Full flush float and ladder

Half flush float and ladder

Fill valve assembly

Flush valve assembly

A dual-flush valve is easier to install than it looks. All the component pieces are seen on the left.

How to Install a Dual-flush Valve

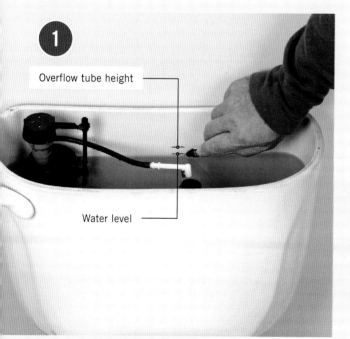

1

Overflow tube height

Water level

Turn off the water supply. Remove the top of the tank and mark both the water level and the top of the overflow tube using a wax pencil. Remove the old assemblies, flush a single time, and mark the level of the remaining water in the bottom of the tank. Hold the toilet handle to flush once more, and remove excess water with a sponge.

Disconnect the supply line from behind the tank. Use channel-lock pliers to remove the lock nut from the valve shank, allowing excess water to drip into a bucket. Next, remove the tank after loosening the flush valve nuts. Remove the old gasket from the flush valve shank, but keep all the old parts together—they may still be needed.

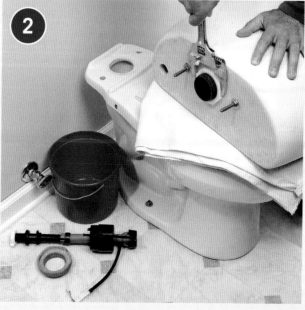

2

(continued)

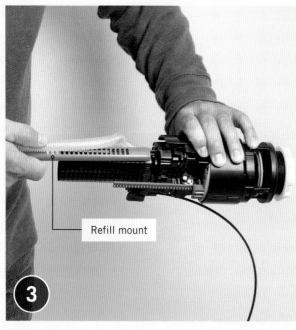

Refill mount

3

After removing the flush valve lock nut from the new flush valve assembly, place the new flush valve assembly into the tank, ensuring it is level and comfortably seated atop the shank. Mark the height of the new overflow tube to match the height of the old tube recorded in step 1; cut the tube to match, removing the assembly from the tank if necessary. Removing the refill mount from the flush valve assembly (above) makes marking and cutting the tube easier.

Re-attach the refill mount, making sure it is low enough to fit inside the tank and high enough to clear the lid. Cut excess refill hose if necessary. To install the entire valve, hand-tighten the lock nut to the threaded shank. Do not over-tighten.

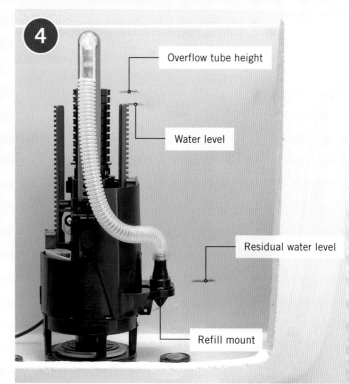

4

Overflow tube height

Water level

Residual water level

Refill mount

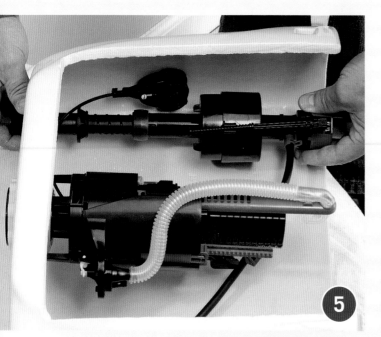

5

Reassemble the tank with bolts, rubber washers, brass washers, and a hex nut. Use the old rubber gasket if necessary and install the fill valve in much the same way as the flush valve; remove the fill valve lock nut and shank washer, and insert the valve onto the fill valve shank adjacent to the flush valve. The height of the fill valve must be approximately 3" greater than the flush valve; adjust as necessary by twisting the threaded shank in and out. When the desired height is reached, hand-tighten the fill valve lock nut to the shank.

The refill hose connects the dual valve assemblies; attach the refill hose from the fill valve to the nipple on the dual flush valve (inset), and ensure both ends are clear of the valve operations. If you need to change the orientation of the flush valve, release the base by turning the assembly counterclockwise until the tabs unlock, lift the valves out, and adjust as needed.

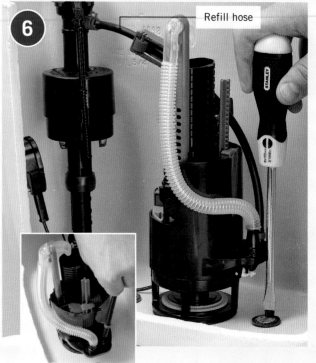

6

Refill hose

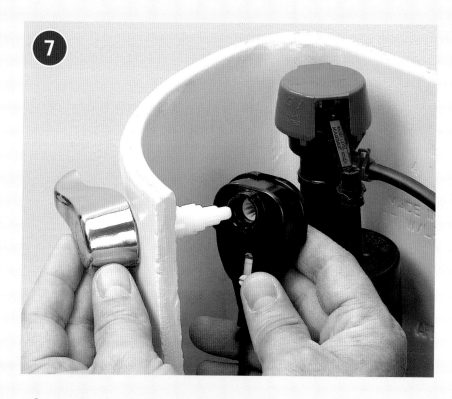

7

Install the dual flush handle to the tank and hand-tighten the lever lock-nut. The nut is reverse-threaded, so be sure the tabs on the collar are oriented vertically and aligned with the handle's tabs. Reconnect and turn on the water supply, checking for leaks. Do not use plumber's putty or thread lubricants to seal the fittings, as they may damage the plastic nut. Teflon tape is a good alternative.

ADJUSTING THE FLUSH AND TANK LEVELS

If the water in the tank is uneven with the original high water mark from step 1, turn the screw near the top of the fill valve clockwise to increase the water level or counterclockwise to decrease it.

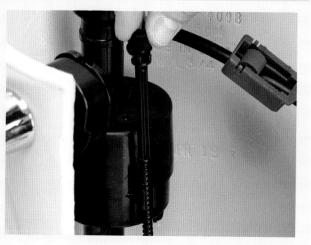

To adjust the level of half or full flushes, look to the flush valve assembly on the right; the higher float near the refill hose adjusts the half flush, while the opposing lower float on the other side of the assembly adjusts the full. Use a small amount of toilet paper and a test flush to gauge the amount of water used; if unsatisfied, adjust the appropriate flush by pulling out each float's stop, and raising or lowering each float to properly adjust the refill level. See the manufacturer's instructions, as the direction of adjustment to raise or lower the water level varies per manufacturer.

ADJUSTING THE REFILL LEVEL IN THE BOWL

The refill tube connects both valve assemblies, and the roller clamp on the tube can be adjusted to monitor the level of water in the bowl. To adjust, add a gallon of water to the bowl and wait 10 minutes, then mark the water level with a wax pencil. Flush the toilet. If the refill valve is still running once the water mark has been reached, decrease the volume of water by moving the roller clamp toward zero. If there's not enough water, do the opposite, moving the clamp toward higher numbers. Continue adjusting until the water reaches the mark in the tank at the same time the valve turns off.

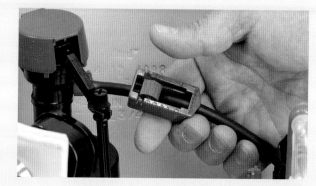

Clogged Toilets

TOOLS & MATERIALS

Towels

Closet auger

Plunger with foldout skirt (force cup)

The toilet is clogged and has overflowed. Have patience. Now is the time for considered action. A second flush is a tempting but unnecessary gamble. First, do damage control. Mop up the water if there's been a spill. Next, consider the nature of the clog. Is it entirely "natural" or might a foreign object be contributing to the congestion? Push a natural blockage down the drain with a plunger. A foreign object should be removed, if possible, with a closet auger. Pushing anything more durable than toilet paper into the sewer may create a more serious blockage in your drain and waste system.

If the tub, sink, and toilet all back up at once, the branch drainline that serves all the bathroom fixtures is probably blocked and your best recourse is to call a drain clearing service.

A blockage in the toilet bowl leaves flush water from the tank nowhere to go but on the floor.

The trap is the most common catching spot for toilet clogs.
Once the clog forms, flushing the toilet cannot generate
enough water power to clear the trap, so flush water backs
up. Traps on modern 1.6-gallon toilets have been redesigned
to larger diameters and are less prone to clogs than the first
generation of 1.6-gallon toilets.

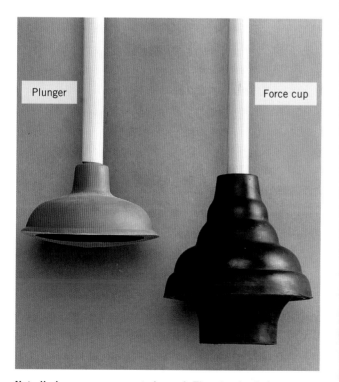

Plunger

Force cup

Not all plungers were created equal. The standard plunger
(left) is simply an inverted rubber cup and is used to plunge
sinks, tubs, and showers. The flanged plunger, also called
a force cup, is designed to get down into the trap of a toilet
drain. You can fold the flange up into the flanged plunger cup
and use it as a standard plunger.

DRAIN CLEARERS

The home repair marketplace is filled with gadgets and
gimmicks, as well as well-established products, that are
intended to clear drains of all types. Some are caustic
chemicals, some are natural enzymes, others are more
mechanical in nature. Some help, some are worthless,
some can even make the problem worse. Nevertheless,
if you are the type of homeowner who is enamored with
new products and the latest solutions, you may enjoy
testing out new drain cleaners as they become available.
In this photo, for example, you'll see a relatively new
product that injects blasts of compressed CO_2 directly
into your toilet, sink, or tub drain to dislodge clogs.
It does not cause any chemicals to enter the waste
stream, and the manufacturers claim the CO_2 blast is
very gentle and won't damage pipes. As with any new
product, use it with caution. But if a plunger or a snake
isn't working, it could save you the cost of a house call.

How to Plunge a Clogged Toilet

Plunging is the easiest way to remove "natural" blockages. Take time to lay towels around the base of the toilet and remove other objects to a safe, dry location, since plunging may result in splashing. Often, allowing a very full toilet to sit for twenty or thirty minutes will permit some of the water to drain to a less precarious level.

There should be enough water in the bowl to completely cover the plunger. Fold out the skirt from inside the plunger to form a better seal with the opening at the base of the bowl. Pump the plunger vigorously half-a-dozen times, take a rest, and then repeat. Try this for four to five cycles.

FORCE CUPS

A flanged plunger (force cup) fits into the mouth of the toilet trap and creates a tight seal so you can build up enough pressure in front of the plunger to dislodge the blockage and send it on its way.

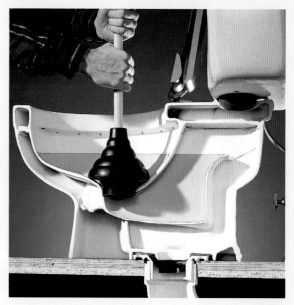

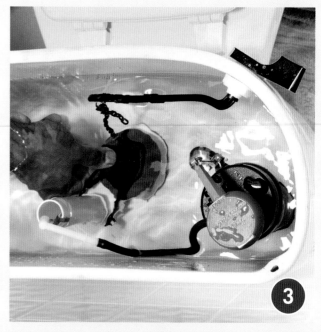

If you force enough water out of the bowl that you are unable to create suction with the plunger, put a controlled amount of water in the bowl by lifting up on the flush valve in the tank. Resume plunging. When you think the drain is clear, you can try a controlled flush, with your hand ready to close the flush valve should the water threaten to spill out of the bowl. Once the blockage has cleared, dump a five-gallon pail of water into the toilet to blast away any residual debris.

How to Clear Clogs with a Closet Auger

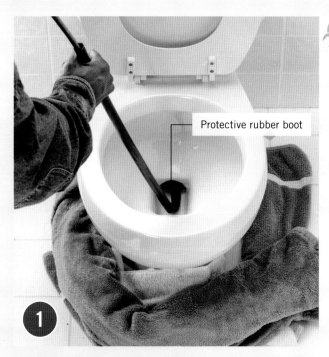

Protective rubber boot

Place the business end of the auger firmly in the bottom of the toilet bowl with the auger tip fully withdrawn. A rubber sleeve will protect the porcelain at the bottom bend of the auger. The tip will be facing back and up, which is the direction the toilet trap takes.

CLOSET AUGERS

A closet auger is a semirigid cable housed in a tube. The tube has a bend at the end so it can be snaked through a toilet trap (without scratching it) to snag blockages.

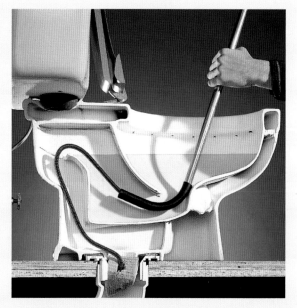

Fully retract the auger until you have recovered the object. This can be frustrating at times, but it is still a much easier task than the alternative—to remove the toilet and go fishing.

Rotate the handle on the auger housing clockwise as you push down on the rod, advancing the rotating auger tip up into the back part of the trap. You may work the cable backward and forward as needed, but keep the rubber boot of the auger firmly in place in the bowl. When you feel resistance, indicating you've snagged the object, continue rotating the auger counterclockwise as you withdraw the cable and the object.

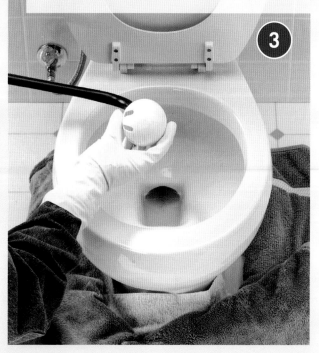

Toilet Flanges

If your toilet rocks, it will eventually leak. The rocking means that the bolts are no longer holding the toilet securely to the floor. If you have tightened the bolts and it still rocks, it is possible that a bolt has broken a piece of the flange off and is no longer able to hold. Rocking might also be because an ongoing leak has weakened the floor and it is now uneven. Whatever the reason, a rocking toilet needs to be fixed.

If your flange is connected to cast-iron piping, use a repair flange. This has a rubber compression ring that will seal the new flange to the cast-iron pipe.

TOOLS & MATERIALS

Drill	#10 stainless-steel flathead wood screws	Solvent-cement
Wrench		Marker
Internal pipe cutter		

Use a flange repair kit for a quick fix to a broken flange. The new flange piece from the kit is simply screwed to the floor after it has been oriented correctly over the broken flange.

TOILET SHIMS

If the toilet is wobbly because of an uneven floor, shims may solve the problem. (Do not install shims if the toilet leaks at the base; they will not solve that problem.) Slip two or more plastic toilet shims under the toilet until it is stabilized. Press the shims with only medium pressure; don't force them too hard. Cut the exposed portions of the shims with a utility knife.

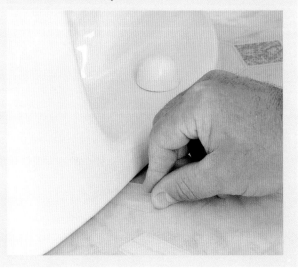

Toilets that rock often only need to have the nuts on the closet bolts tightened. But if you need to tighten the bolts on an ongoing basis, you very likely have a problem with the closet flange.

How to Replace a PVC Closet Flange

1

Begin by removing the toilet and wax ring. Cut the pipe just below the bottom of the flange using an internal pipe cutter (inset, available at plumbing supply stores). Remove the flange.

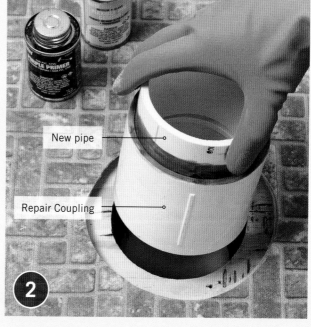

New pipe

Repair Coupling

2

If your flange is attached to a closet bend, you will need to open up the floor around the toilet to get at the horizontal pipe connecting the bend to the stack to make the repair. If it is connected to a length of vertical plastic pipe, use a repair coupling and a short length of pipe to bring the pipe back up to floor level. Cement the new pipe into the repair coupling first and allow it to set. Clean the old pipe thoroughly before cementing.

3

Cut the replacement pipe flush with the floor. Dry-fit the new flange into the pipe. Turn the flange until the side cut-out screw slots are parallel to the wall. (Do not use the curved keyhole slots, as they are not as strong.) Draw lines to mark the location of the slots on the floor.

4

Prime and solvent-cement the pipe and flange, inserting the flange slightly off the marks and twisting it to proper alignment. Secure the flange to the floor with #10 stainless-steel flathead wood screws.

Toilet Drain Lines

If your existing toilet drain line is heavily deteriorated, replace it. You will also need to replace the drain line if you are relocating and replacing the main drain stalk or if you are moving the toilet to a different spot in the bathroom.

Replacing a toilet drain is sometimes a troublesome task, mostly because the cramped space makes it difficult to route the large, 3" or 4" pipe. You likely will need to remove flooring around the toilet and wall surface behind the toilet.

Replacing a toilet drain may require framing work, as well, if you find it necessary to cut into joists in order to route the new pipes. When possible, plan your project to avoid changes to the framing members.

Replacing a toilet drain usually requires that you remove flooring and wall surface to gain access to the pipes.

TOOLS & MATERIALS

Drill	Pipe
Circular saw	Exterior-grade plywood
Reciprocating saw	Screws

How to Replace a Toilet Drain Line

1

Remove the toilet, then unscrew the toilet flange from the floor and remove it from the drain pipe. You can also use an internal pipe cutter to cut plastic drain pipe (see previous page, top left).

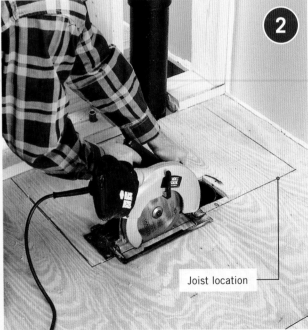

2

Joist location

Cut away the flooring around the toilet drain along the center of the floor joists, using a circular saw with the blade set to a depth ⅛" more than the thickness of the subfloor. The exposed joist will serve as a nailing surface when the subfloor is replaced.

Cut away the old closet bend as close as possible to the old drainage stack, cutting first with a grinder equipped with a metal-cutting blade, then finishing with a reciprocating saw.

If a joist obstructs the route to a new drainage stack, cut away a section of the floor joist. Install double headers and metal joist hangers to support the ends of the cut joist.

Closet bend

Create a new toilet drain running to the drainage stack, using a closet bend and a straight length of pipe. Position the drain so there will be at least 15" of space between the center of the bowl and side wall surfaces when the toilet is installed. Make sure the drain slopes at least ¼" per ft. toward the stack, then support the pipe with plastic pipe strap attached to framing members. Insert a 6" length of pipe in the top inlet of the closet bend; once the new drain pipes have been tested, this pipe will be cut off with a handsaw and fitted with a toilet flange.

Cut a piece of exterior-grade plywood to fit the cutout floor area, and use a jigsaw to cut an opening for the toilet drain stub-out. Position the plywood, and attach it to joists and blocking with 2" screws.

Sink Faucets

TOOLS & MATERIALS

Pliers
Needlenose pliers
Heatproof grease
Channel-type pliers
Utility knife
White vinegar
Old toothbrush
Tape measure
Repair kit (exact type varies)
Teflon tape
Screwdrivers
Pipe joint compound
Plumber's putty
Rag

It's not surprising that sink faucets leak and drip. Any fitting that contains moving mechanical parts is susceptible to failure. But add to the equation the persistent force of water pressure working against the parts, and the real surprise is that faucets don't fail more quickly or often. It would be a bit unfair to say that the inner workings of a faucet are regarded as disposable by manufacturers, but it is safe to say that these parts have become more easy to remove and replace.

The older your faucet, the more likely you can repair it by replacing small parts like washers and O-rings. Many newer faucets can be repaired only by replacing the major inner components, like a ceramic disk or a cartridge that encapsulates all the washers and O-rings that could possibly wear out.

The most important aspect of sink faucet repair is identifying which type of faucet you own. In this chapter we show all of the common types and provide instructions on repairing them. In every case, the easiest and most reliable repair method is to purchase a replacement kit with brand-new internal working parts for the model and brand of faucet you own.

Eventually, just about every faucet develops leaks and drips. Repairs can usually be accomplished simply by replacing the mechanical parts inside the faucet body (the main trick is figuring out which kind of parts your faucet has).

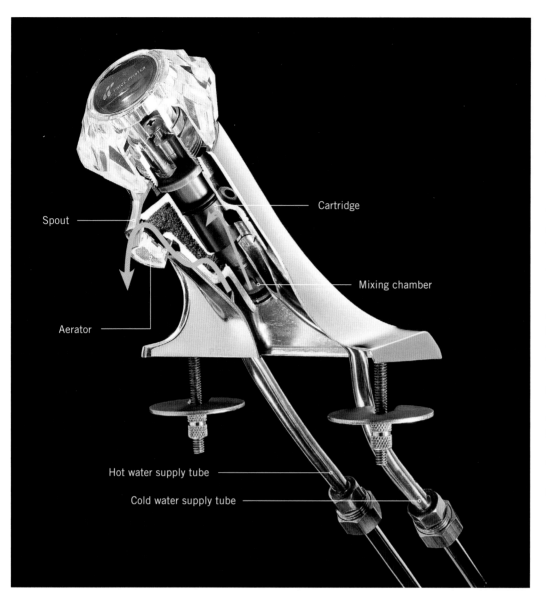

Spout

Aerator

Cartridge

Mixing chamber

Hot water supply tube

Cold water supply tube

All faucets, no matter the type, have valves that move many thousands of times to open and close hot- and cold-water ports. These valves—or the rubber or plastic parts that rub against other parts when the faucet is being adjusted—wear out in time. Depending on the faucet, you may be able to fix the leak by cleaning or replacing small parts, such as washers or O-rings; or you may need to buy a repair kit and replace a number of parts; or the only solution may be to replace a self-enclosed "cartridge" that contains all the moving parts.

COMMON PROBLEMS AND REPAIRS

PROBLEMS	REPAIRS
Faucet drips from the end of the spout or leaks around the base.	1. Identify the faucet design (page 214), then install replacement parts, using directions on the following pages.
Old worn-out faucet continues to leak after repairs are made.	1. Replace the old faucet (page 54).
Water pressure at spout seems low, or water flow is partially blocked.	1. Clean faucet aerator (page 214). 2. Replace corroded galvanized pipes with copper or PEX.
Water pressure from sprayer seems low, or sprayer leaks from handle.	1. Clean sprayer head (page 223). 2. Fix diverter valve (page 224).
Water leaks onto floor underneath faucet.	1. Replace cracked sprayer hose (page 225). 2. Tighten water connections, or replace supply tubes and shutoff valves. 3. Fix leaky sink strainer.
Hose bib or valve drips from spout or leaks around handle.	1. Take valve apart and replace washers and O-rings.

Identifying Your Faucet and the Parts You Need

A leaky faucet is the most common home plumbing problem. Fortunately, repair parts are available for almost every type of faucet, from the oldest to the newest, and installing these parts is usually easy. But if you don't know your make and model, the hardest part of fixing a leak may be identifying your faucet and finding the right parts. Don't make the common mistake of thinking that any similar-looking parts will do the job; you've got to get exact replacements.

There are so many faucet types that even experts have trouble classifying them into neat categories. Two-handle faucets are either compression (stem) or washerless two-handle. Single-handle faucets are classified as mixing cartridge; ball; disc; or disc/cartridge.

A single-handle faucet with a rounded, dome-shaped cap is often a ball type. If a single-handle faucet has a flat top, it is likely a cartridge or a ceramic disc type. An older two-handle faucet is likely of the compression type; newer two-handle models use washerless cartridges. Shut off the water, and test to verify that the water is off. Dismantle the faucet carefully. Look for a brand name: it may be clearly visible on the baseplate, or may be printed on an inner part, or it may not be printed anywhere. Put all the parts into a reliable plastic bag and take them to your home center or plumbing supply store. A knowledgeable salesperson can help you identify the parts you need.

If you cannot find what you are looking for at a local store, check online faucet sites or the manufacturers' sites; they often have step-by-step instruction for identifying what you need. Note that manufacturers' terminology may not match the terms we use here. For example, the word "cartridge" may refer to a ceramic-disc unit.

Most faucets have repair kits, which include all the parts you need, and sometimes a small tool as well. Even if some of the parts in your faucet look fine, it's a good idea to install the parts provided by the kit, to ensure against future wear.

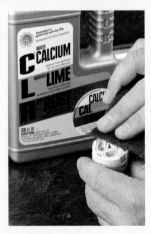

REPAIR TIPS

If water flow is weak, unscrew the aerator at the tip of the spout. If there is sediment, then dirty water is entering the faucet, which could damage the faucet's inner workings.

To remove handles and spouts, work carefully and look for small screw heads. You often need to first pry off a cap on top, but not always. Parts may be held in place with small setscrews.

Cleaning and removing debris can sometimes solve the problem of low water flow, and occasionally can solve a leak as well.

Apply plumber's grease (also known as faucet grease or valve grease), to new parts before installing them. Be especially sure to coat rubber parts like O-rings and washers.

Compression Faucets

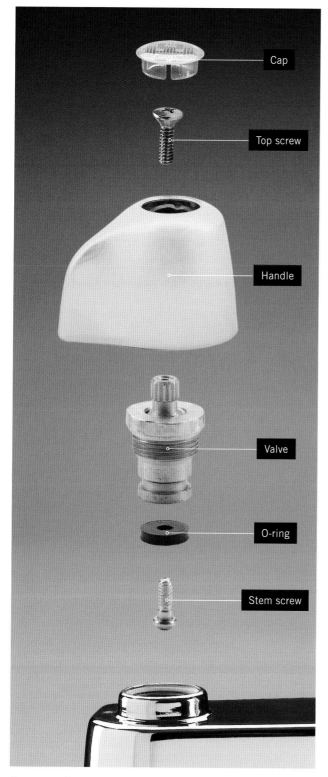

Pry off the cap on top of the handle and remove the screw that holds the cap onto the stem. Pull the handle up and out. Use an adjustable wrench or pliers to unscrew the stem and pull it out.

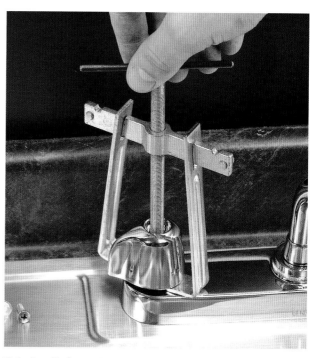

A compression faucet has a stem assembly that includes a retaining nut, threaded spindle, O-ring, stem washer, and stem screw. Dripping at the spout occurs when the washer becomes worn. Leaks around the handle are caused by a worn O-ring.

If the handle is stuck, try applying mineral cleaner from above. If that doesn't work, you may need to buy a handle puller. With the cap and the hold-down screw removed, position the wings of the puller under the handle and tighten the puller to slowly pull the handle up.

Remove the screw that holds the rubber washer in place, and pry out the washer. Replace a worn washer with an exact replacement—one that is the same diameter, thickness, and shape.

Replace any O-rings. A worn O-ring can cause water to leak out the handle. Gently pry out the old O-ring and reinstall an exact replacement. Apply plumber's grease to the rubber parts before reinstalling the stem.

If washers wear out quickly, the seat is likely worn. Use a seat wrench to unscrew the seat from inside the faucet. Replace it with an exact duplicate. If replacing the washer and O-ring doesn't solve the problem, you may need to replace the entire stem.

Washerless Two-Handle Faucet

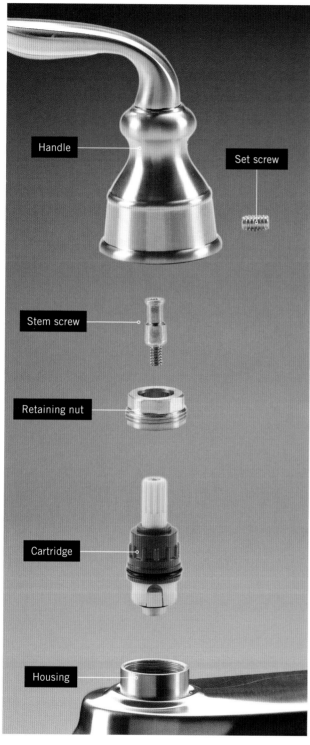

Handle

Set screw

Stem screw

Retaining nut

Cartridge

Housing

Remove the faucet handle and withdraw the old cartridge. Make a note of how the cartridge is oriented before you remove it. Purchase a replacement cartridge.

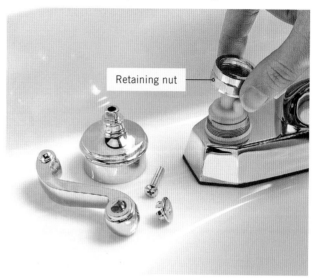

Retaining nut

Install the replacement cartridge. Clean the valve seat first and coat the valve seat and O-rings with faucet grease. Be sure the new cartridge is in the correct position, with its tabs seated in the slotted body of the faucet. Re-assemble the valve and handles.

Almost all two-handle faucets made today are "washerless." Instead of an older-type compression stem, there is a cartridge, usually with a plastic casing. Many of these cartridges contain ceramic discs, while others have metal or plastic pathways. No matter the type of cartridge, the repair is the same; instead of replacing small parts, you simply replace the entire cartridge.

One-Handle Cartridge Faucets

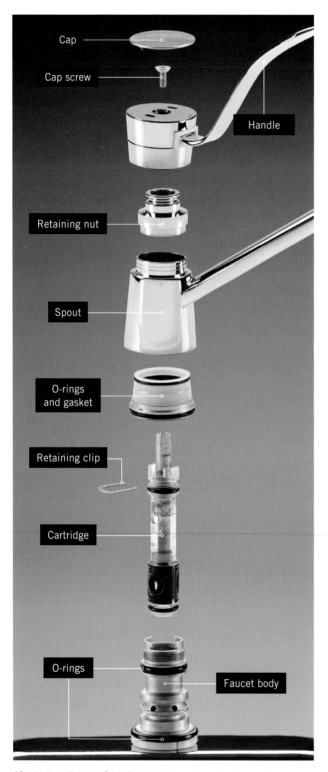

Cap

Cap screw

Handle

Retaining nut

Spout

O-rings and gasket

Retaining clip

Cartridge

O-rings

Faucet body

Single-handle cartridge faucets like this work by moving the cartridge up and down and side to side, which opens up pathways to direct varying amounts of hot and cold water to the spout. Moen, Price-Pfister, Delta, Peerless, Kohler, and others make many types of cartridges, some of which look very different from this one.

To remove the spout, pry off the handle's cap and remove the screw below it. Pull the handle up and off. Use a crescent wrench to remove the pivot nut.

Lift out the spout. If the faucet has a diverter valve, remove it as well. Use a screwdriver to pry out the retainer clip, which holds the cartridge in place.

Remove the cartridge. If you simply pull up with pliers, you may leave part of the stem in the faucet body. If that happens, replace the cartridge and buy a stem puller made for your model.

Gently pry out and replace all O-rings on the faucet body. Smear plumber's grease onto the new replacement cartridge and the new O-rings, and reassemble the faucet.

Here is one of many other types of single-handle cartridges. In this model, all the parts are plastic except for the stem, and it's important to note the direction in which the cartridge is aligned. If you test the faucet and the hot and cold are reversed, disassemble and realign the cartridge.

Ball Faucets

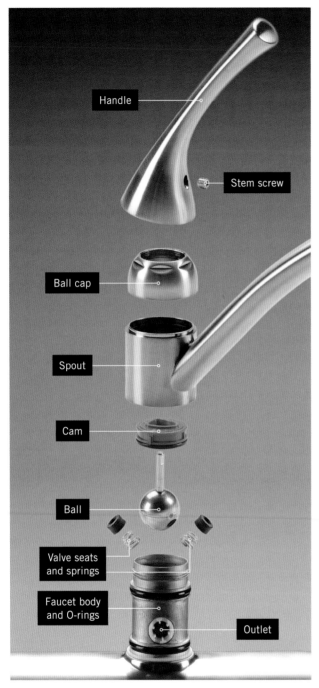

Handle

Stem screw

Ball cap

Spout

Cam

Ball

Valve seats and springs

Faucet body and O-rings

Outlet

Ball

Cam

Remove the old ball and cam after removing the faucet handle and ball cap. Some faucets may require a ball faucet tool to remove the handle. Otherwise, simply use a pair of channel-type pliers to twist off the ball cap.

Pry out the neoprene valve seals and springs. Place thick towels around the faucet. Slowly turn on the water to flush out any debris in the faucet body. Replace the seals and springs with new parts. Also replace the O-rings on the valve body. You may want to replace the ball and cam, too, especially if you're purchasing a repair kit. Coat all rubber parts in faucet grease, and reassemble the faucet.

The ball-type faucet is used by Delta, Peerless, and a few others. The ball fits into the faucet body and is constructed with three holes (not visible here)—a hot inlet, a cold inlet, and the outlet, which fills the valve body with water that then flows to the spout or sprayer. Depending on the position of the ball, each inlet hole is open, closed, or somewhere in-between. The inlet holes are sealed to the ball with valve seats, which are pressed tight against the ball with springs. If water drips from the spout, replace the seats and springs. Or go ahead and purchase an entire replacement kit and replace all or most of the working parts.

Disc Faucets

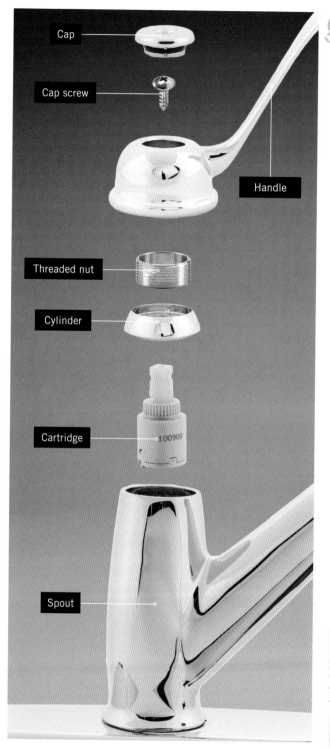

- Cap
- Cap screw
- Handle
- Threaded nut
- Cylinder
- Cartridge — 100908
- Spout

Disc-type faucets are the most common single-handle faucets currently being made. A pair of ceramic discs encased in a cylinder often referred to as a "cartridge" rub together as they rotate to open ports for hot and cold water. The ceramic discs do wear out in time, causing leaks, and there is only one solution—replace the disc unit (or "cartridge"). This makes for an easy—through comparatively expensive—repair.

OTHER CARTRIDGES

Many modern cartridges do not have seals or O-rings that can be replaced, and some have a ball rather than a ceramic disk inside. For the repair, the cartridge's innards do not matter; just replace the whole cartridge.

Replace the cylinder with a new one, coating the rubber parts with faucet grease before installing the new cylinder. Make sure the rubber seals fit correctly in the cylinder openings before you install the cylinder. Assemble the faucet handle.

Kitchen Sprayers

If water pressure from a sink sprayer seems low, or if water leaks from the handle, it is usually because lime buildup and sediment have blocked small openings inside the sprayer head. To fix the problem, first take the sprayer head apart and clean the parts. If cleaning the sprayer head does not help, the problem may be caused by a faulty diverter valve. The diverter valve inside the faucet body shifts water flow from the faucet spout to the sprayer when the sprayer handle is pressed. Cleaning or replacing the diverter valve may fix water pressure problems.

Whenever making repairs to a sink sprayer, check the sprayer hose for kinks or cracks. A damaged hose should be replaced.

If water pressure from a faucet spout seems low, or if the flow is partially blocked, take the spout aerator apart and clean the parts. The aerator is a screw-on attachment with a small wire screen that mixes tiny air bubbles into the water flow. Make sure the wire screen is not clogged with sediment and lime buildup. If water pressure is low throughout the house, it may be because galvanized steel water pipes are corroded. Corroded pipes should be replaced with copper.

TOOLS & MATERIALS

Screwdriver	Vinegar
Channel-type pliers	Universal washer kit
Needlenose pliers	Heatproof grease
Small brush	Replacement sprayer hose

Kitchen sprayers are very convenient and, in theory, quite simple. Yet, they break down with surprising regularity. Fixing or replacing one is an easy job, however.

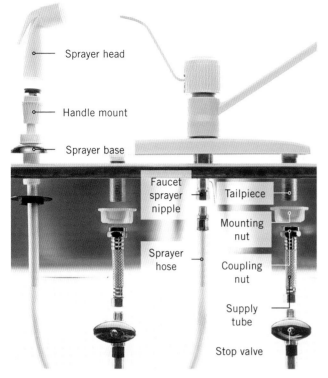

The standard sprayer hose attachment is connected to a nipple at the bottom of the faucet valve. When the lever of the sprayer is depressed, water flows from a diverter valve in the faucet body out to the sprayer. If your sprayer stream is weak or doesn't work at all, the chances are good that the problem lies in the diverter valve.

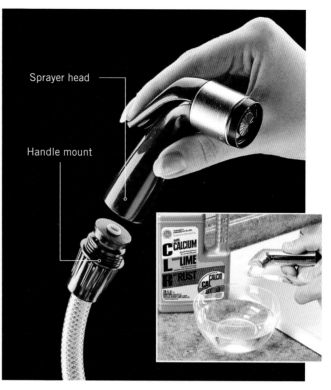

Sprayer heads can be removed from the sprayer hose, usually by loosening a retaining nut. A sprayer's head can get clogged with minerals. Unscrew the sprayer from the hose and remove any parts at its tip. Soak it in mineral cleaner, and use a small brush to open any clogged orifices.

How to Repair a Sprayer

Shut off the water at the stop valves and remove the faucet handle to gain access to the faucet parts. Disassemble the faucet handle and body to expose the diverter valve. Ball-type faucets like the one shown here require that you also remove the spout to get at the diverter.

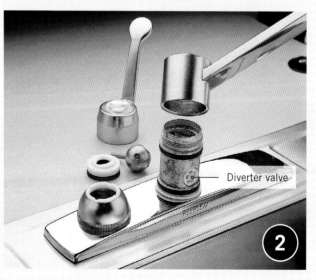

Locate the diverter valve, seen here at the base of the valve body. Because different types and brands of faucets have differently configured diverters, do a little investigating beforehand to try and locate information about your faucet. The above faucet is a ball type.

(continued)

Pull the diverter valve from the faucet body with needlenose pliers. Use a toothbrush dipped in white vinegar to clean any lime buildup from the valve. If the valve is in poor condition, bring it to the hardware store and purchase a replacement.

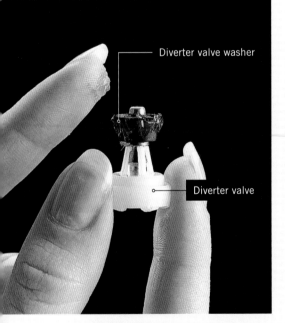

Diverter valve washer

Diverter valve

Coat the washer or O-ring on the new or cleaned diverter valve with faucet grease. Insert the diverter valve back into the faucet body. Reassemble the faucet. Turn on the water and test the sprayer. If it still isn't functioning to your satisfaction, remove the sprayer tip and run the sprayer without the filter and aerator in case any debris has made its way into the sprayer line during repairs.

FINDING THE DIVERTER ON A TWO-HANDLE FAUCET

On a two-handle faucet, the diverter is usually located in a vertical position just under the spout. Remove the spout. You may need to use longnose pliers to pull out the diverter. Try cleaning out any debris. If that does not restore operation, replace the valve.

Diverter

How to Replace a Kitchen Sprayer

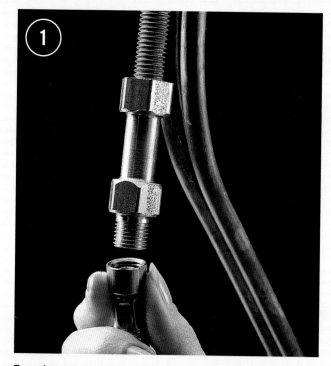

To replace a sprayer hose, start by shutting off the water at the shutoff valves. Clear out the cabinet under your sink and put on eye protection. Unthread the coupling nut that attaches the old hose to a nipple or tube below the faucet spout. Use a basin wrench if you can't get your channel-type pliers on the nut.

Unscrew the mounting nut of the old sprayer from below and remove the old sprayer body. Clean the sink deck and then apply plumber's putty to the base of the new sprayer. Insert the new sprayer tailpiece into the opening in the sink deck.

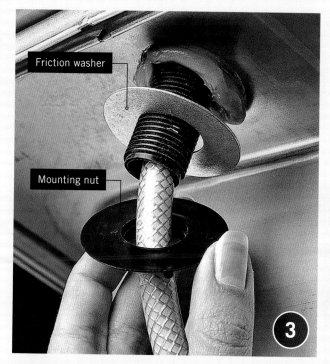

Friction washer

Mounting nut

From below, slip the friction washer up over the sprayer tailpiece. Screw the mounting nut onto the tailpiece and tighten with a basin wrench or channel-type pliers. Do not overtighten. Wipe away any excess plumber's putty.

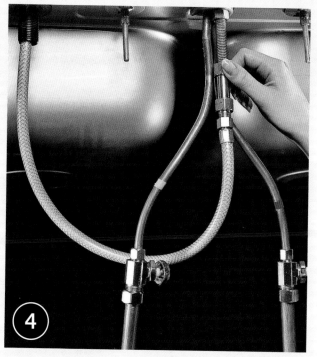

Screw the coupling for the sprayer hose onto the hose nipple underneath the faucet body. For a good seal, apply pipe joint compound to the nipple threads first. Tighten the coupling with a basin wrench, turn on the water supply at the shutoff valves, and test the new sprayer.

Fixing Leaky Tubs & Shower Faucets

Tub and shower faucets have the same basic designs as sink faucets, and the techniques for repairing leaks are the same as described in the faucet repair section of this book (pages 212 to 221). To identify your faucet design, you may have to take off the handle and disassemble the faucet.

When a tub and shower are combined, the showerhead and the tub spout share the same hot and cold water supply lines and handles. Combination faucets are available as three-handle, two-handle, or single-handle types (next page). The number of handles gives clues as to the design of the faucets and the kinds of repairs that may be necessary.

With combination faucets, a diverter valve or gate diverter is used to direct water flow to the tub spout or the showerhead. On three-handle faucet types, the middle handle controls a diverter valve. If water does not shift easily from tub to showerhead, or if water continues to run out the spout when the shower is on,

the diverter valve probably needs to be cleaned and repaired (pages 240 to 241).

Two-handle and single-handle types use a gate diverter that is operated by a pull lever or knob on the tub spout. Although gate diverters rarely need repair, the lever occasionally may break, come loose, or refuse to stay in the up position. To repair a gate diverter set in a tub spout, replace the entire spout.

Tub and shower faucets and diverter valves may be set inside wall cavities. Removing them may require a deep-set ratchet wrench.

If spray from the showerhead is uneven, clean the spray holes. If the showerhead does not stay in an upright position, remove the head and replace the O-ring.

To add a shower to an existing tub, install a flexible shower adapter. Several manufacturers make complete conversion kits that allow a shower to be installed in less than one hour.

Tub/shower plumbing is notorious for developing drips from the tub spout and the showerhead. In most cases, the leak can be traced to the valves controlled by the faucet handles.

Tub & Shower Combination Faucets

Showerhead

Showerhead

Showerhead

Diverter valve

Cold water supply line

Cold water supply line

Cold water supply line

Gate diverter

Hot water supply line

Tub spout

Hot water supply line

Tub spout

Hot water supply line

Tub spout

Three-handle faucet (page 228) has valves that are either compression or cartridge design.

Two-handle faucet (page 230) has valves that are either compression or cartridge design.

Single-handle faucet (page 232) has valves that are cartridge, ball-type, or disc design.

Fixing Three-Handle Tub & Shower Faucets

A three-handle faucet type has two handles to control hot and cold water, and a third handle to control the diverter valve and direct water to either a tub spout or a shower head. The separate hot and cold handles indicate cartridge or compression faucet designs.

If a diverter valve sticks, if water flow is weak, or if water runs out of the tub spout when the flow is directed to the showerhead, the diverter needs to be repaired or replaced. Most diverter valves are similar to either compression or cartridge faucet valves. Compression-type diverters can be repaired, but cartridge types should be replaced.

Remember to turn off the water before beginning work.

TOOLS & MATERIALS

Screwdriver

Adjustable wrench or channel-type pliers

Deep-set ratchet wrench

Small wire brush

Replacement diverter cartridge or universal washer kit

Faucet grease

Vinegar

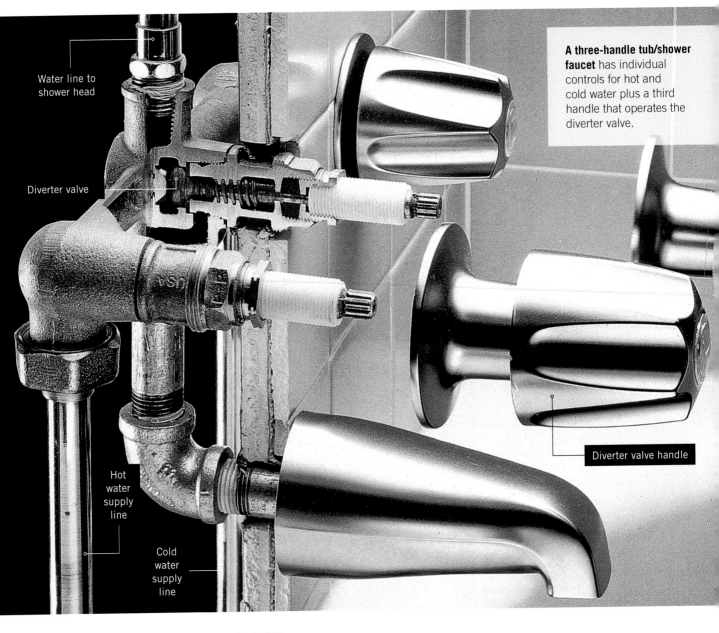

A three-handle tub/shower faucet has individual controls for hot and cold water plus a third handle that operates the diverter valve.

Water line to shower head

Diverter valve

Hot water supply line

Cold water supply line

Diverter valve handle

How to Repair a Compression Diverter Valve

Escutcheon

Diverter handle

Remove the diverter valve handle with a screwdriver. Unscrew or pry off the escutcheon.

Bonnet nut

Remove bonnet nut with an adjustable wrench or channel-type pliers.

Unscrew the stem assembly, using a deep-set ratchet wrench. If necessary, chip away any mortar surrounding the bonnet nut.

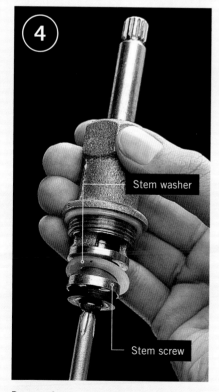

Stem washer

Stem screw

Remove brass stem screw. Replace stem washer with an exact duplicate. If stem screw is worn, replace it.

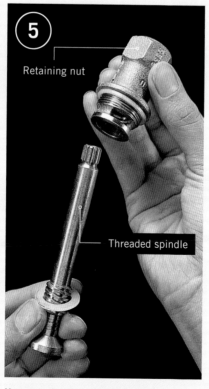

Retaining nut

Threaded spindle

Unscrew the threaded spindle from the retaining nut.

Clean sediment and lime buildup from nut, using a small wire brush dipped in vinegar. Coat all parts with faucet grease and reassemble diverter valve.

Fixing Two-Handle Tub & Shower Faucets

Two-handle tub and shower faucets are either cartridge or compression design. Because the valves of two-handle tub and shower faucets may be set inside the wall cavity, a deep-set socket wrench may be required to remove the valve stem.

Two-handle tub and shower designs have a gate diverter. A gate diverter is a simple mechanism located in the tub spout. A gate diverter closes the supply of water to the tub spout and redirects the flow to the shower head. Gate diverters seldom need repair. Occasionally, the lever may break, come loose, or refuse to stay in the up position.

If the diverter fails to work properly, replace the tub spout. Tub spouts are inexpensive and easy to replace.

Remember to turn off the water before beginning any work.

TOOLS & MATERIALS

Screwdriver
Allen wrench
Pipe wrench
Channel-type pliers
Small cold chisel
Ball-peen hammer
Deep-set ratchet wrench
Masking tape or cloth
Pipe joint compound
Replacement faucet parts, as needed

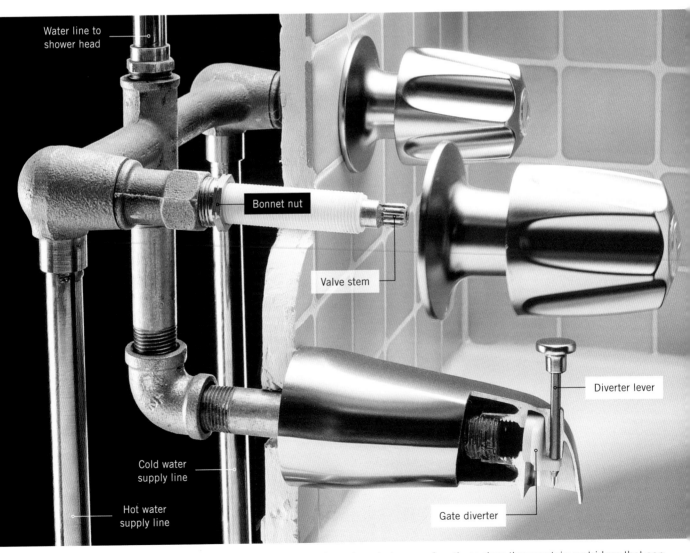

A two-handle tub/shower faucet can operate with compression valves, but more often these days they contain cartridges that can be replaced. Unlike a three-handled model, the diverter is a simple gate valve that is operated by a lever.

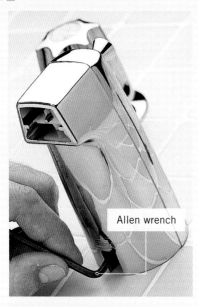

Unscrew faucet spout. Use a pipe wrench, or insert a large screwdriver or hammer handle into the spout opening and turn spout counterclockwise.

Spout nipple

Check underneath tub spout for a small access slot. The slot indicates the spout is held in place with an Allen screw. Remove the screw, using an Allen wrench. Spout will slide off.

Allen wrench

Spread pipe joint compound on threads of spout nipple before replacing spout. If you have a copper pipe or a short pipe, buy a spout retrofit kit, which can attach a spout to most any pipe.

How to Remove a Deep-set Faucet Valve

1

Escutcheon

Masking tape

Stem nipple

2

Bonnet nut

3

Remove handle and unscrew the escutcheon with channel-type pliers. Pad the jaws of the pliers with masking tape to prevent scratching the escutcheon.

Chip away any mortar surrounding the bonnet nut using a ball-peen hammer and a small cold chisel.

Unscrew the bonnet nut with a deep-set ratchet wrench. Remove the bonnet nut and stem from the faucet body.

Fixing Single-Handle Tub & Shower Faucets

A single-handle tub and shower faucet has one valve that controls both water flow and temperature. Single-handle faucets may be ball-type, cartridge, or disc designs.

If a single-handle control valve leaks or does not function properly, disassemble the faucet, clean the valve, and replace any worn parts. Repairing a single-handle cartridge faucet is shown on the opposite page.

Direction of the water flow to either the tub spout or the showerhead is controlled by a gate diverter. Gate diverters seldom need repair. Occasionally, the lever may break, come loose, or refuse to stay in the up position. Remember to turn off the water before beginning any work; the shower faucet shown here has built-in shutoff valves, but many other valves do not. Open an access panel in an adjoining room or closet, behind the valve, and look for two shutoffs. If you can't find them there, you may have to shut off intermediate valves or the main shutoff valve.

TOOLS & MATERIALS

Screwdriver
Adjustable wrench
Channel-type pliers

Replacement faucet parts, as needed

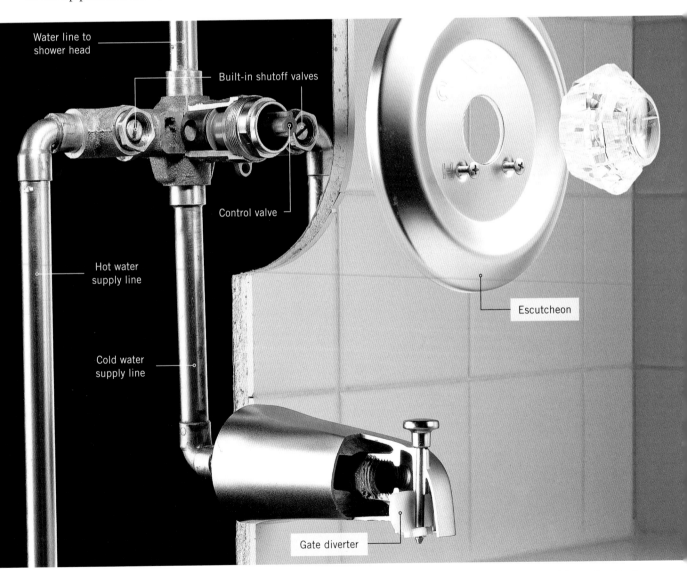

Water line to shower head

Built-in shutoff valves

Control valve

Hot water supply line

Cold water supply line

Escutcheon

Gate diverter

A single-handle tub/shower faucet is the simplest type to operate and to maintain. The handle controls the mixing ratio of both hot and cold water, and the diverter is a simple gate valve.

How to Repair a Single-Handle Cartridge Tub & Shower Faucet

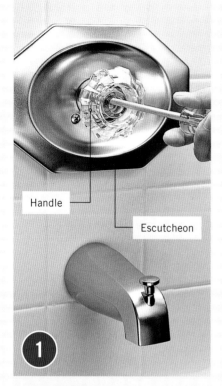

Handle

Escutcheon

1

Use a screwdriver to remove the handle and escutcheon.

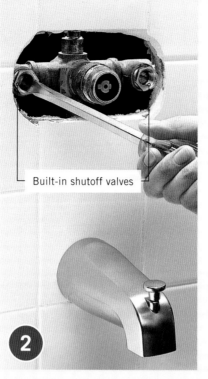

Built-in shutoff valves

2

Turn off water supply at the built-in shutoff valves or the main shutoff valve.

Bonnet nut

3

Unscrew and remove the retaining ring or bonnet nut using adjustable wrench.

O-ring

Cartridge

4

Remove the cartridge assembly by grasping the end of the valve with channel-type pliers and pulling gently.

5

Flush the valve body with clean water to remove sediment. Replace any worn O-rings. Reinstall the cartridge and test the valve. If the faucet fails to work properly, replace the cartridge.

Single-Handle Tub & Shower Faucet with Scald Control

In many plumbing systems, if someone flushes a nearby toilet or turns on the cold water of a nearby faucet while someone else is taking a shower, the shower water temperature can suddenly rise precipitously. This is not only uncomfortable; it can actually scald you. For that reason, many one-handle shower valves have a device, called a "balancing valve" or an "anti-scald valve," that keeps the water from getting too hot.

The temperature of your shower may drastically rise to dangerous scalding levels if a nearby toilet is flushed. A shower fixture equipped with an anti-scald valve prevents this sometimes dangerous situation.

 ## How to Adjust the Shower's Temperature

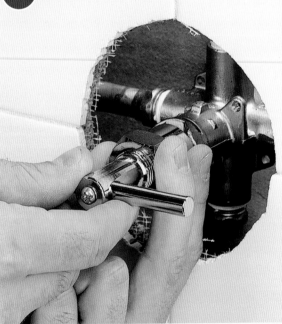

To reduce or raise the maximum temperature, remove the handle and escutcheon. Some models have an adjustment screw, others have a handle that can be turned by hand.

To remove a balancing valve, you may need to buy a removal tool made for your faucet. Before replacing, slowly turn on water to flush out any debris; use a towel or bucket to keep water from entering inside the wall.

Fixing & Replacing Showerheads

If spray from the showerhead is uneven, clean the spray holes. The outlet or inlet holes of the showerhead may get clogged with mineral deposits. Showerheads pivot into different positions. If a showerhead does not stay in position, or if it leaks, replace the O-ring that seals against the swivel ball.

A tub can be equipped with a shower by installing a flexible shower adapter kit. Complete kits are available at hardware stores and home centers.

TOOLS & MATERIALS

Adjustable wrench or channel-type pliers

Pipe wrench

Drill

Glass and tile bit

Mallet

Screwdriver

Masking tape

Thin wire (paper clip)

Faucet grease

Rag

Replacement O-rings

Masonry anchors

Flexible shower adapter kit (optional)

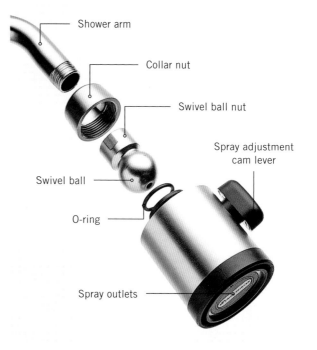

Shower arm

Collar nut

Swivel ball nut

Spray adjustment cam lever

Swivel ball

O-ring

Spray outlets

A typical showerhead can be disassembled easily for cleaning and repair. Some showerheads include a spray adjustment cam lever that is used to change the force of the spray.

How to Clean & Repair a Showerhead

Swivel ball nut

Collar nut

①

Unscrew the swivel ball nut, using an adjustable wrench or channel-type pliers. Wrap jaws of the tool with masking tape to prevent marring the finish. Unscrew collar nut from the showerhead.

Inlet holes

②

Clean outlet and inlet holes of showerhead with a thin wire. Flush the head with clean water.

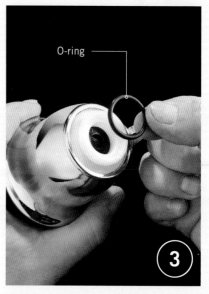

O-ring

③

Replace the O-ring, if necessary. Lubricate the O-ring with faucet grease before installing.

How to Install a Flexible Shower Adapter

Remove old tub spout. Install new tub spout from kit, using a pipe wrench. New spout will have an adapter hose outlet. Wrap the tub spout with a rag to prevent damage to the chrome finish.

Adapter hose outlet

1

Adapter hose outlet

Flexible shower hose

Attach flexible shower hose to the adaptor hose outlet. Tighten with an adjustable wrench or channel-type pliers.

2

Flexible shower hose

3

Determine location of showerhead hanger. Use hose length as a guide and make sure showerhead can be easily lifted off hanger.

4

Mark hole locations. Use a glass and tile bit to drill holes in ceramic tile for masonry anchors.

5

Insert anchors into holes and tap into place with a wooden or rubber mallet.

6

Fasten showerhead holder to the wall and hang showerhead.

Variation: Shower Conversion Kit

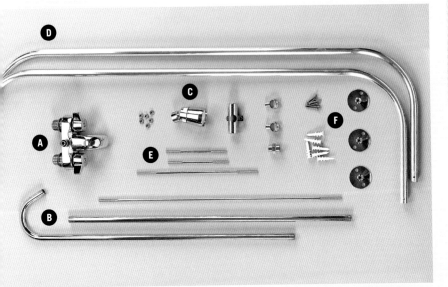

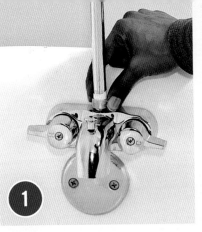

A packaged kit for adding a shower to your tub features a faucet with diverter (A), shower riser plumbing (B), showerhead (C), and a frame for the shower curtain (D) that mounts on the wall and ceiling with threaded rods (E), and fasteners and fittings (F).

1 **Remove the old tub faucet** and replace it with the new diverter-type faucet from the kit. Fit the assembled shower riser into the top of the faucet and hand-tighten. Apply Teflon tape to the threads before making the connection. This assembly includes one straight and one curved section, joined by a coupling. The top, curved pipe includes a connector to a wall brace. Shorten the straight section using a tubing cutter to lower the showerhead height, if desired. Slip the compression nut and washer onto the bottom end of the shower riser and attach the riser to the top of the faucet, hand-tightening for the time being.

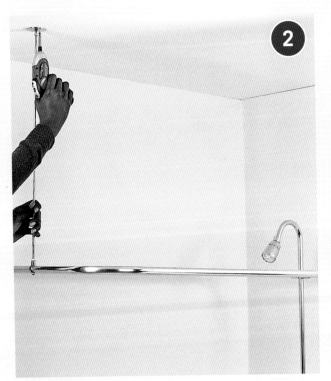

2 **With a helper,** assemble the curtain frame, securing with setscrews. Hold the frame level and measure to the ceiling to determine the ceiling brace pipe length. Cut the pipe and complete the ceiling brace assembly. Set the shower riser to the desired height and connect the brace to the wall (ensure strong connections by driving the mounting screws into a wall stud and ceiling joist, if possible.)

3 **After the curtain frame is completely assembled and secured,** tighten the faucet connection with a wrench. Full-size shower kits require one shower curtain on each side of the curtain frame. The hooks seen here feature roller bearings on the tops so they can be operated very smoothly with minimal resistance.

Tubs & Showers

Tub or shower not draining? First, make sure it's only the tub or shower. If your sink is plugged, too, it may be a coincidence or it may be that a common branch line is plugged. A sure sign of this is when water drains from the sink into the tub. This could require the help of a drain cleaning service.

If the toilet also can't flush (or worse, water comes into the tub when you flush the toilet), then the common drain to all your bathroom fixtures is plugged. Call a drain cleaning service. If you suspect the problem is only with your tub or shower, then read on. We'll show you how to clear drainlines and clean and adjust two types of tub stopper mechanisms. Adjusting the mechanism can also help with the opposite problem: a tub that drains when you're trying to take a bath.

As with bathroom sinks, tub and shower drain pipes may become clogged with soap and hair. The drain stopping mechanisms can also require cleaning and adjustment.

TOOLS & MATERIALS

Phillips screwdriver	Toothbrush
Plunger	Needlenose pliers
Scrub brush	Dishwashing brush
White vinegar	Faucet grease

MAINTENANCE TIP

Like bathroom sinks, tubs and showers face an ongoing onslaught from soap and hair. When paired, this pesky combination is a sure-fire source of clogs. The soap scum coagulates as it is washed down the drain and binds the hair together in a mass that grows larger with every shower or bath. To nip these clogs in the bud, simply pour boiling hot clean water down the drain from time to time to melt the soapy mass and wash the binder away.

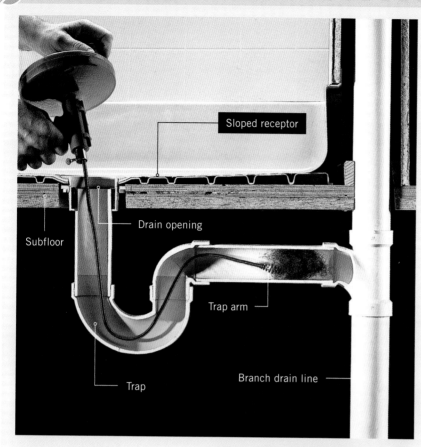

Sloped receptor

Drain opening

Subfloor

Trap arm

Trap

Branch drain line

On shower drains, feed the head of a hand-crank or drill-powered auger in through the drain opening after removing the strainer. Crank the handle of the auger to extend the cable and the auger head down into the trap and, if the clog is farther downline, toward the branch drain. When clearing any drain, it is always better to retrieve the clog than to push it farther downline.

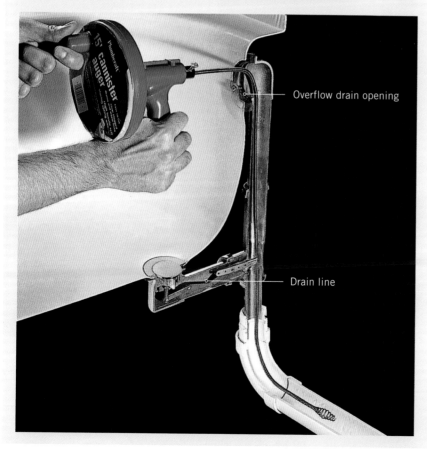

Overflow drain opening

Drain line

On combination tub/showers, it's generally easiest to insert the auger through the overflow opening after removing the coverplate and lifting out the drain linkage. Crank the handle of the auger to extend the cable and the auger head down into the trap and, if the clog is farther downline, toward the branch drain. When clearing any drain, it is always better to retrieve the clog than to push it farther downline.

How to Fix a Plunger-Type Drain

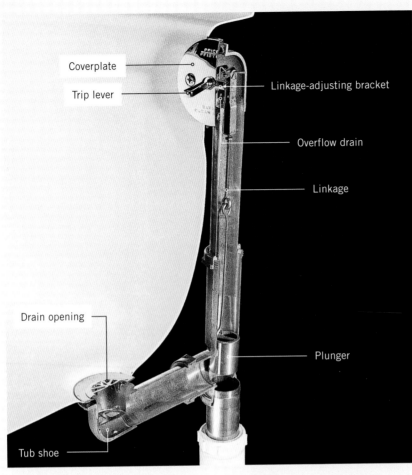

Coverplate

Trip lever

Linkage-adjusting bracket

Overflow drain

Linkage

Drain opening

Plunger

Tub shoe

1

A plunger-type tub drain has a simple grate over the drain opening and a behind-the-scenes plunger stopper. Remove the screws on the overflow coverplate with a slotted or Phillips screwdriver. Pull the coverplate, linkage, and plunger from the overflow opening.

Clean hair and soap off the plunger with a scrub brush. Mineral buildup is best tackled with white vinegar and a toothbrush or a small wire brush.

2

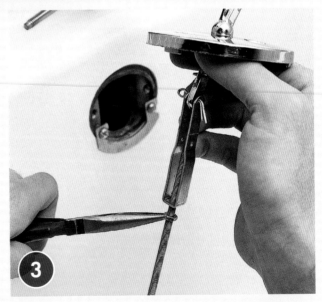

3

Adjust the plunger. If your tub isn't holding water with the plunger down, it's possible the plunger is hanging too high to fully block water from the tub shoe. Loosen the locknut with needlenose pliers, then screw the rod down about ⅛". Tighten the locknut down. If your tub drains poorly, the plunger may be set too low. Loosen the locknut and screw the rod in ⅛" before retightening the locknut.

How to Fix a Pop-up Drain

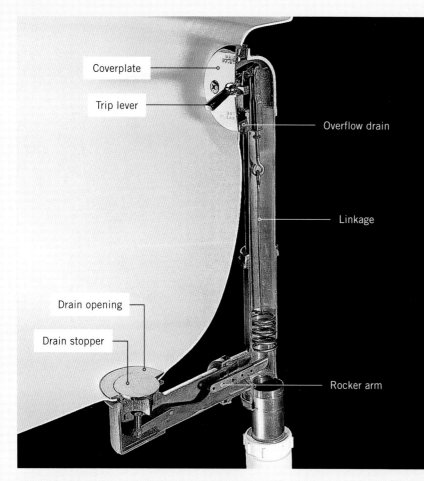

Coverplate

Trip lever

Overflow drain

Linkage

Drain opening

Drain stopper

Rocker arm

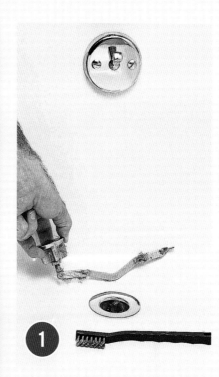

Raise the trip lever to the open position.
Pull the stopper and rocker arm assembly from the drain. Clean off soap and hair with a dishwashing brush in a basin of hot water. Clean off mineral deposits with a toothbrush or small wire brush and white vinegar.

Remove the screws from the cover plate. Pull the trip lever and the linkage from the overflow opening. Clean off soap and hair with a brush in a basin of hot water. Remove mineral buildup with white vinegar and a wire brush. Lubricate moving parts of the linkage and rocker arm mechanism with faucet grease.

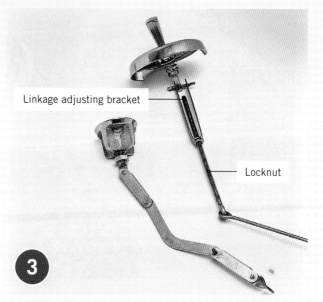

Linkage adjusting bracket

Locknut

Adjust the pop-up stopper mechanism by first loosening the locknut on the lift rod. If the stopper doesn't close all the way, shorten the linkage by screwing the rod ⅛" farther into the linkage-adjusting bracket. If the stopper doesn't open wide enough, extend the linkage by unscrewing the rod ⅛". Tighten the locknut before replacing the mechanism and testing your adjustment.

Sink Drains

Every sink has a drain trap and a fixture drain line. Sink clogs usually are caused by a buildup of soap and hair in the trap or fixture drain line. Remove clogs by using a plunger, disconnecting and cleaning the trap (this page), or using a hand auger (page 239).

Many sinks hold water with a mechanical plug called a pop-up stopper. If the sink will not hold standing water, or if water in the sink drains too slowly, the pop-up stopper must be cleaned and adjusted.

TOOLS & MATERIALS

Plunger	Screwdriver	Bucket
Channel-type pliers	Flashlight	Replacement gaskets
Small wire brush	Rag	Teflon tape

Clogged lavatory sinks can be cleared with a plunger (not to be confused with a flanged force-cup). Remove the pop-up drain plug and strainer first, and plug the overflow hole by stuffing a wet rag into it, allowing you to create air pressure with the plunger.

How to Clear a Sink Trap

Place bucket under trap to catch water and debris. Loosen slip nuts on trap bend with channel-type pliers. Unscrew nuts by hand and slide away from connections. Pull off trap bend.

Dump out debris. Clean trap bend with a small wire brush. Inspect slip nut washers for wear and replace if necessary. Reinstall trap bend and tighten slip nuts.

How to Clear a Kitchen Sink

Drainline from dishwasher

Plunging a kitchen sink is not difficult, but you need to create an uninterrupted pressure lock between the plunger and the clog. If you have a dishwasher, the drain tube needs to be clamped shut and sealed off at the disposer or drainline. The pads on the clamp should be large enough to flatten the tube across its full diameter (or you can clamp the tube ends between small boards).

If there is a second basin, have a helper hold a basket strainer plug in its drain or put a large pot or bucket full of water on top of it. Unfold the skirt within the plunger and place this in the drain of the sink you are plunging. There should be enough water in the sink to cover the plunger head. Plunge rhythmically for six repetitions with increasing vigor, pulling up hard on the last repitition. Repeat this sequence until the clog is removed. Flush out a cleared clog with plenty of hot water.

How to Use a Hand Auger at the Trap Arm

If you suspect the clog is downstream of the trap, remove the trap arm from the fitting at the wall. Look in the fixture drain with a flashlight. If you see water, that means the fixture drain is plugged. Clear it with a hand-crank or drill-powered auger (see page 239).

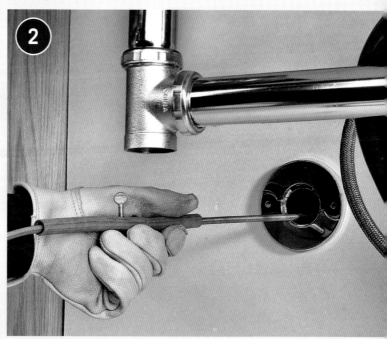

If plunging doesn't work, remove the trap and clean it out (see previous page). With the trap off, see if water flows freely from both sinks (if you have two). Sometimes clogs will lodge in the tee fitting or one of the waste pipes feeding it. These may be pulled out manually or cleared with a bottlebrush or wire. When reassembling the trap, apply Teflon tape clockwise to the male threads of metal waste pieces. Tighten with your channel-type pliers. Plastic pieces need no tape and should be hand tightened only.

Branch & Main Drains

TOOLS & MATERIALS

Adjustable wrench or pipe wrench	Rags
Hand auger	Penetrating oil
Cold chisel	Cleanout plug (if needed)
Ball-peen hammer	Pipe joint compound
Bucket	Electrical drum auger
Ladder	Gloves
Phillips screwdriver	Teflon Tape

If using a plunger or a hand auger does not clear a clog in a fixture drain line, it means that the blockage may be in a branch line, the main waste-vent stack, or the sewer service line.

First, use a hand-crank or drill-powered auger to clear the branch drain line closest to any stopped-up fixtures. Branch drain lines may be serviced through the cleanout fittings located at the end of the branch. Because waste water may be backed up in the drain lines, always open a cleanout with caution. Place a bucket and rags under the opening to catch waste water. Never position yourself directly under a cleanout opening while unscrewing the plug or cover.

If using an auger on the branch line does not solve the problem, then the clog may be located in a main drainage stack. To clear the stack, run an auger cable down through the roof vent. Make sure that the cable of your auger is long enough to reach down the entire length of the stack. If it is not, you may want to rent or borrow another auger. Always use extreme caution when working on a ladder or on a roof.

If no clog is present in the main stack, the problem may be located in the sewer service line. Locate the main cleanout, usually a wye-shaped fitting at the bottom of the main drainage stack. Remove the plug and push the cable of a hand auger into the opening.

Some sewer service lines in older homes have a house trap. The house trap is a U-shaped fitting located at the point where the sewer line exits the house. Most of the fitting will be beneath the floor surface, but it can be identified by its two openings. Use a hand auger to clean a house trap.

If the auger meets solid resistance in the sewer line, retrieve the cable and inspect the bit. Fine, hair-like roots on the bit indicate the line is clogged with tree roots. Dirt on the bit indicates a collapsed line.

Use a power auger to clear sewer service lines that are clogged with tree roots. Power augers (page 246) are available at rental centers. However, a power auger is a large, heavy piece of equipment. Before renting, consider the cost of rental and the level of your do-it-yourself skills versus the price of a professional sewer cleaning service. If you rent a power auger, ask the rental dealer for complete instructions on how to operate the equipment.

Always consult a professional sewer cleaning service if you suspect a collapsed line.

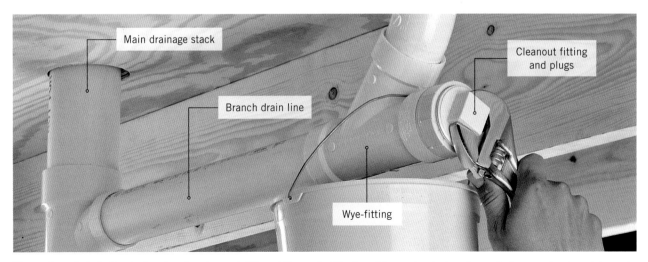

Clear a branch drain line by locating the cleanout fitting at the end of the line. Place a bucket underneath the opening to catch waste water, then slowly unscrew the cleanout plug with an adjustable wrench. Clear clogs in the branch drain line with a hand auger.

How to Clear a Branch Drain Line

Street side

House side

Clear the house trap in a sewer service line using a hand auger. Slowly remove only the plug on the "street side" of the trap. If water seeps out the opening as the plug is removed, the clog is in the sewer line beyond the trap. If no water seeps out, auger the trap. If no clog is present in the trap, replace the street-side plug and remove the house-side plug. Use the auger to clear clogs located between the house trap and main stack.

If all else fails, you can try to clear the main drainage stack by running the cable of a hand-crank or drill-powered auger down through the roof vent. Always use extreme caution while working on a ladder or roof.

How to Replace a Main Drain Cleanout Plug

Cleanout plug

Remove the cleanout plug, using a large wrench. If the plug does not turn out, apply penetrating oil around the edge of the plug, wait 10 minutes, and try again. Place rags and a bucket under fitting opening to catch any water that may be backed up in the line.

Remove stubborn plugs by placing the cutting edge of a cold chisel on the edge of the plug. Strike the chisel with a ball-peen hammer to move plug counterclockwise. If the plug does not turn out, break it into pieces with the chisel and hammer. Remove all broken pieces.

Cleanout fitting

Replace the old plug with a new plug. Apply pipe joint compound to the threads of the replacement plug and screw into the cleanout fitting.

Wing nut

Metal plates

ALTERNATE: Replace the old plug with an expandable rubber plug. A wing nut squeezes the rubber core between two metal plates. The rubber bulges slightly to create a watertight seal.

How to Power-Auger a Floor Drain

1

Remove the cover from the floor drain using a slotted or Phillips screwdriver. On one wall of the drain bowl you'll see a cleanout plug. Remove the cleanout plug from the drain bowl with your largest channel-type pliers. This cleanout allows you to bypass the trap. If it's stuck, apply penetrating oil to the threads and let it sit a half an hour before trying to free it again. If the wrench won't free it, rent a large pipe wrench from your home center or hardware store. You can also auger through the trap if you have to.

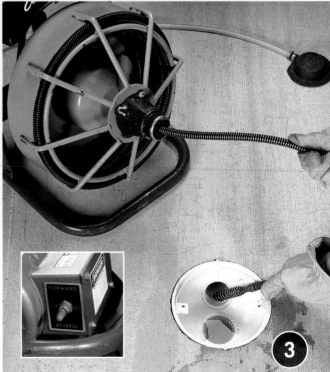

POWER AUGER LARGE LINES

If you choose to auger a larger line, you may find yourself opening a cleanout with 10 or 20 vertical feet of waste water behind it. Be careful. The cap may unexpectedly burst open when it's loose enough, spewing noxious waste water uncontrollably over anything in its path, including you! Here are some precautions:

Whenever possible, remove a trap or cleanout close to the top of the backed-up water level. Run your auger through this. Make sure the auger and its electric connections will not get wet should waste water spew forcefully from the cleanout opening.

Use the spear tool on the power auger first, to let the water drain out through a smaller hole before widening it with a larger cutting tool. If you are augering through a 3" or 4" cleanout, use three bits: the spear, a small cutter, and then a larger cutter to do the best job.

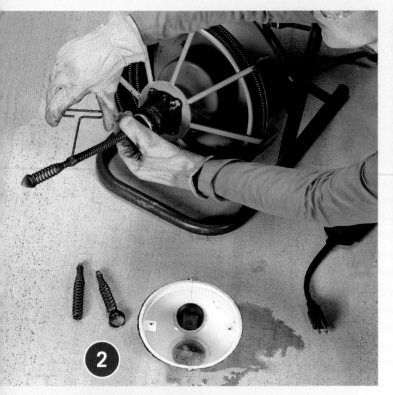

2

Rent an electric drum auger with at least 50 ft. of ½" cable. The rental company should provide a properly sized, grounded extension cord, heavy leather gloves, and eye protection. The auger should come with a spear tool, cutter tool, and possibly a spring tool suitable for a 2" drainline. Attach the spearhead first (with the machine unplugged).

3

Wear close-fitting clothing and contain long hair. Place the power auger machine in a dry location within 3 ft. of the drain opening. Plug the tool into a grounded, GFI-protected circuit. Wear eye protection and gloves. Position the footswitch where it is easy to actuate. Make sure the FOR/REV switch is in the Forward position (inset photo). Hand feed the cleaning tool and some cable into the drain or cleanout before turning the machine on.

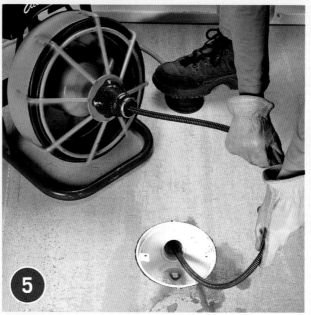

Stationary power augers (as opposed to pistol-grip types) are controlled by a foot pedal called an actuator so you can turn the power on and off hands-free.

With both gloved hands on the cable, depress the foot actuator to start the machine. Gradually push the rotating cable into the drain opening. If the rotation slows or you cannot feed more cable into the drain, pull back on the cable before pushing it forward again. Don't force it. The cable needs to be rotating whenever the motor is running or it can kink and buckle. If the cleaning tool becomes stuck, reverse it, back the tool off the obstruction, and switch back to Forward.

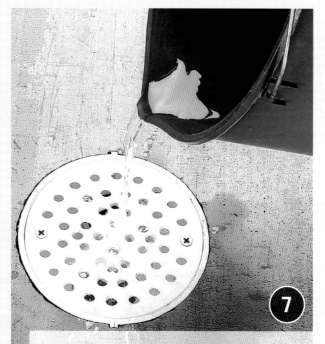

Gradually work through the clog by pulling back on the cable whenever the machine starts to bog down and push it forward again when it gains new momentum. Never let the cable stop turning when the motor is running. When you have broken through the clog or snagged an object, withdraw the cable from the line. Manually pull the cable from the drain line while continuing to run the drum Forward. When the cleaning tool is close to the drain opening, release the foot actuator and let the cable come to a stop before feeding the last 2 or 3 ft. of cable into the drum by hand.

After clearing the drain pipe, run the auger through the trap. Finish cleaning the auger. Wrap Teflon tape clockwise onto the plug threads and replace the plug. Run hot water through a hose from the laundry sink or use a bucket to flush remaining debris through the trap and down the line.

Supply Pipes

When replacing old water supply pipes, we recommend that you use Type M rigid copper or PEX. Use ¾" pipe for the main distribution pipes and ½" pipes for the branch lines running to individual fixtures.

For convenience, run hot and cold water pipes parallel to one another, between 3" and 6" apart. Use the straightest, most direct routes possible when planning the layout, because too many bends in the pipe runs can cause significant resistance and reduce water flow.

It is a good idea to remove old supply pipes that are exposed, but pipes hidden in walls can be left in place unless they interfere with the installation of the new supply pipes.

Support copper supply pipes at least every 10 ft. along vertical runs and 6 ft. along horizontal runs (check local codes). Always use copper or plastic support materials with copper; never use steel, which can interact with copper and cause corrosion.

TOOLS & MATERIALS

Male-threaded adapter	Copper pipes
Full-bone control valve	Tee fittings

How to Replace Water Supply Pipes

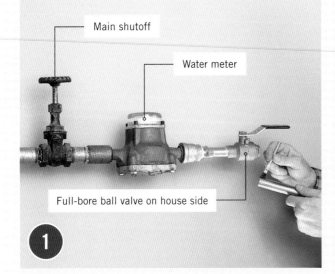

Shut off the water on the street side of the water meter, then disconnect and remove the old water pipes from the house side. Solder a ¾" male-threaded adapter and full-bore control valve to a short length of ¾" copper pipe, then attach this assembly to the house side of the water meter. Extend the ¾" cold-water distribution pipe toward the nearest fixture, which is usually the water heater.

At the water heater, install a ¾" tee fitting in the cold-water distribution pipe. Use two lengths of ¾" copper pipe and a full-bore control valve to run a branch pipe to the water heater. From the outlet opening on the water heater, extend a ¾" hot water distribution pipe. Continue the hot and cold supply lines on parallel routes toward the next group of fixtures in your house.

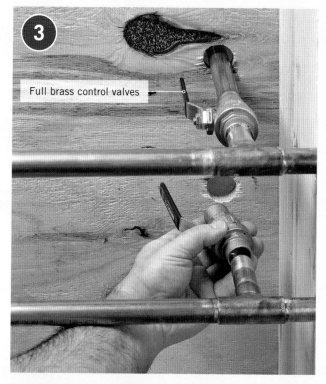

Establish routes for branch supply lines by drilling holes located in stud cavities. Install tee fittings, then begin the branch lines by installing brass control valves. Branch lines should be made with ¾" pipe if they are supplying more than one fixture; ½" if they are supplying only one fixture.

Extend the branch lines to the fixtures. In our project, we ran ¾" vertical branch lines up through the framed chase to the bathroom. Route pipes around obstacles, such as a main waste-vent stack, by using 45° and 90° elbows and short lengths of pipe.

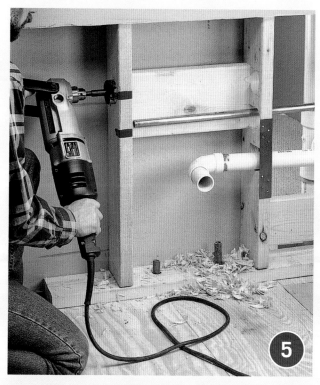

Where branch lines run through studs or floor joists, drill holes or cut notches in the framing members, then insert the pipes. For long runs of pipe, you may need to join two or more shorter lengths of pipe, using couplings as you create the runs.

Install ¾" to ½" reducing tee fittings and elbows to extend the branch lines to individual fixtures. In our bathroom, we installed a hot and cold stubout for the bathtub and sink, and a cold-water stubout for the toilet. Cap each stubout until your work has been inspected and the wall surfaces have been completed.

Noisy Pipes

TOOLS & MATERIALS

Reciprocating saw or hacksaw

Propane torch (for sweating copper)

Pipe wrenches (for galvanized steel)

Adjustable wrench

Foam rubber pipe insulation

Pipe and fittings, as needed

Utility knife

Teflon tape

Pipes can make a loud banging noise when faucets are turned off or when valves on washing machines (or other automatic appliances) shut abruptly. The sudden stop of flowing water traps air and creates a shock wave, called water hammer, that slams through the water supply system. Some pipes may knock against wall studs or joists, creating additional noise.

Water hammer can be more than an annoyance. The shockwave can cause damage and eventually failure in pipes and fittings. If a pressure-relief valve on your water heater leaks, it may not be a faulty valve, but a pressure surge in the supply system.

You can eliminate water hammer by installing a simple device called a water hammer arrester in the supply line. Inexpensive point-of-use arresters are small enough to be installed easily near the noisy valve or appliance (the closer the better). They can be positioned horizontally or vertically or at an angle without any change in effectiveness. Unlike with old-style air chambers, water cannot fill a water hammer arrester, so they should be effective for the life of the system.

Pipes that bang against studs or joists can be quieted by cushioning them with pieces of pipe insulation. Make sure pipe hangers are snug and that pipes are well supported.

Clattering pipes can be a major annoyance, but they also should alert you of a problem with the supply system.

Loose pipes may bang or rub against joist hangers, creating noise. Use pieces of foam rubber pipe insulation to cushion pipes.

A "Sioux strap" holds pipe away from a framing member. Just snap the strap on and drive a nail.

How to Install a Water Hammer Arrester

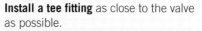

Install a tee fitting as close to the valve as possible.

Shut off the water supply and drain the pipes. Use a tubing cutter or reciprocating saw to cut out a section of horizontal pipe long enough for a tee fitting.

Short pipe

Branch arm

T-fitting

Install a short piece of pipe in the branch arm of the tee fitting. This short pipe will be used to attach a threaded fitting.

Install a threaded fitting. Use a fitting recommended by the manufacturer of your arrester.

Wrap the threads of the arrester in Teflon tape. Thread the arrester onto the fitting by hand. Tighten by holding the fitting with one adjustable wrench and turning the arrester with the other. Do not overtighten. Turn the water on and check for leaks.

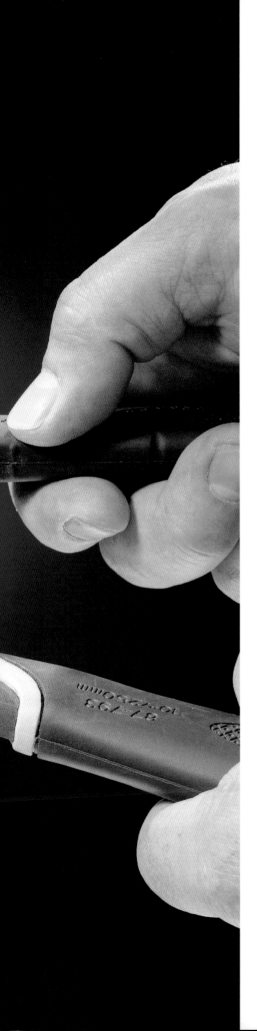

Plumbing Tools, Materials & Skills

Most home plumbing projects can be completed using a fairly inexpensive set of tools. So don't hesitate to buy a high-quality tool even if it costs a bit more. Some tools, like a basin wrench or spud wrench, get used seldom but are usually worth their modest price even if you only use them once. Large and expensive tools, such as a power drain auger, can be rented.

The type of plumbing material you employ has a profound effect on how you do the job. Plastic pipes are joined by solvent cement, while copper sweated and pieces of PEX are joined with crimping rings. Each type of material carries with it a small army of fittings and adapters and handling tools. Here, you'll see how to match the parts correctly.

Finally, good work comes down to good technique and patience. We can't teach you patience, but here we show you the techniques you'll need to become an accomplished home plumber.

In this chapter:
- Plumbing Tools
- Plumbing Materials
- Copper
- Rigid Plastic Pipe
- Working with Outdoor Flexible Plastic Pipe
- Cross-Linked Polyethylene (PEX)
- Cast Iron
- Pipe Fittings
- Shutoff Valves
- Valves & Hose Bibs
- Compression Fittings

Plumbing Tools

Many plumbing projects and repairs can be completed with basic hand tools you probably already own. Adding a few simple plumbing tools will prepare you for all the projects in this book. Specialty tools, such as a snap cutter or appliance dolly, are available at rental centers. When buying tools, invest in quality products.

Always care for tools properly. Clean tools after using them, wiping them free of dirt and dust with a soft rag. Prevent rust on metal tools by wiping them with a rag dipped in household oil. If a metal tool gets wet, dry it immediately, and then wipe it with an oiled rag. Keep toolboxes and cabinets organized. Make sure all tools are stored securely.

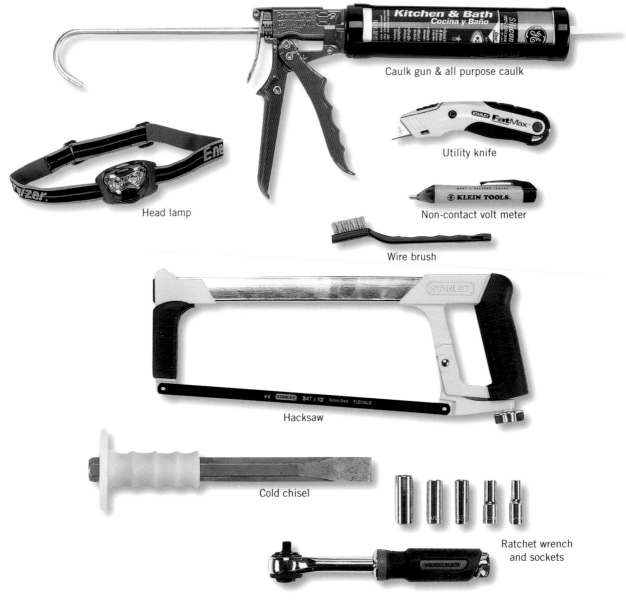

Caulk gun & all purpose caulk

Utility knife

Non-contact volt meter

Head lamp

Wire brush

Hacksaw

Cold chisel

Ratchet wrench and sockets

Tape measure

Metal files

Strainer wrench

Seat wrench

Adjustable wrenches

Screwdriver

Putty knife

Channel-type pliers

Needlenose pliers

Basin wrench

Level

(continued)

Plumbing Tools (continued)

Drill-powered auger is stronger than a hand-crank auger for removing larger pipe obstructions. This auger can be cranked by hand or attached to a standard ⅜" power drill.

Force cup clears drain clogs with water and air pressure. The force cup is used for toilet bowls. The flange usually can be folded up into the cup for use as a standard plunger.

Pipe wrench has a movable jaw that adjusts to fit a variety of pipe diameters. Pipe wrench is used for tightening and loosening pipes, pipe fittings, and large nuts. Two pipe wrenches often are used together to prevent damage to pipes and fittings.

Spud wrench is specially designed for removing or tightening large nuts that are 2" to 4" in diameter. Hooks on the ends of the wrench grab onto the lugs of large nuts for increased leverage.

Blow bag, sometimes called an expansion nozzle, is used to clear drains. It attaches to a garden hose and removes clogs with large spurts of water. The blow bag is best used on floor drains.

Plastic tubing cutter works like a gardener's pruners to cut flexible plastic pipes quickly.

Tubing cutters make straight, smooth cuts in plastic and copper pipe. A tubing cutter usually has a triangular blade for removing burrs from the insides of pipes.

Closet auger is used to clear toilet clogs. It is a slender tube with a crank handle on one end of a flexible auger cable. A special bend in the tube allows the auger to be positioned in the bottom of the toilet bowl. The bend is usually protected with a rubber sleeve to prevent scratching the toilet.

MAPP torch (left) is used for soldering fittings to copper pipes. Light the torch quickly and safely using a spark lighter.

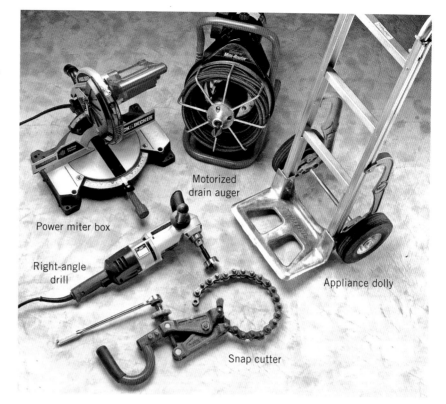

Power miter box

Motorized drain auger

Right-angle drill

Appliance dolly

Snap cutter

Rental tools may be needed for large jobs and special situations. A power miter saw makes fast, accurate cuts in a wide variety of materials, including plastic pipes. A motorized drain auger clears tree roots from sewer service lines. Use an appliance dolly to move heavy objects like water heaters. A snap cutter is designed to cut tough cast-iron pipes. The right-angle drill is useful for drilling holes in hard-to-reach areas.

Power drills and bits

Reciprocating saw

Flame-resistant pad helps keep wood and other underlying materials safe from the torch's flame.

Power hand tools can make any job faster, easier, and safer. Cordless power tools offer added convenience. Use a cordless ⅜" power drill for virtually any drilling task.

Plumbing Materials

COMMON PIPE & TUBE TYPES

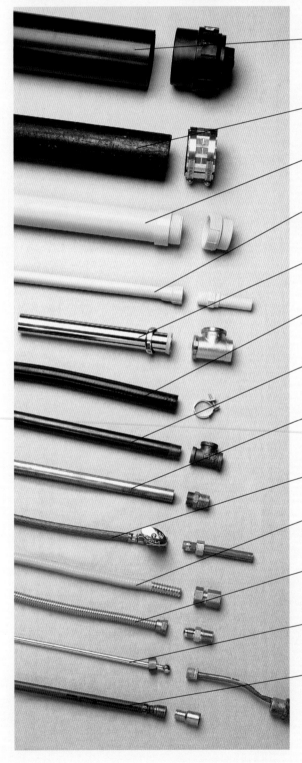

BENEFITS & CHARACTERISTICS

ABS (acrylonitrile butadiene styrene) ABS is an approved DWV pipe (although it has its detractors) and is commonly used in many markets, especially in the western U.S.

Cast iron is strong but hard to work with. Repairs should be made with plastic pipe, if allowed.

PVC (polyvinyl chloride) is rigid plastic that resists heat and chemicals. Schedule 40 is the minimum thickness for use as DWV pipe and water service pipe.

CPVC (chlorinated polyvinyl chloride) rigid plastic is inexpensive and withstands high temperature and pressure.

Chromed brass has an attractive shiny surface and is used for drain traps where appearance is important.

PE (polyethylene) plastic is a black or bluish flexible pipe sometimes used for main water service lines as well as irrigation systems.

Black pipe (iron pipe) generally is threaded at the ends to accept female-threaded fittings. Not for potable water.

Rigid copper is used for water supply pipes. It resists corrosion and has smooth surfaces for good water flow.

Braided metal is used for water supply tubes that connect shutoff valves to fixtures.

Flexible stainless-steel (protective coated) connectors are used to attach gas appliances to supply stopcocks.

Flexible stainless-steel (uncoated) connectors are used to attach gas appliances to supply stopcocks

Chromed copper supply tube is used in areas where appearance is important. Easy to bend and fit.

PEX (cross-linked polyethylene) is flexible and is approved by major building codes for water supply.

Flexible copper tubing (not shown) bends easily and requires fewer couplings than rigid copper.

COMMON USES	LENGTHS	DIAMETERS	FITTING METHODS	TOOLS USED FOR CUTTING
DWV pipes, sewer pipes, drain traps	10 ft.	1¼, 1½, 2, 3, 4"	Solvent cement or threaded fittings	Tubing cutter, miter box or hacksaw
DWV pipes, sewer pipes	5 ft., 10 ft.	1½, 2, 3, 4"	Oakum & lead, banded neoprene couplings	Snap cutter or hacksaw
DWV pipes, sewer pipes, drain traps	10 ft., 20 ft.; or sold by linear ft.	1¼", 1½", 2", 3", 4"	Solvent cement, threaded fittings	Tubing cutter, miter box, or hacksaw
Hot & cold water supply pipes	10 ft.	⅜", ½", ¾", 1"	Solvent cement and plastic fittings, or with compression fittings	Tubing cutter, miter box, or hacksaw
Valves & shutoffs; drain traps, supply risers	Lengths vary	1¼", ½", ¾", 1¼", 1½"	Compression fittings, or with metal solder	Tubing cutter, hacksaw, or reciprocating saw
Outdoor cold water supply pipes	Sold in coils of 25 to hundreds of ft.	¼" to 1"	Rigid PVC fittings and stainless steel hose clamps	Ratchet-style plastic pipe cutter or miter saw
Gas supply pipe	Sold in lengths up to 10 ft.	⅜, 1, 1¼, 1½"	Threaded connectors	Hacksaw, power cutoff saw or reciprocating saw with bi-metal blade
Hot & cold water supply pipes	10 ft., 20 ft.; or sold by linear ft.	⅜", ½", ¾", 1"	Metal solder, compression fittings, threaded fittings, press connect fittings, push connect fittings, flared fittings	Tubing cutter, hacksaw, or jigsaw
Supply tubes	12" or 20"	⅜, ½, ¾	Attached threaded fittings	Do not cut
Gas ranges, dryers, water heaters	12" to 60"	⅝", ½" (OD)	Attached threaded fittings	Do not cut
Gas ranges, dryers, water heaters	12" to 60"	⅝", ½" (OD)	Attached threaded fittings	Do not cut
Supply tubing	12", 20", 30"	⅜"	Brass compression fittings	Tubing cutter or hacksaw
Hot & cold water supply; PEX-AL-PEX (usually orange) is used in radiant floors	Sold in coils of 25 ft. to hundreds of ft.	¼" to 1"	Crimp fittings, push connect fittings	Tubing cutter
Gas supply; hot & cold water supply	30-ft., 60-ft. coils; or by ft.	¼", ⅜", ½", ¾", 1"	Brass flare fittings, solder, compression fittings	Tubing cutter or hacksaw

Copper

Copper is an ideal material for water supply pipes. It resists corrosion and has smooth surfaces that provide good water flow. Copper pipes are available in several diameters, but most home water supply systems use ½" or ¾" pipe. Copper pipe is manufactured in rigid and flexible forms.

Rigid copper, sometimes called hard copper, is approved for home water supply systems by all local codes. It comes in three wall-thickness grades: Types M, L, and K. Type M is the thinnest, the least expensive, and a good choice for do-it-yourself home plumbing.

Rigid Type L usually is required by code for commercial plumbing systems. Because it is strong and solders easily, Type L may be preferred by some professional plumbers and do-it-yourselfers for home use. Type K has the heaviest wall thickness and is used most often for underground water service lines.

Flexible copper, also called soft copper, comes in two wall-thickness grades: Types L and K. Both are approved for most home water supply systems, although flexible Type L copper is used primarily for gas service lines. Because it is bendable and will resist a mild frost, Type L may be installed as part of a water supply system in unheated indoor areas, like crawl spaces. Type K is used for underground water service lines.

A third form of copper, called DWV, is used for drain systems. Because most codes now allow low-cost plastic pipes for drain systems, DWV copper is seldom used.

Copper pipes are connected with soldered, compression, or flare fittings (see chart below). Always follow your local code for the correct types of pipes and fittings allowed in your area.

Soldered fittings, also called sweat fittings, often are used to join copper pipes. Correctly soldered fittings are strong and trouble-free. Copper pipe can also be joined with compression fittings or flare fittings. See chart below.

COPPER PIPE & FITTING CHART

FITTING METHOD	RIGID COPPER			FLEXIBLE COPPER		GENERAL COMMENTS
	TYPE M	TYPE L	TYPE K	TYPE L	TYPE K	
Soldered	yes	yes	yes	yes	yes	Inexpensive, strong, and trouble-free fitting method. Requires some skill.
Compression	yes	not applicable		no	no	Makes repairs and replacement easy. More expensive than solder. Best used on flexible copper.
Flare	no	no	no	yes	yes	Use only with flexible copper pipes. Usually used as a gas-line fitting. Requires some skill.
Push-connect fittings	no	yes	yes	no	no	

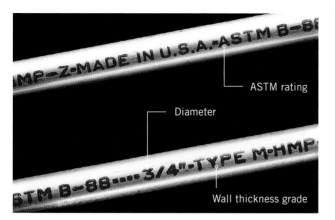

Grade stamp information includes the pipe diameter, the wall-thickness grade, and a stamp of approval from the ASTM (American Society for Testing and Materials). Type M pipe is identified by red lettering, Type L by blue lettering.

Bend flexible copper pipe with a coil-spring tubing bender to avoid kinks. Select a bender that matches the outside diameter of the pipe. Slip bender over pipe using a twisting motion. Bend pipe slowly until it reaches the correct angle, but not more than 90º.

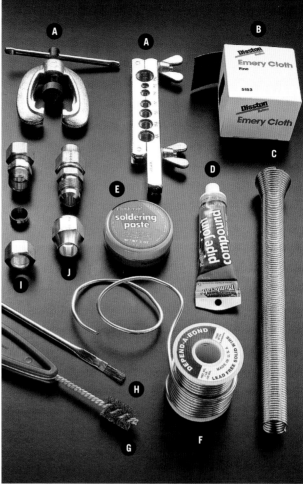

Specialty tools and materials for working with copper include: flaring tools (A), emery cloth (B), coil-spring tubing bender (C), pipe joint compound (D), soldering paste (flux) (E), lead-free solder (F), wire brush (G), flux brush (H), compression fitting (I), flare fitting (J).

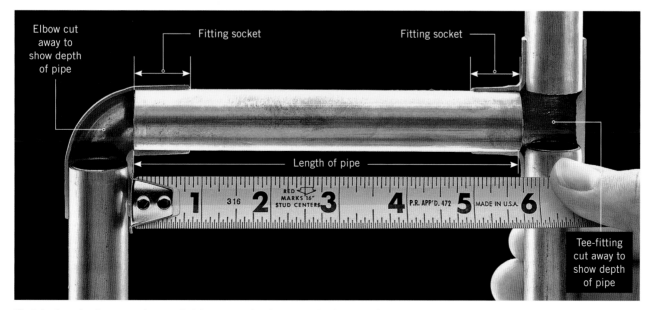

Find the length of copper pipe needed by measuring between the bottom of the copper fitting sockets (fittings shown in cutaway). Mark the length on the pipe with a felt-tipped pen.

Cutting & Soldering Copper

The best way to cut rigid and flexible copper pipe is with a tubing cutter. A tubing cutter makes a smooth, straight cut, an important first step toward making a watertight joint. Remove any metal burrs on the cut edges with a reaming tool or round file.

Copper can be cut with a hacksaw. A hacksaw is useful in tight areas where a tubing cutter will not fit. Take care to make a smooth, straight cut when cutting with a hacksaw.

A soldered pipe joint, also called a sweated joint, is made by heating a copper or brass fitting with a propane torch until the fitting is just hot enough to melt metal solder. The heat draws the solder into the gap between the fitting and pipe to form a watertight seal. A fitting that is overheated or unevenly heated will not draw in solder. Copper pipes and fittings must be clean and dry to form a watertight seal.

SOLDERING TIPS

Use caution when soldering copper. Pipes and fittings become very hot and must be allowed to cool before handling.

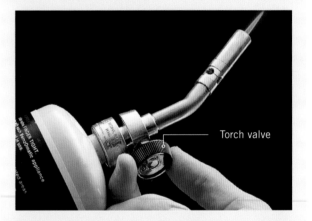

Torch valve

Prevent accidents by shutting off propane torch immediately after use. Make sure valve is closed completely.

TOOLS & MATERIALS

Tubing cutter
   with reaming tip
   (or hacksaw
   and round file)
Wire brush
Flux brush
Propane torch
Spark lighter (or matches)
Round file
Cloth

Adjustable wrench
Channel-type pliers
Copper pipe
Copper fittings
Emery cloth
Soldering paste (flux)
Sheet metal
Lead-free solder
Rag

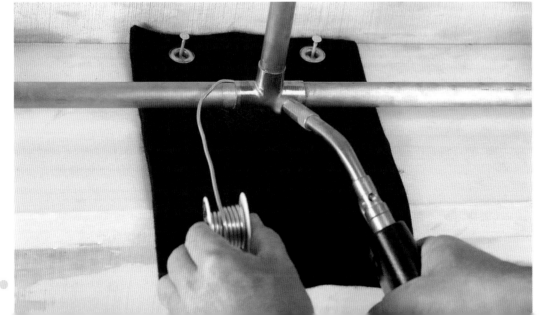

Protect wood from the heat of the torch flame while soldering. Use an old cookie sheet, two sheets of 26-gauge metal, or a fiber shield, as shown.

How to Cut Rigid & Flexible Copper Pipe

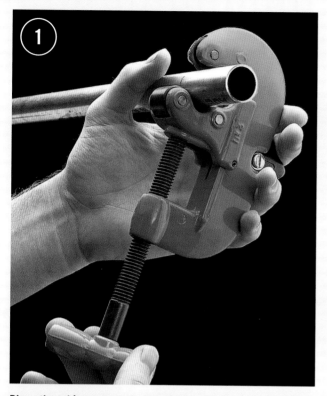

Place the tubing cutter over the pipe and tighten the handle so that the pipe rests on both rollers and the cutting wheel is on the marked line.

Turn the tubing cutter one rotation so that the cutting wheel scores a continuous straight line around the pipe.

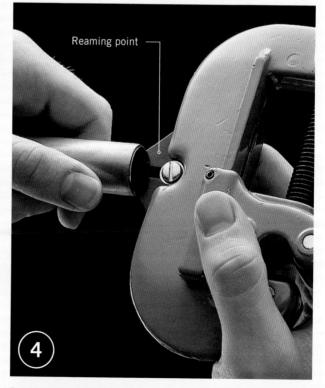

Rotate the cutter in the opposite direction, tightening the handle slightly after every two rotations, until the cut is complete.

Remove sharp metal burrs from the inside edge of the cut pipe, using the reaming point on the tubing cutter, or a round file.

How to Solder Copper Pipes & Fittings

Clean the end of each pipe by sanding with emery cloth. Ends must be free of dirt and grease to ensure that the solder forms a good seal.

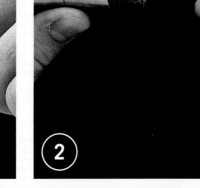

Clean the inside of each fitting by scouring with a wire brush or emery cloth.

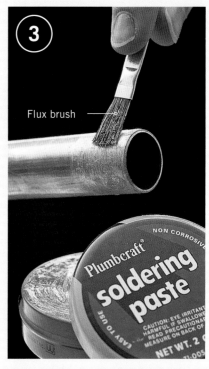

Apply a thin layer of soldering paste (flux) to end of each pipe, using a flux brush. Soldering paste should cover about 1" of pipe end. Don't use too much flux.

Apply a thin layer of flux to the inside of the fitting.

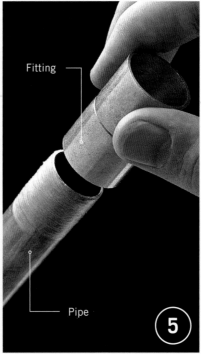

Assemble each joint by inserting the pipe into the fitting so it is tight against the bottom of the fitting sockets. Twist each fitting slightly to spread soldering paste.

Use a clean dry cloth to remove excess flux before soldering the assembled fitting.

Prepare the wire solder by unwinding 8" to 10" of wire from spool. Bend the first 2" of the wire to a 90º angle.

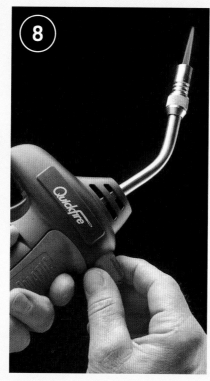

Open the gas valve and trigger the spark lighter to ignite the torch. Adjust the torch valve until the inner portion of the flame is 1" to 2" long.

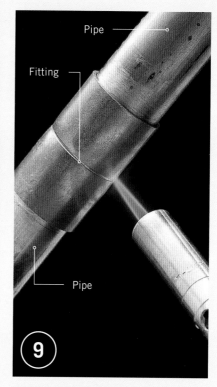

Pipe

Fitting

Pipe

Move the torch flame back and forth and around the pipe and the fitting to heat the area evenly.

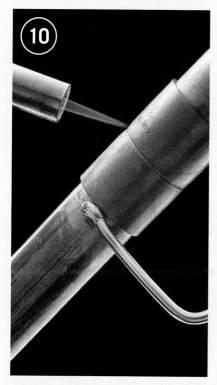

Heat the other side of the copper fitting to ensure that heat is distributed evenly. Touch solder to pipe. Solder will melt when the pipe is at the right temperature.

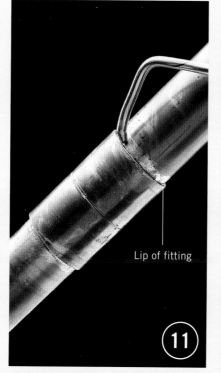

Lip of fitting

When solder melts, remove the torch and quickly push ½" to ¾" of solder into each joint. Capillary action fills the joint with liquid solder. A correctly soldered joint should show a thin bead of solder around the lips of the fitting.

Allow the joint to cool briefly, then wipe away excess solder with a dry rag.

CAUTION: Pipes will be hot. If joints leak after water is turned on, disassemble and resolder.

How to Solder Brass Valves

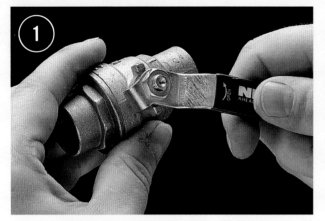

Valves should be fully open during all stages of the soldering process. If a valve has any plastic or rubber parts, remove them prior to soldering.

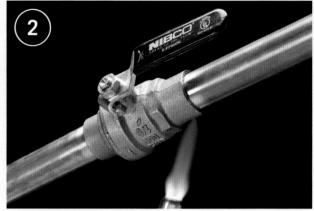

To prevent valve damage, quickly heat the pipe and the flanges of the valve, not the valve body. After soldering, cool the valve by spraying with water.

How to Take Apart Soldered Joints

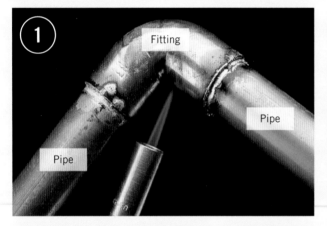

Fitting

Pipe

Pipe

Turn off the water and drain the pipes by opening the highest and lowest faucets in the house. Light your torch. Hold the flame tip to the fitting until the solder becomes shiny and begins to melt.

Use channel-type pliers to separate the pipes from the fitting.

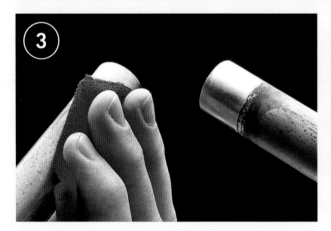

Remove old solder by heating the ends of the pipe with your torch. Use a dry rag to wipe away melted solder quickly. Caution: Pipes will be hot.

Use emery cloth to polish the ends of the pipe down to bare metal. Never reuse fittings.

PUSH FITTINGS

Push fittings make water supply connections about as easy as possible. They are expensive, so you won't want to use them for all connections on a large installation. But even professional plumbers use them in tight spots where sweating or welding would be difficult. They are also an ideal material for making a quick repair.

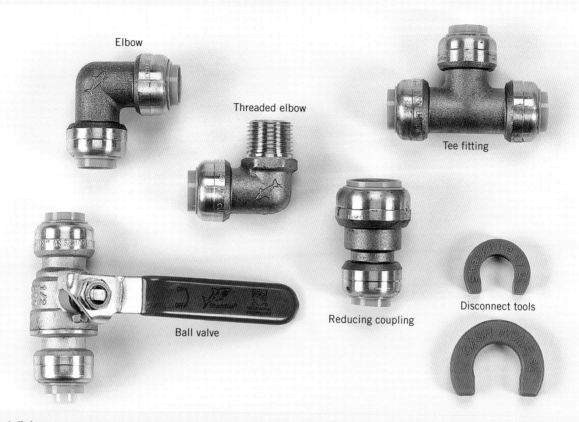

Elbow

Threaded elbow

Tee fitting

Ball valve

Reducing coupling

Disconnect tools

Push fittings are available as couplings tees, elbows, and even shutoff valves. They connect to hard copper, CPVC, and PEX pipe, but not to PVC or galvanized or black steel pipe. In most areas they are approved for use inside covered walls.

Cut the pipe square, and remove any burrs and rough edges. Draw a mark 1" from the cut end.

To remove a pipe from a push fitting, slip the disconnect tool over the pipe, slide it over the fitting, and press against the fitting's release collar as you pull the pipe out.

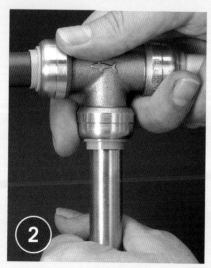

Push the pipe into the fitting an inch or so until you hear it click. Tug to make sure you have a strong connection. It may not seem like it, but the connection is indeed watertight and durable. You may rotate it to the desired position.

Rigid Plastic Pipe

Cut rigid ABS, PVC, or CPVC plastic pipes with a tubing cutter or with any saw. Cuts must be straight to ensure watertight joints.

Rigid plastics are joined with plastic fittings and solvent cement. Use a solvent cement that is made for the type of plastic pipe you are installing. For example, do not use ABS solvent on PVC pipe. Some solvent cements, called "all-purpose" or "universal" solvents, may be used on all types of plastic pipe.

Solvent cement hardens in about 30 seconds, so test-fit all plastic pipes and fittings before cementing the first joint. For best results, the surfaces of plastic pipes and fittings should be dulled with emery cloth and liquid primer before they are joined.

Liquid solvent cements and primers are toxic and flammable. Provide adequate ventilation when fitting plastics, and store the products away from any source of heat.

Plastic grip fittings can be used to join rigid or flexible plastic pipes to copper plumbing pipes.

Solvent welding is a chemical bonding process used to permanently join PVC pipes and fittings.

TOOLS & MATERIALS

Tape measure	Utility knife	Fittings	Rag
Felt-tipped pen	Channel-type pliers	Emery cloth	Petroleum jelly
Tubing cutter (or miter box or hacksaw)	Gloves	Plastic pipe primer	
	Plastic pipe	Solvent cement	

Primer and solvent cement are specific to the plumbing material being used. Do not use all-purpose or multi-purpose products. Light to medium body cements are appropriate for DIYers as they allow the longest working time and are easiest to use. When working with large pipe, 3 or 4" in diameter, buy a large-size can of cement, which has a larger dauber. If you use the small dauber (which comes with the small can), you may need to apply twice, which will slow you down and make connections difficult. (The smaller can of primer is fine for any other size pipe, since there's no rush in applying primer.) Cement (though not primer) goes bad in the can within a month or two after opening, so you may need to buy a new can for a new project.

How to Cut Rigid Plastic Pipe

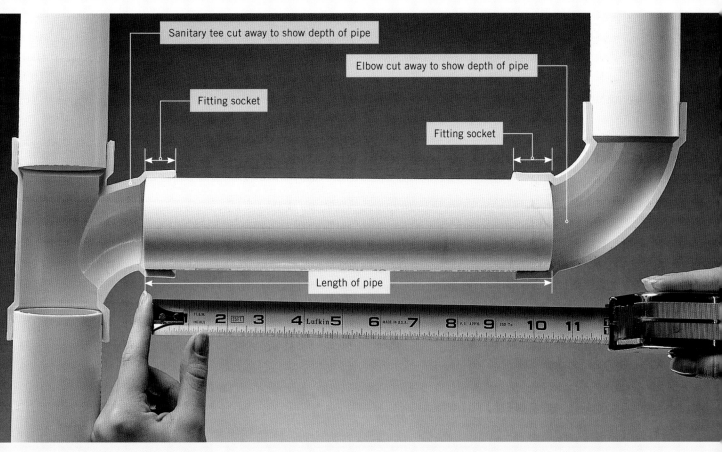

Sanitary tee cut away to show depth of pipe

Elbow cut away to show depth of pipe

Fitting socket

Fitting socket

Length of pipe

Find the length of plastic pipe needed by measuring between the bottoms of the fitting sockets (fittings shown in cutaway). Mark the length on the pipe with a felt-tipped pen.

Plastic tubing cutters do a fast, neat job of cutting. You'll probably have to go to a professional plumbing supply store to find one, however. They are not interchangeable with metal tubing cutters.

The best cutting tool for plastic pipe is a power miter saw with a fine tooth woodworking blade or a plastic-specific blade.

A ratcheting plastic-pipe cutter can cut smaller diameter PVC and CPVC pipe in a real hurry. They also are sold only at plumbing supply stores.

How to Solvent-Cement Rigid PVC Pipe

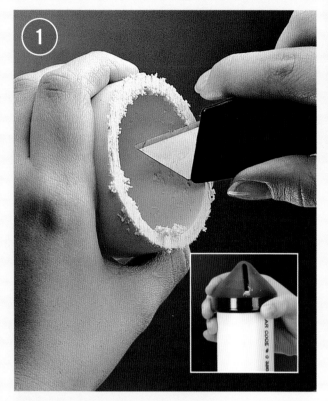

Remove rough burrs on cut ends of plastic pipe, using a utility knife or deburring tool (inset).

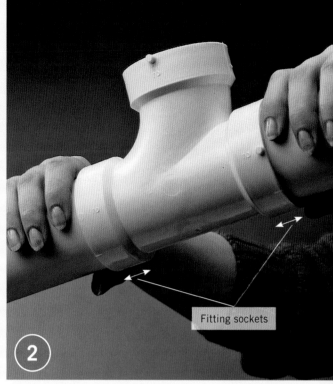

Fitting sockets

Test-fit all pipes and fittings. Pipes should fit tightly against the bottom of the fitting sockets.

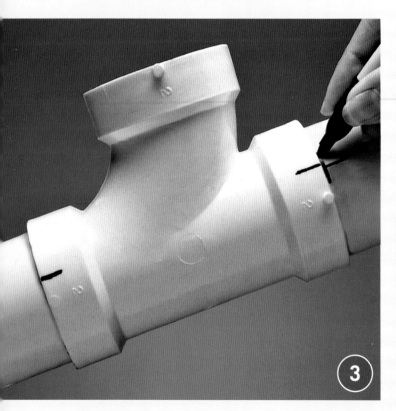

Mark the depth of the fitting sockets on the pipes. Take pipes apart. Clean the ends of the pipes and fitting sockets with emery cloth.

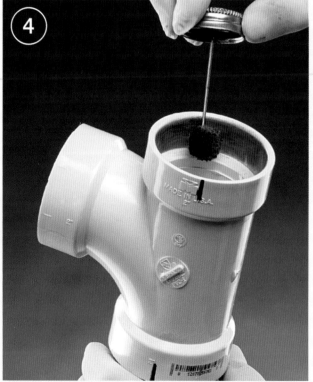

Apply a light coat of plastic pipe primer to the ends of the pipes and to the insides of the fitting sockets. Primer dulls glossy surfaces and ensures a good seal.

Solvent-cement each joint by applying a thick coat of solvent cement to the end of the pipe. Apply a thin coat of solvent cement to the inside surface of the fitting socket. Work quickly: solvent cement hardens in about 30 seconds.

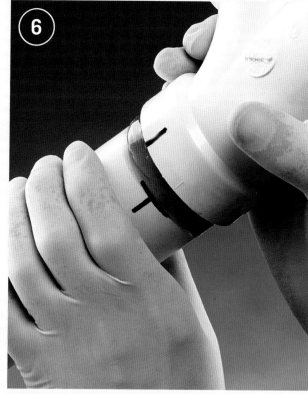

Quickly position the pipe and fitting so that the alignment marks are offset by about 2". Force the pipe into the fitting until the end fits flush against the bottom of the socket.

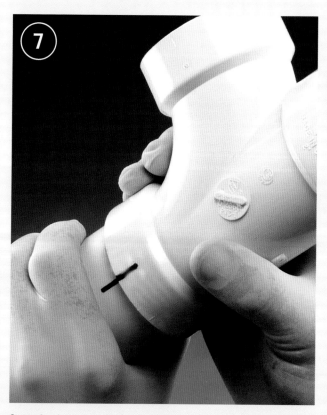

Spread solvent by twisting the pipe until the marks are aligned. Hold the pipe in place for about 20 seconds to prevent the joint from slipping.

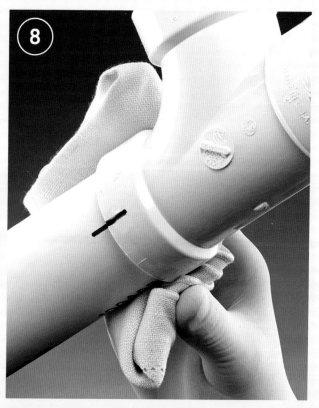

Wipe away excess solvent cement with a rag. Do not disturb the joint for 30 minutes after gluing.

Working with Outdoor Flexible Plastic Pipe

Flexible PE (polyethylene) pipe is used for underground cold water lines. Very inexpensive, PE pipe is commonly used for automatic lawn sprinkler systems and for extending cold water supply to utility sinks in detached garages and sheds.

Unlike other plastics, PE is not solvent-cemented, but is joined using "barbed" rigid PVC fittings and stainless-steel hose clamps. In cold climates, outdoor plumbing lines should be shut off and drained for winter.

TOOLS & MATERIALS

Tape measure	Flexible pipe
Tubing cutter	Fittings
Screwdriver or wrench	Hose clamps
Pipe joint compound	Utility knife

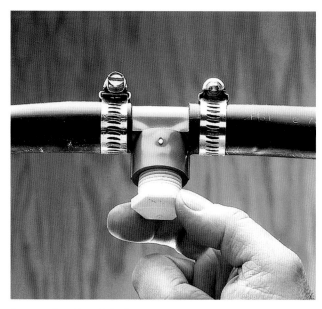

Connect lengths of PE pipe with a barbed PVC fitting. Secure the connection with stainless steel hose clamps.

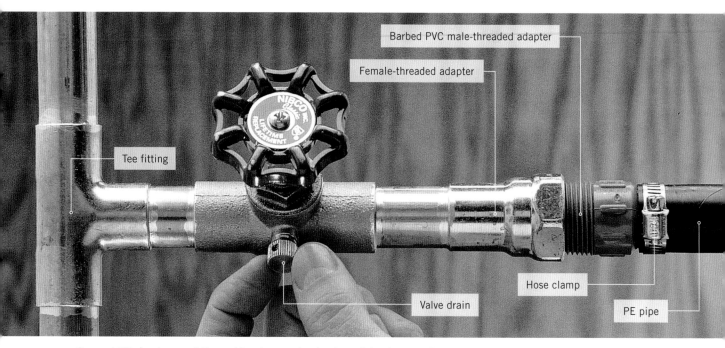

Barbed PVC male-threaded adapter

Female-threaded adapter

Tee fitting

Valve drain

Hose clamp

PE pipe

Connect PE pipe to an existing cold water supply pipe by splicing in a tee fitting to the copper pipe and attaching a drain-and-waste shutoff valve and a female-threaded adapter. Screw a barbed PVC male-threaded adapter into the copper fitting, then attach the PE pipe. The drain-and-waste valve allows you to blow the PE line free of water when winterizing the system.

How to Cut & Join Outdoor Flexible Plastic Pipe

Cut flexible PE pipe with a plastic tubing cutter, or use a miter box or sharp knife. Remove any rough burrs with a utility knife.

Fit stainless-steel hose clamps over the ends of the flexible pipes being joined.

Slide the band clamps over the joint ends. Hand tighten each clamp with a screwdriver or wrench.

OPTION: To ensure a tighter fit, dab some pipe joint compound onto the barbs so they are easier to slide into the flexible plastic pipe. Apply pipe joint compound to the barbed ends of the tee fitting. Work each end of PE pipe over the barbed portions of the fitting and into position.

Cross-Linked Polyethylene (PEX)

Cross-linked polyethylene (PEX) is growing quickly in acceptance as a supply pipe for residential plumbing. It's not hard to understand why. Developed in the 1960s but relatively new to the United States, this supply pipe combines the ease of use of flexible tubing with the durability of rigid pipe. It can withstand a wide temperature range (from subfreezing to 180°F); it is inexpensive; and it's quieter than rigid supply pipe.

PEX is flexible plastic (polyethylene, or PE) tubing that's reinforced by a chemical reaction that creates long fibers to increase the strength of the material. It has been allowed by code in Europe and the southern United States for many years, but has won approval for residential supply use in most major plumbing codes only recently. It's frequently used in manufactured housing and recreational vehicles and in radiant heating systems (use PEX-AL-PEX, a different material now used in radiant systems). Because it is so flexible, PEX can easily be bent to follow corners and make other changes in direction. From the water main and heater, it is connected into manifold fittings that redistribute the water in much the same manner as a lawn irrigation system.

For standard residential installations, PEX can be joined with very simple fittings and tools. Unions are generally made with a crimping tool and a crimping ring. You simply insert the ends of the pipe you're joining into the ring, then clamp down on the ring with the crimping tool. PEX pipe, tools, and fittings can be purchased from most wholesale plumbing suppliers and at many home centers. Coils of PEX are sold in several diameters from ¼-inch to 1 inch. PEX tubing and fittings from different manufacturers are not interchangeable. Any warranty coverage will be voided if products are mixed.

TOOLS & MATERIALS

Tape measure	Manifolds
Felt-tipped pen	Protector plates
Full-circle crimping tool	PEX fittings
Go/no-go gauge	Utility knife
Tubing cutter	Plastic hangers
PEX pipe	Crimp ring

PEX pipe is a relatively new water supply material that's growing in popularity in part because it can be installed with simple mechanical connections.

PEX Tools & Materials

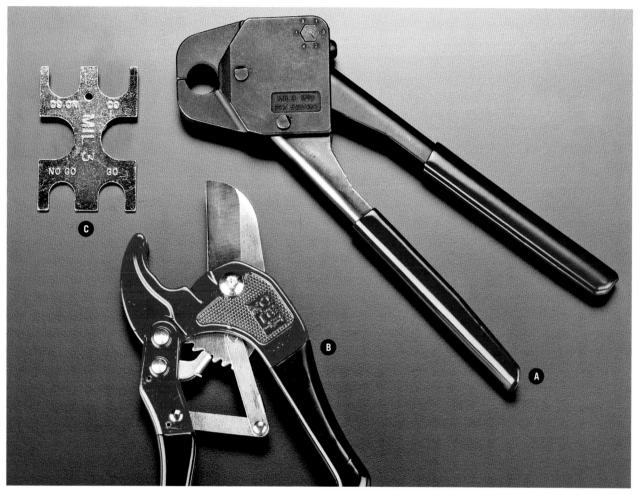

Specialty tools for installing PEX are available wherever PEX is sold. The basic set includes a full-circle crimping tool (A), a tubing cutter (B), and a go/no-go gauge (C) to test connections after they've been crimped. Competing manufacturers make several types of fittings, with proprietary tools that only work with their fittings. The tools and fittings you use may differ from those shown on these pages.

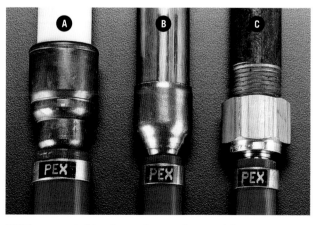

PEX is connected to other water supply materials with transition fittings, including CPVC-to-PEX (A), copper-to-PEX (B), and iron-to-PEX (C).

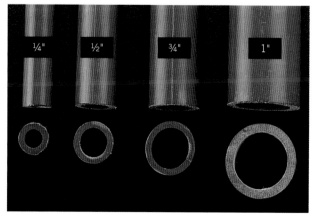

Generally, you should use the same diameter PEX as is specified for rigid supply tubing, but in some "home run" installations (see next page) you can use ⅜" PEX where ½" rigid copper would normally be used.

PEX Installation

Check with your local plumbing inspector to verify that PEX is allowed in your municipality. PEX has been endorsed by all major plumbing codes in North America, but your municipality may still be using an older set of codes. Follow the guidelines below when installing PEX:

- Do not install PEX in above-ground exterior applications because it degrades quickly from UV exposure.

- Do not use PEX for gas lines.

- Do not use plastic solvents or petroleum-based products with PEX (they can dissolve the plastic).

- Keep PEX at least 12" away from recessed light fixtures and other potential sources of high heat.

- Do not attach PEX directly to a water heater. Make connections at the heater with metallic tubing (either flexible water-heater connector tubing or rigid copper) at least 18" long; then join it to PEX with a transition fitting.

- Do not install PEX in areas where there is a possibility of mechanical damage or puncture. Always fasten protective plates to wall studs that house PEX.

- Always leave some slack in installed PEX lines to allow for contraction and in case you need to cut off a bad crimp.

- Use the same minimum branch and distribution supply-pipe dimensions for PEX that you'd use for copper or CPVC, according to your local plumbing codes.

- You can use push fittings to join PEX to itself or to CPVC or copper. See page 275.

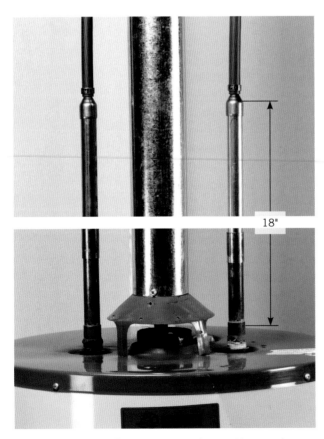

Do not connect PEX directly to a water heater. Use metal connector tubes. Solder the connector tubes to the water heater before attaching PEX. Never solder metal tubing that is already connected to PEX lines.

Bundle PEX together with plastic ties when running pipe through wall cavities. PEX can contract slightly, so leave some slack in the lines.

Buying PEX

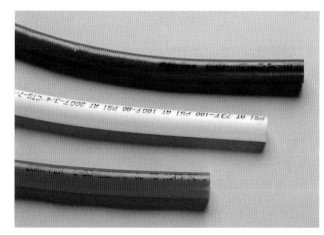

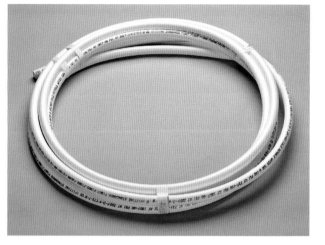

PEX combines the flexibility of plastic tubing with the durability of rigid supply pipe. It is sold in coils of common supply-pipe diameters.

Color coding is a practice many PEX manufacturers have embraced to make identification easier. Because the material is identical except for the color, you can buy only one color (red is more common) and use it for both hot and cold supply lines.

THE PEX ADVANTAGE

PEX supply tubing offers a number of advantages over traditional rigid supply tubing:

- Easy to install. PEX does not require coupling joints for long runs or elbows and sweeps for turns. The mechanical connections do not require solvents or soldering.

- Easy to transport. Large coils are lightweight and much easier to move around than 10-ft. lengths of pipe.

- Good insulation. The PEX material has better thermal properties than copper for lessened heat loss.

- Quiet. PEX will not rattle or clang from trapped air or kinetic energy.

- Good for retrofit jobs. PEX is easier to snake through walls than rigid supply tubing and is compatible with copper, PVC, or iron supply systems if the correct transition fittings are used. If your metal supply tubes are used to ground your electrical system, you'll need to provide a jumper if PEX is installed in midrun. Check with a plumber or electrician.

- Freeze resistance. PEX retains some flexibility in sub-freezing conditions and is less likely to be damaged than rigid pipe, but it is not frostproof.

GENERAL CODES FOR PEX

PEX has been endorsed for residential use by all major building codes, although some municipal codes may be more restrictive. The specific design standards may also vary, but here are some general rules:

- For PEX, maximum horizontal support spacing is 32" and maximum vertical support spacing is 10 ft.

- Maximum length of individual distribution lines is 60 ft.

- PEX is designed to withstand 210°F water for up to 48 hours. For ongoing use, most PEX is rated for 180 degree water up to 100 pounds per square inch of pressure.

- Directional changes of more than 90 degrees require a guide fitting.

- A mid-story guide is required for most PEX installations in walls. The guide should prevent movement perpendicular to the pipe direction.

System Designs

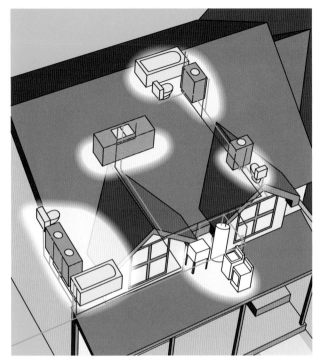

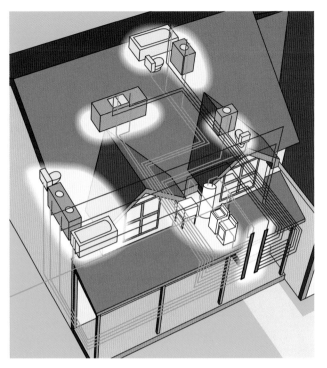

Trunk-and-branch systems are configured in much the same way as traditional rigid copper or PVC supply systems. A main supply line (the trunk line) carries water to all of the outlets via smaller branch lines that tie into the trunk and serve a few outlets in a common location.

Home run systems rely on one or two central manifolds to distribute the hot and cold water very efficiently. Eliminating the branch fittings allows you to use thinner supply pipe in some situations.

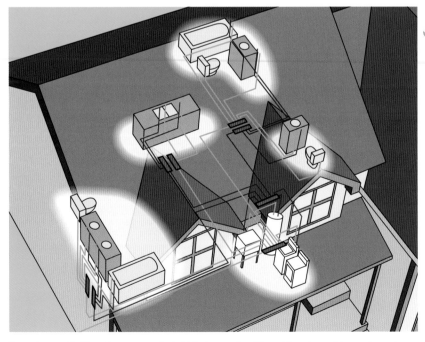

Remote manifold systems are a hybrid between traditional trunk-and-branch systems and home run systems. Instead of relying on just one or two manifolds, they employ several smaller manifolds downline from a larger manifold. Each smaller manifold services a group of fixtures, as in a bathroom or kitchen.

CHOOSING A PEX SYSTEM

- For maximum single-fixture water pressure: Trunk and branch

- For economy of materials: Trunk and branch or remote manifold

- For minimal wait times for hot water (single fixture): Home run

- For minimal wait times for hot water (multiple fixtures used at same approximate time): Trunk and branch or remote manifold

- For ease of shutoff control: Home run

- For lowest number of fittings and joints: Home run

How to Make PEX Connections

Cut the pipe to length, making sure to leave enough extra material so the line will have a small amount of slack once the connections are made. A straight, clean cut is very important. For best results, use a tubing cutter.

Inspect the cut end to make sure it is clean and smooth. If necessary, deburr the end of the pipe with a sharp utility knife. Slip a crimp ring over the end.

Align the jaws of a full-circle crimping tool over the crimp ring and squeeze the handles together to apply strong, even pressure to the ring.

Insert the barbed end of the fitting into the pipe until it is snug against the cut edges. Position the crimp ring so it is 1/8" to 1/4" from the end of the pipe, covering the barbed end of the fitting. Pinch the fitting to hold it in place.

Test the connection to make sure it is mechanically acceptable, using a go/no-go gauge. If the ring does not fit into the gauge properly, cut the pipe near the connection and try again.

How to Plumb a PEX Water-Supply System

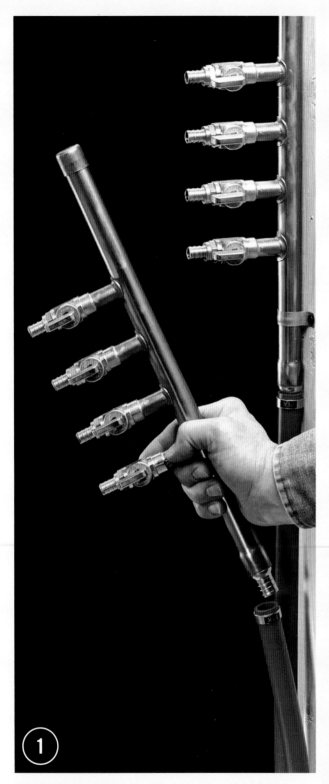

Install copper manifolds (one for hot and one for cold) in an accessible location central to the fixtures. The manifold should have one outlet for each supply line it will support (fixtures that require hot and cold supply will need a separate outlet for each). Run supply lines from the water heater and water main to the copper manifolds. Connect the supply pipes to the manifolds with crimp fittings.

A manifold may be attached vertically or horizontally, but it must be anchored with correctly sized hangers screwed to the framing members.

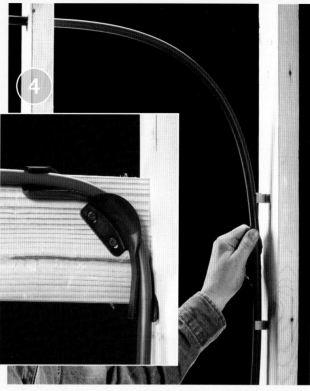

Starting at each fixture (and leaving at least 12" of extra pipe exposed), run appropriately sized PEX through holes in the framing to the manifolds. Pipes may be bundled together loosely with plastic ties. Protect the line with a nailing plate at each stud location. Be sure to leave some slack in the supply lines.

Support the pipe with a plastic hanger near every floor or ceiling and midway up vertical runs. Also use hangers to guide pipe near the beginnings and ends of curves and near fittings. Use a plastic guide for sharp curves (inset). Do not bend PEX so sharply that it kinks.

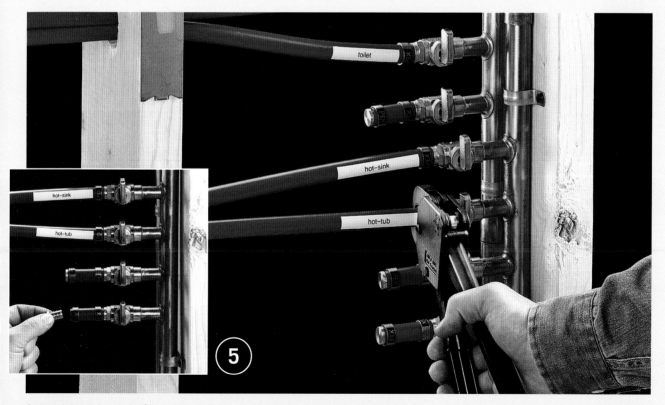

Cut each branch supply line to length (leave some extra in case you need to recrimp). Install shutoff valves for each outlet (most manifolds come with preattached valves). Connect the PEX branch supply lines to the shutoff valves. Label each pipe. Use a short length of PEX and a plug to seal any unused outlets (inset).

Cast Iron

Cast-iron pipe often is found in older homes, where it is used for large DWV pipes, especially the main stack and sewer service lines. It can be identified by its dark color, rough surface, and large size. Cast-iron pipes in home drains usually are 3 inches or more in diameter.

Cast-iron pipes may rust through or hubbed fittings (below) may leak. If your house is more than 30 years old, you may find it necessary to replace a cast-iron pipe or joint.

Cast iron is heavy and difficult to cut and fit. For this reason, leaky cast-iron pipe usually is replaced with PVC of the same diameter. PVC can be joined to cast iron easily, using a banded coupling (below).

Snap cutters are the traditional tool of choice for cutting cast iron, but today's variable-speed reciprocating saws do the job easily and safely. Use a long metal-cutting blade and set the saw at low speed. Wear eye and ear protection when cutting cast iron pipe.

Cast-iron pipe was used almost exclusively for drain systems until the introduction of heavy-duty PVC drain pipes. It is tough to work with and in most cases replacing it makes sense.

TOOLS & MATERIALS

Tape measure	Riser clamps
Chalk	or strap hangers
Adjustable wrenches	Two wood blocks
Reciprocating saw	2½" wallboard screws
(or rented snap cutter)	Banded couplings
Ratchet wrench	Plastic replacement pipe
Screwdriver	

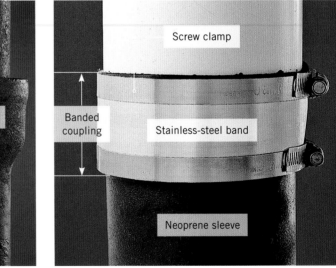

Hubbed fittings (shown cutaway, left) were used to join cast-iron pipe. Hubbed pipe has a straight end and a flared end. The straight end of one pipe fits inside the hub of the next pipe. In the old days, joints were sealed with packing material (oakum) and lead. Repair leaky joints by cutting out the entire hubbed fitting and replacing with plastic pipe.

Banded couplings may be used to replace leaky cast iron with a PVC or ABS plastic pipe. The new plastic pipe is connected to the remaining cast-iron pipe with a banded coupling. Banded coupling has a neoprene sleeve that seals the joint. Pipes are held together with stainless steel bands and screw clamps.

Cutting Cast-Iron Pipe

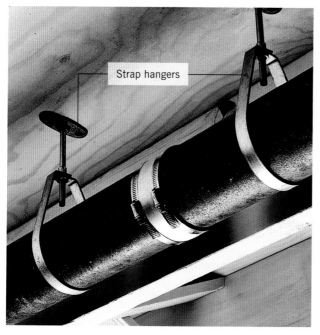

Before cutting a horizontal run of cast-iron drain pipe, make sure it is supported with strap hangers every 5 ft. and at every joint connection.

Before cutting a vertical run of cast-iron pipe, make sure it is supported at every floor level with a riser clamp. Never cut through pipe that is not supported.

How to Remove & Replace a Section of Cast-Iron Pipe

Support the upper section of pipe by installing a riser clamp 6" above the pipe section to be replaced. Attach wood blocks to the studs with 2½" deck screws, so that the riser clamp rests on tops of blocks.

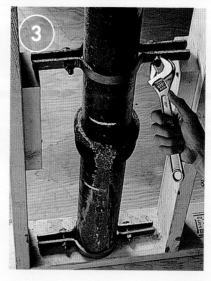

Use chalk to mark cut lines on the cast-iron pipe. If replacing a leaky hub, mark at least 6" on each side of hub.

Support lower section of pipe by installing a riser clamp flush against the bottom plate or floor.

(continued)

Wrap the chain of the snap cutter around the pipe, so that the cutting wheels are against the chalkline.

Tighten the chain and snap the pipe according to the tool manufacturer's directions.

Repeat cutting at the other chalkline. Remove cut section of pipe.

Screw clamp

Banded clamp

Neoprene sleeve

Cut a length of PVC plastic pipe to be ½" shorter than the section of cast-iron pipe that has been cut away.

Slip a banded coupling and a neoprene sleeve onto each end of the cast-iron pipe.

Make sure the cast-iron pipe is seated snugly against the rubber separator ring molded into the interior of the sleeve.

Fold back the end of each neoprene sleeve until the molded separator ring on the inside of the sleeve is visible.

Position the new plastic pipe so it is aligned with the cast-iron pipes.

Roll the ends of the neoprene sleeves over the ends of the new plastic pipe.

Slide stainless-steel bands and clamps over the neoprene sleeves.

Tighten the screw clamps with a ratchet wrench or screwdriver.

Pipe Fittings

Use the photos on these pages to identify the plumbing fittings specified in the project how-to directions found in this book. Each fitting shown is available in a variety of sizes to match your needs. Always use fittings made from the same material as your pipes.

Pipe fittings come in a variety of shapes to serve different functions within the plumbing system. DWV fittings include:

Vents: In general, the fittings used to connect vent pipes have very sharp bends with no sweep. Vent fittings include the vent tee and vent 90° elbow. Standard drain pipe fittings can also be used to join vent pipes.

Horizontal-to-vertical drains: To change directions in a drain pipe from the horizontal to the vertical, use fittings with a noticeable sweep. Standard fittings for this use include waste tee fittings and 90° elbows. Wye fittings and 45° and 22½° elbows can also be used for this purpose.

Vertical-to-horizontal drains: To change directions from the vertical to the horizontal, use fittings with a very pronounced, gradual sweep. Common fittings for this purpose include the long-radius wye tee fitting and some wye fittings with 45° elbows.

Horizontal offsets in drains: wye fittings, 45° elbows, 22½° elbows, and long sweep 90° elbows are used when changing directions in horizontal pipe runs. Whenever possible, horizontal drain pipes should use gradual, sweeping bends rather than sharp turns.

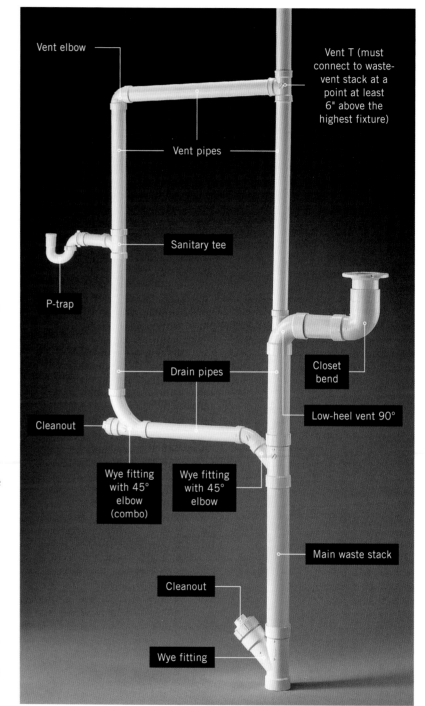

Basic DWV tree shows the correct orientation of drain and vent fittings in a plumbing system. Bends in the vent pipes can be very sharp, but drain pipes should use fittings with a noticeable sweep. Fittings used to direct falling waste water from a vertical to a horizontal pipe should have bends that are even more sweeping. Your local plumbing code may require that you install cleanout fittings where vertical drain pipes meet horizontal runs.

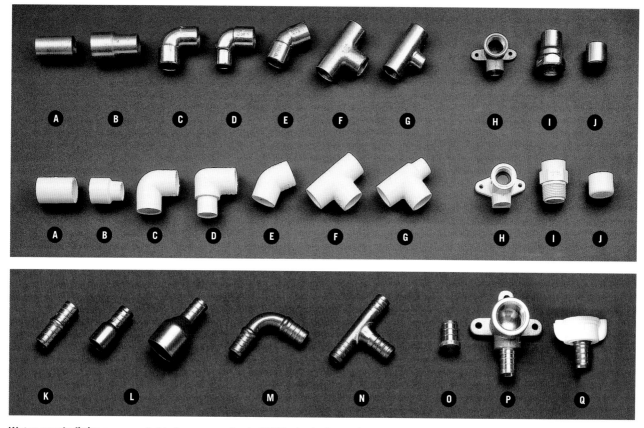

Water supply fittings are available for copper (top), CPVC plastic (center), and PEX (bottom). Fittings for CPVC and copper are available in many shapes, including: unions (A), reducers (B), 90° elbows (C), reducing elbows (D), 45° elbows (E), tee fittings (F), reducing tee fittings (G), drop-ear elbows (H), threaded adapters (I), and caps (J). Common PEX fittings (bottom) include unions (K), PEX-to-copper unions (L), 90° elbows (M), tee fittings (N), plugs (O), drop-ear elbows (P), and threaded adapters (Q). Easy-to-install push fittings are also available.

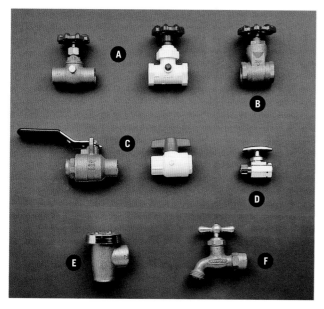

Water supply valves are available in brass or plastic and in a variety of styles, including: drain-and-waste valves (A), gate valve (B), full-bore ball valves (C), fixture shutoff valve (D), vacuum breaker (E), and hose bib (F).

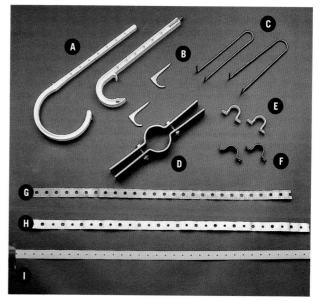

Support materials for pipes include: plastic pipe hangers (A), copper J-hooks (B), copper wire hangers (C), riser clamp (D), plastic pipe straps (E), copper pipe straps (F), flexible copper, steel, and plastic pipe strapping (G, H, I). Do not mix metal types when supporting metal pipes; use copper support materials for copper pipe, and steel for steel and cast-iron pipes.

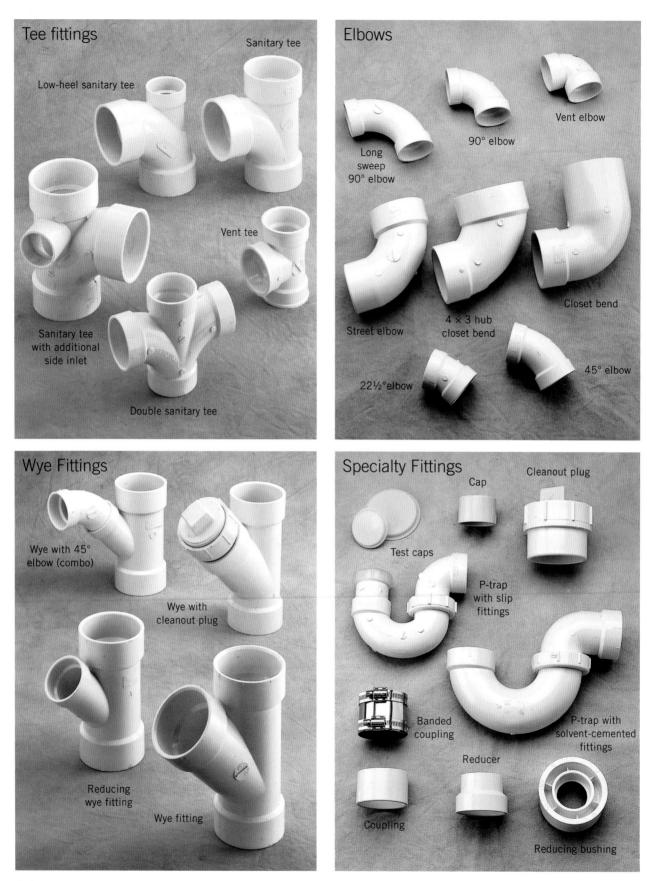

Tee fittings

Sanitary tee

Low-heel sanitary tee

Vent tee

Sanitary tee with additional side inlet

Double sanitary tee

Elbows

Vent elbow

90° elbow

Long sweep 90° elbow

Street elbow

4 × 3 hub closet bend

Closet bend

22½° elbow

45° elbow

Wye Fittings

Wye with 45° elbow (combo)

Wye with cleanout plug

Reducing wye fitting

Wye fitting

Specialty Fittings

Cap

Cleanout plug

Test caps

P-trap with slip fittings

Banded coupling

P-trap with solvent-cemented fittings

Coupling

Reducer

Reducing bushing

Fittings for DWV pipes are available in many configurations, with openings ranging from 1¼" to 4" in diameter. When planning your project, buy plentiful numbers of DWV and water supply fittings from a reputable retailer with a good return policy. It is much more efficient to return leftover materials after you complete your project than it is to interrupt your work each time you need to shop for a missing fitting.

How to Use Transition Fittings

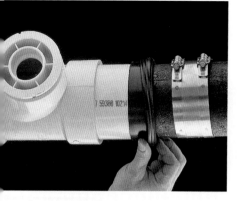

Connect plastic to cast iron with banded couplings. Rubber sleeves cover ends of pipes and ensure a watertight joint.

Make transitions in DWV pipes with rubber couplings. The two products shown here (Mission-brand fittings, see Resources page 298) can be used to connect pipes of different materials.

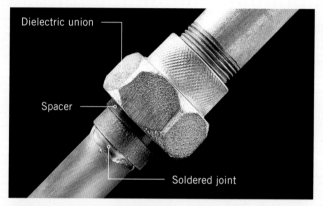

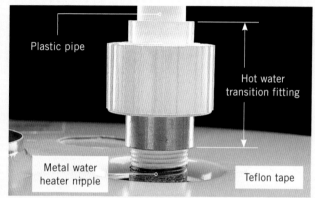

Connect copper to galvanized steel with a dielectric union. A dielectric union is threaded onto iron pipe and is soldered to copper pipe. A dielectric union has a plastic spacer that prevents corrosion caused by an electrochemical reaction between dissimilar metals.

Connect metal hot water pipe to plastic with a hot water transition fitting that prevents leaks caused by different expansion rates of materials. Metal pipe threads are wrapped with Teflon tape. Plastic pipe is solvent-cemeted to fitting.

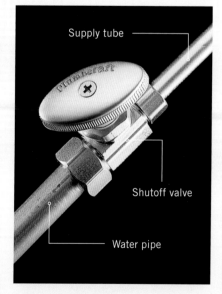

Connect any supply tube to a fixture tailpiece with a coupling nut. The coupling nut compresses the bell-shaped end of the supply tube against the fixture tailpiece.

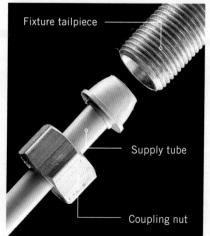

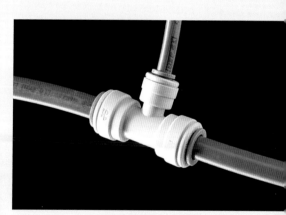

Connect a water pipe to any fixture supply tube using a shutoff valve.

Specialty supply fittings can be used to supply portable water fixtures such as icemakers and hot water dispensers. The John-Guest Speed-Fit fitting shown here (see Resources, page 298) is designed to connect to clear tubing or the manufacturer's proprietary plastic supply tubing.

Shutoff Valves

Worn-out shutoff valves or supply tubes can cause water to leak underneath a sink or other fixture. First, try tightening the fittings with an adjustable wrench. If this does not fix the leak, replace the shutoff valves and supply tubes.

Shutoff valves are available in several fitting types. For copper pipes, valves with compression-type fittings are easiest to install. For plastic pipes, use grip-type valves. For galvanized steel pipes, use valves with female threads.

Older plumbing systems often were installed without fixture shutoff valves. When repairing or replacing plumbing fixtures, you may want to install shutoff valves if they are not already present.

TOOLS & MATERIALS

Hacksaw	Felt-tipped pen
Tubing cutter	Shutoff valves
Adjustable wrench	Supply tubes
Tubing bender	Pipe joint compound

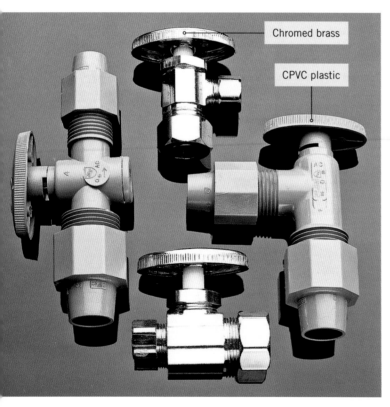

Shutoff valves allow you to shut off the water to an individual fixture so it can be repaired. They can be made from durable chromed brass or lightweight plastic. Shutoff valves come in ½" and ¾" diameters to match common water pipe sizes.

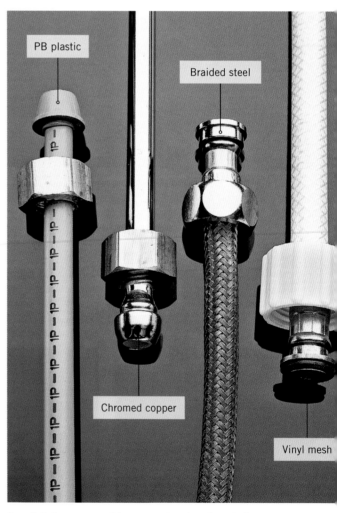

Supply tubes are used to connect water pipes to faucets, toilets, and other fixtures. They come in 12", 20", and 30" lengths. PB plastic and chromed copper tubes are inexpensive. Braided steel and vinyl mesh supply tubes are easy to install.

How to Install Shutoff Valves & Supply Tubes

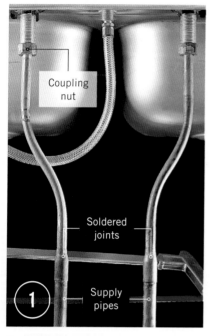

Coupling nut

Soldered joints

Supply pipes

1

Turn off water at the main shutoff valve. Remove old supply pipes. If pipes are soldered copper, cut them off just below the soldered joint, using a hacksaw or tubing cutter. Make sure the cuts are straight. Unscrew the coupling nuts and discard the old pipes.

Slide a compression nut and a compression ring over the copper water pipe. Threads of the nut should face the end of the pipe.

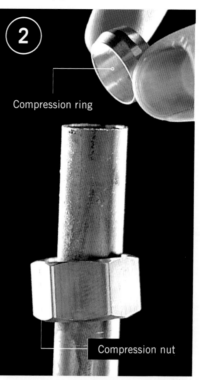

2

Compression ring

Compression nut

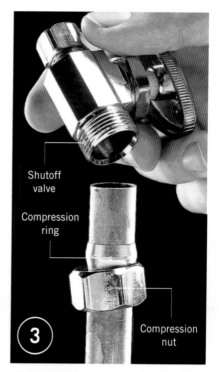

Shutoff valve

Compression ring

3

Compression nut

Apply pipe joint compound to the threads of the shutoff valve or compression nut. Screw the compression nut onto the shutoff valve and tighten with an adjustable wrench.

4

Bend chromed copper supply tube to reach from the tailpiece of the fixture to the shutoff valve, using a tubing bender. Bend the tube slowly to avoid kinking the metal.

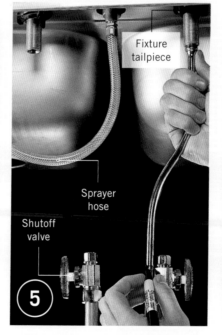

Fixture tailpiece

Sprayer hose

Shutoff valve

5

Position the supply tube between fixture tailpiece and the shutoff valve, and mark the tube to length. Cut the supply tube with a tubing cutter.

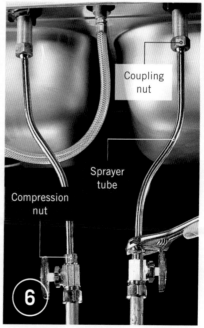

Coupling nut

Sprayer tube

Compression nut

6

Attach the bell-shaped end of the supply tube to the fixture tailpiece with a coupling nut, then attach the other end to the shutoff valve with compression ring and nut. Tighten all fittings with an adjustable wrench.

Valves & Hose Bibs

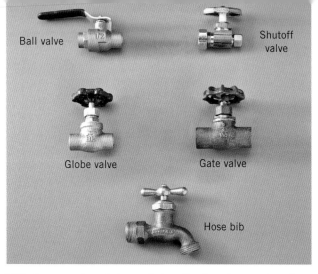

Valves make it possible to shut off water at any point in the supply system. If a pipe breaks or a plumbing fixture begins to leak, you can shut off water to the damaged area so that it can be repaired. A hose bib is a faucet with a threaded spout, often used to connect rubber utility or appliance hoses.

Valves and hose bibs leak when washers or seals wear out. Replacement parts can be found in the same universal washer kits used to repair compression faucets. Coat replacement washers with faucet grease to keep them soft and prevent cracking.

If you have the opportunity to replace a shutoff valve, install a ball valve, which has proved itself to be the most reliable type.

Remember to turn off the water before beginning work.

With the exception of chromed shutoff valves that are installed at individual fixtures (see previous pages), valves and hose bibs are heavy-duty fittings, usually with a brass body they are installed in-line to regulate water flow. Gate valves and globe valves are similar and are operated with a wheel-type handle that spins. Ball valves are operated with a handle much like a gas pipe stopcock and are considered by pros to be the most reliable. Hose bibs are spigots with a threaded end designed to accept a female hose coupling.

TOOLS & MATERIALS

Screwdriver	Universal washer kit
Adjustable wrench	Faucet grease

How to Fix a Leaky Hose Bib

Remove the handle screw and lift off the handle. Unscrew the packing nut with an adjustable wrench.

Unscrew the spindle from the valve body. Remove the stem screw and replace the stem washer. Replace the packing washer and reassemble the valve.

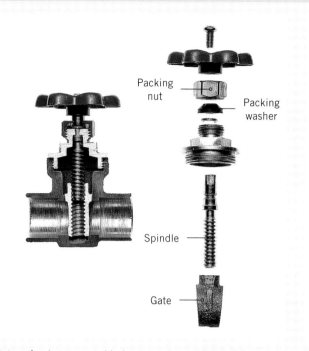

Gate valve has a movable brass wedge, or "gate," that screws up and down to control water flow. Gate valves may develop leaks around the handle. Repair leaks by replacing the packing washer or packing string found underneath the packing nut.

Globe valve has a curved chamber. Repair leaks around the handle by replacing the packing washer. If valve does not fully stop water flow when closed, replace the stem washer.

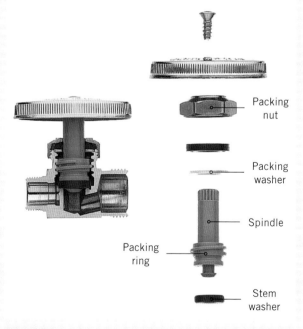

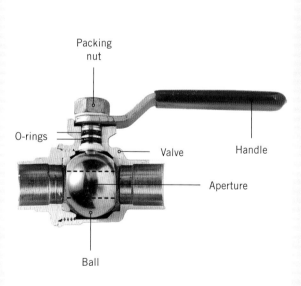

Shutoff valve controls water supply to one or more fixtures. A shutoff valve has a plastic spindle with a packing washer and a snap-on stem washer. Repair leaks around the handle by replacing the packing washer. If a valve does not fully stop water flow when closed, replace the stem washer. Shutoff valves with multiple outlets are available to supply several fixtures from a single supply.

Ball valve contains a metal ball with an aperture (or controlled hole) in the center. The ball is controlled by a handle. When the handle is turned the hole is positioned parallel to the valve (open) or perpendicular (closed).

Compression Fittings

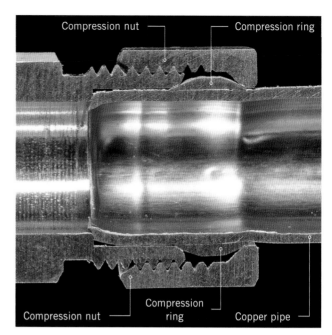

Compression nut — Compression ring

Compression nut — Compression ring — Copper pipe

Compression fitting (shown in cutaway) shows how threaded compression nut forms seal by forcing the compression ring against the copper pipe. Compression ring is covered with pipe joint compound before assembling to ensure a perfect seal.

Compression fittings are used to make connections that may need to be taken apart. Compression fittings are easy to disconnect and are often used to install supply tubes and fixture shutoff valves. Use compression fittings in places where it is unsafe or difficult to solder, such as in crawl spaces.

Compression fittings are used most often with flexible copper pipe. Flexible copper is soft enough to allow the compression ring to seat snugly, creating a watertight seal. Compression fittings also may be used to make connections with Type M rigid copper pipe.

TOOLS & MATERIALS

Felt-tipped pen
Tubing cutter or hacksaw

Adjustable wrenches
Brass compression fittings

Pipe joint compound or Teflon tape

How to Attach Supply Tubes to Fixture Shutoff Valves with Compression Fittings

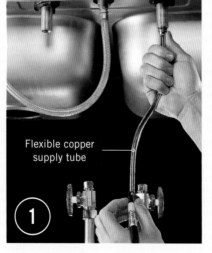

Flexible copper supply tube

(1)

Bend flexible copper supply tube and mark to length. Include ½" for portion that will fit inside valve. Cut tube.

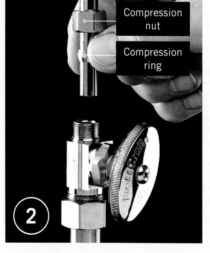

Compression nut

Compression ring

(2)

Slide the compression nut and then the compression ring over the end of the pipe. The threads of the nut should face the valve.

(3)

Apply a small amount of pipe joint compound to the threads. This lubricates the threads.

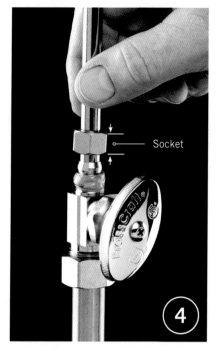

Insert the end of the pipe into the fitting so it fits flush against the bottom of the fitting socket.

Slide the compression ring and nut against the threads of the valve. Hand tighten the nut onto the valve.

Tighten the compression nut with adjustable wrenches. Do not overtighten. Turn on the water and watch for leaks. If the fitting leaks, tighten the nut gently.

How to Join Two Copper Pipes with a Compression Union Fitting

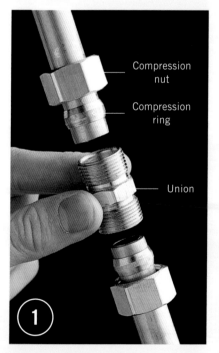

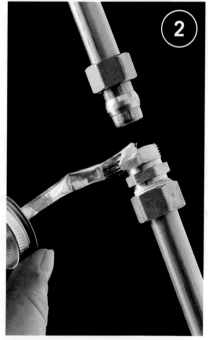

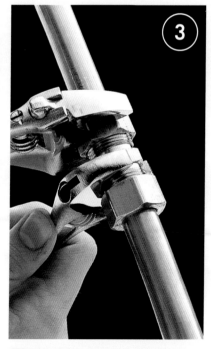

Slide compression nuts and rings over the ends of pipes. Place a threaded union between the pipes.

Apply a layer of pipe joint compound or Teflon tape to the union's threads, then screw compression nuts onto the union.

Hold the center of the union fitting with an adjustable wrench and use another wrench to tighten each compression nut one complete turn. Turn on the water. If the fitting leaks, tighten the nuts gently.

Glossary

Access panel — Opening in a wall or ceiling that provides access to the plumbing system

Air admittance valve — A valve that allows air into a drain line in order to protect the trap water seal from being drained. Often used where traditional vent pipe would be difficult to install

Appliance — Powered device that uses water, such as a dishwasher, washing machine, whirlpool, or water softener

Auger — Flexible tool used for clearing obstructions in drain lines

Ballcock — Valve that controls the water supply entering a toilet tank

Blow bag — Expanding rubber device that attaches to a garden hose; used for clearing floor drains

Branch drain line — Pipe that connects additional lines to a drain system

Branch line — Pipe that connects additional lines to a water supply system

Cleanout — Cover in a waste pipe or trap that provides access for cleaning

Closet auger — Flexible rod used to clear obstructions in toilets

Closet bend — Curved fitting that fits between a closet flange and a toilet drain

Closet flange — Ring at the opening of a toilet drain, used as the base for a toilet

Coupling — Fitting that connects two pieces of pipe

DWV — Drain, waste, and vent; the system for removing water from a house

DWV stack — Pipe that connects house drain system to a sewer line at the bottom and vents air to outside of house at the top

Elbow — Angled fitting that changes the direction of a pipe

Fixture — Device that uses water, such as a sink, tub, shower, sillcock, or toilet

Flapper (tank ball) — Rubber seal that controls the flow of water from a toilet tank to a toilet bowl

Flux (soldering paste) — Paste applied to metal joints before soldering to increase joint strength

Hand auger (snake) — Hand tool with flexible shaft, used for clearing clogs in drain lines

Hose bib — Any faucet spout that is threaded to accept a hose

I.D. — Inside diameter; plumbing pipes are classified by I.D.

Loop vent — A special type of vent configuration used in island installations

Main shutoff valve — Valve that controls water supply to an entire house

Motorized auger — Power tool with flexible shaft, used for clearing tree roots from sewer lines

Nipple — Pipe with threaded ends

O.D. — Outside diameter

Plumber's putty — A soft material used for sealing joints between fixtures and supply or drain parts

Reducer — A fitting that connects pipes of different sizes

Riser — 1) A pipe that extends one or more stories 2) A vertical pipe that connects a valve to a faucet or fitting

Run — Assembly of pipes that extends from water supply to fixture, or from drain to stack

Saddle valve — Fitting clamped to copper supply pipe, with hollow spike that punctures the pipe to divert water to another device, usually a dishwasher or refrigerator icemaker

Sanitary fitting — Fitting that joins DWV pipes; allows solid material to pass through without clogging

Shutoff valve — Valve that controls the water supply for one fixture or appliance

Sillcock — Compression faucet used on the outside of a house

Soil stack — Main vertical drain line, which carries waste from all branch drains to a sewer line

Solder — Metal alloy used for permanently joining metal (usually copper) pipes

Tee fitting — Fitting shaped like the letter *t* used for creating or joining branch lines

Trap — A plumbing fitting, usually curved, that is filled with standing water, that prevents sewer gases from entering a house

Union — Fitting that joins two sections of pipe but can be disconnected without cutting

Vacuum breaker — Attachment for outdoor and below-ground fixtures that prevents waste water from entering supply lines if water supply pressure drops

Wet vent — Pipe that serves as a drain for one fixture and as a vent for another

Wye fitting — Fitting shaped like the letter *y* used for creating or joining branch lines

Measurement Conversions

LUMBER DIMENSIONS

NOMINAL - U.S.	ACTUAL - U.S. (IN INCHES)	METRIC
1 × 2	¾ × 1½	19 × 38 mm
1 × 3	¾ × 2½	19 × 64 mm
1 × 4	¾ × 3½	19 × 89 mm
1 × 5	¾ × 4½	19 × 114 mm
1 × 6	¾ × 5½	19 × 140 mm
1 × 7	¾ × 6¼	19 × 159 mm
1 × 8	¾ × 7¼	19 × 184 mm
1 × 10	¾ × 9¼	19 × 235 mm
1 × 12	¾ × 11¼	19 × 286 mm
1¼ × 4	1 × 3½	25 × 89 mm
1¼ × 6	1 × 5½	25 × 140 mm
1¼ × 8	1 × 7¼	25 × 184 mm
1¼ × 10	1 × 9¼	25 × 235 mm
1¼ × 12	1 × 11¼	25 × 286 mm

NOMINAL - U.S.	ACTUAL - U.S. (IN INCHES)	METRIC
1½ × 4	1¼ × 3½	32 × 89 mm
1½ × 6	1¼ × 5½	32 × 140 mm
1½ × 8	1¼ × 7¼	32 × 184 mm
1½ × 10	1¼ × 9¼	32 × 235 mm
1½ × 12	1¼ × 11¼	32 × 286 mm
2 × 4	1½ × 3½	38 × 89 mm
2 × 6	1½ × 5½	38 × 140 mm
2 × 8	1½ × 7¼	38 × 184 mm
2 × 10	1½ × 9¼	38 × 235 mm
2 × 12	1½ × 11¼	38 × 286 mm
3 × 6	2½ × 5½	64 × 140 mm
4 × 4	3½ × 3½	89 × 89 mm
4 × 6	3½ × 5½	89 × 140 mm

METRIC CONVERSIONS

TO CONVERT:	TO:	MULTIPLY BY:
Inches	Millimeters	25.4
Inches	Centimeters	2.54
Feet	Meters	0.305
Yards	Meters	0.914
Square inches	Square centimeters	6.45
Square feet	Square meters	0.093
Square yards	Square meters	0.836
Ounces	Milliliters	30.0
Pints (U.S.)	Liters	0.473 (Imp. 0.568)
Quarts (U.S.)	Liters	0.946 (Imp. 1.136)
Gallons (U.S.)	Liters	3.785 (Imp. 4.546)
Ounces	Grams	28.4
Pounds	Kilograms	0.454

TO CONVERT:	TO:	MULTIPLY BY:
Millimeters	Inches	0.039
Centimeters	Inches	0.394
Meters	Feet	3.28
Meters	Yards	1.09
Square centimeters	Square inches	0.155
Square meters	Square feet	10.8
Square meters	Square yards	1.2
Milliliters	Ounces	.033
Liters	Pints (U.S.)	2.114 (Imp. 1.76)
Liters	Quarts (U.S.)	1.057 (Imp. 0.88)
Liters	Gallons (U.S.)	0.264 (Imp. 0.22)
Grams	Ounces	0.035
Kilograms	Pounds	2.2

COUNTERBORE, SHANK & PILOT HOLE DIAMETERS

SCREW SIZE	COUNTERBORE DIAMETER FOR SCREW HEAD (IN INCHES)	CLEARANCE HOLE FOR SCREW SHANK (IN INCHES)	PILOT HOLE DIAMETER	
			HARD WOOD (IN INCHES)	SOFT WOOD (IN INCHES)
#1	.146 (⁹⁄₆₄)	⁵⁄₆₄	³⁄₆₄	¹⁄₃₂
#2	¼	³⁄₃₂	³⁄₆₄	¹⁄₃₂
#3	¼	⁷⁄₆₄	¹⁄₁₆	³⁄₆₄
#4	¼	⅛	¹⁄₁₆	³⁄₆₄
#5	¼	⅛	⁵⁄₆₄	¹⁄₁₆
#6	⁵⁄₁₆	⁹⁄₆₄	³⁄₃₂	⁵⁄₆₄
#7	⁵⁄₁₆	⁵⁄₃₂	³⁄₃₂	⁵⁄₆₄
#8	⅜	¹¹⁄₆₄	⅛	³⁄₃₂
#9	⅜	¹¹⁄₆₄	⅛	³⁄₃₂
#10	⅜	³⁄₁₆	⅛	⁷⁄₆₄
#11	½	³⁄₁₆	⁵⁄₃₂	⁹⁄₆₄
#12	½	⁷⁄₃₂	⁹⁄₆₄	⅛

Resources

Accessibility Resource Center (ARC)
Shower and wet room kits, Aging in Place
    and accessibility accessories
715-743-2771
www.arcfirst.net

American Standard
800 442 1902
www.americanstandard-us.com

Black+Decker
Power tools and accessories
800-544-6986
www.blackanddecker.com

International Assoc. of Plumbing
    & Mechanical Officials
909 472 4100
www.iapmo.org

International Code Council
800 284 4406
www.iccsafe.org

John Guest Co.
Speedfit push-in fittings
www.johnguest.com

Kleer Drain
www.kleerdrain.com

Kohler
800 4 KOHLER
www.kohlerco.com

Laticrete
Floor-warming mats and supplies
800-243-4788
www.laticrete.com

Moen
Bathroom faucets, shower fixtures, safety
    and accessibility accessories
800-289-6636
www.moen.com

MTI
Tubs, shower bases and enclosures,
    sinks, accessories
800-783-8827
mtibaths.com

National Kitchen & Bathroom Assoc. (NKBA)
800 843 6522
www.nkba.com

Plumbing and Drainage Institute
978 557 0720
www.pdionline.org

Plumbing, Heating, Cooling Contractors
    Association (PHCC)
Producers of the National Standard
    Plumbing Code
www.phccweb.org
800-533-7694

Price Pfister
800 624 2120
www.pricepfister.com

Swanstone
800 325 7008
www.swanstone.com

Toto
800 350 8686
www.totousa.com

Water Sense
www.SaveWaterAmerica.com

World Plumbing Council
+44 17 08 47 27 91
email: secretariat@worldplumbing.org
www.worldplumbing.org

Photo Credits

Page 17 photo Terry J Alcorn / www.istock.com

Page 22 photo courtesy of Kohler

Page 23 photos courtesy of Price Pfister

Page 54 (top) courtesy of iStock

Page 54 (bottom) courtesy of Price Pfister

Page 70 photo courtesy of shutterstock

Page 77 photos courtesy of shutterstock

Page 90 photo courtesy of photolibrary

Page 110 bidet courtesy of Kohler

Page 111 courtesy of Toto

Page 115 courtesy Jennifer Morgan / www.istock.com

Page 134 photo courtesy of Kohler

Page 136 courtesy of GE

Page 146 photo courtesy of Nicola Gavin / www.istock.com

Page 151 (lower left & right) photos courtesy of Kohler

Page 151 (top right) photo courtesy of Ceramic Tiles of Italy

Page 168 (bottom) photo courtesy of Symmons

Page 200 photo courtesy of Kohler

Page 222 photo courtesy of Kohler

Index